DATE DUE			
NOV 3 0 '92 S			
MAR 06 1995 S			

Welfare and the Poor
in the Nineteenth-Century City

"Crazy Nora" (*Courtesy of The Historical Society of Pennsylvania*). This painting by William E. Winner (1815–83) depicts Honora Power, an Irish, immigrant Catholic, who peddled her wares in nineteenth-century Philadelphia and eventually died in the Friends' almshouse in 1865.

Welfare and the Poor in the Nineteenth-Century City

PHILADELPHIA, 1800–1854

Priscilla Ferguson Clement

Rutherford • Madison • Teaneck
Fairleigh Dickinson University Press
London and Toronto: Associated University Presses

© 1985 by Associated University Presses, Inc.

Associated University Presses
440 Forsgate Drive
Cranbury, NJ 08512

Associated University Presses
25 Sicilian Avenue
London WC1A 2QH, England

Associated University Presses
2133 Royal Windsor Drive
Unit 1
Mississauga, Ontario
Canada L5J 1K5

Library of Congress Cataloging in Publication Data

Clement, Priscilla Ferguson, 1942–
    Welfare and the poor in the nineteenth-century city.

    Bilbliography: p.
    Includes index.
    1. Public welfare—Pennsylvania—Philadelphia—
History—19th century. 2. Poor—Pennsylvania—
Philadelphia—History—19th century. I. Title.
HV99.P5C64 1985   362.5′09748′11   83-49357
ISBN 0-8386-3216-5

Printed in the United States of America

To the scholar I most admire,
my father, William J. Ferguson

Contents

Illustrations

Tables and Figures

Acknowledgments

I am indebted to my dissertation adviser at the University of Pennsylvania, Charles E. Rosenberg, for understanding my limitations on travel (a husband and children in Philadelphia), for finding me an intriguing topic near home, and most of all, for wisely directing me through the writing of the first version of this book. For reading portions of various revisions and for their trenchant criticism of same, I thank George Franz, David Kennedy, and Richard McLeod. I am also deeply grateful to Sara Whildin, librarian at the Pennsylvania State University, Delaware County campus, and my father, William J. Ferguson (to whom this book is dedicated), for reading the entire manuscript and providing me not only with useful suggestions for change, but also with much needed moral support.

Without the fine records at the Philadelphia City Archives, this book could not have been written. For guiding me through the maze of data on nineteenth-century poor relief and for responding so cheerfully and optimistically to all my questions, I thank Ward Childs, archivist.

The College of Liberal Arts Research Office and the Commonwealth Campus Scholarly Activity Fund at the Pennsylvania State University extended me needed financial support to complete various portions of the manuscript. Parts of chapters 2 and 3 appeared in the *Pennsylvania Magazine of History and Biography* and are reprinted here with permission of the editor. DeeDee Beebe and Ursula Livesay deserve credit for deciphering my scribbles and typing portions of this book.

Finally, many thanks to my husband, John, and my three children, Andy, Jenny, and Laura, for uncomplainingly accepting my frequent disappearances to research and to write.

Welfare and the Poor
in the Nineteenth-Century City

The Poor

And wherefore do the poor complain?
    The rich man asked of me!
Come walk abroad with me I said,
    And I will answer thee.

Twas winter, and the frozen streets
    Were cheerless to behold,
And we were wrapped and coated well,
    And yet were very cold.

We met an old bareheaded man,
    And his locks were thin and white—
We asked him what he did abroad
    In that cold winter's night?

Twas bitter cold, indeed! he said;—
    At home no fire had he,
And therefore he had come abroad,
    To ask for charity.

We met a young barefooted child,
    And she begged loud and bold—
We asked her why she went abroad
    When the night was so cold?

She said her father could not work,
    For he lay sick in bed;
And therefore was it she had come
    Abroad to beg for bread.

We went into a cabin then,
    To shield us from the storm,
And hoped to find some friendly blaze,
    Our frozen limbs to warm.

We found three shivering little girls,
    with their wretched mother there,
And in their haggard eyes we read
    COLD, HUNGER, and DESPAIR

She said for her suffering bairns
    No bed nor fire had she,
For she had been abroad, in VAIN
    to beg for charity....

From a pamphlet published in 1829 by Mathew Carey, Philadelphia publisher and a reformer interested in poverty and welfare in the city. The pamphlet is entitled "Address to the Liberal and Humane."

Introduction

Today, public welfare is an established part of the American social and economic system, and yet it is the subject of much controversy. Periodically since the New Deal Era, when the federal government assumed primary responsibility for welfare, major revisions of the public-relief program have been suggested and some of them implemented. In the 1960s, John F. Kennedy first proposed and Lyndon Johnson ultimately initiated the war on poverty. Subsequently, Richard Nixon dismantled that program and put forth his own Family Assistance Plan, which was, after all, never adopted. Some years later, along came Jimmy Carter with his Better Jobs and Income Plan, which also never came to fruition. In the 1980s, President Ronald Reagan suggested and Congress implemented a series of cutbacks in a number of welfare programs.[1]

Not only is public-welfare policy much in the news, so, too, are analyses of America's poor. Data about the country's least affluent citizens have become readily available as such government agencies as the Department of Health and Human Services and the Social Security Administration have, in the last several decades, gathered extensive statistics about welfare and the poor.[2]

While studies of the composition of our poor population and the welfare programs on which they depend may be fairly commonplace today, they were not so in the past. Until very recently, historians have largely ignored pre-twentieth-century welfare programs and the poor who relied on them.[3] Consequently, most Americans have little sense of the continuity of welfare reform.

The paucity of historical surveys of pre-twentieth-century public welfare and the poor it serviced can in part be attributed to the very real obstacles to conducting such studies. There is no central repository of data on public welfare prior to the creation of the Social Security Administration in 1935. From the seventeenth through the early twentieth centuries, most public poor relief programs were locally administered, and so the study of public assistance is inevitably the study of local history—often a tedious exercise.[4] North America's first settlers shared the English conviction that communities, acting through their local governments, had responsibility for the well-being of all their members. This pattern of local administration

19

of welfare, which began two centuries ago, has actually continued to the present, for although the federal government funds most welfare programs, some of them, such as unemployment insurance and aid to families with dependent children (AFDC), are still locally administered. Up until the 1930s, local communities both paid for and administered public welfare.

Not surprisingly, the best records of past poor relief programs exist where there were the most indigent—in urban areas. One of the largest American cities in the eighteenth and nineteenth centuries, Philadelphia, has preserved some of America's best public-welfare records.[5]

The locus of this study of poor relief is Philadelphia in the first half of the nineteenth century, although I begin with a brief description of eighteenth-century welfare practices and end just past midcentury in 1854, when the governmental structure of the city altered considerably, as did its method of dispensing welfare.[6] I also refer frequently to relief practices in other cities in this era as well. I define public welfare as aid given by citizens through their government to individuals who cannot adequately support themselves. I do not include as public assistance either educational expenditures or outlays for the apprehension and punishment of criminals.

Some students of past American-welfare practices feel that relief policies gradually became more benevolent over time. While conceding that there were occasional lapses when aid programs were reduced or even eliminated, some historians believe that assistance to the poor has and will become progressively more beneficial.[7] There are, in contrast, others who have stressed the repressive nature of many past relief programs. These historians contend that welfare policies were often designed to restrain or control the poor rather than improve their lot.[8] Both viewpoints have merit. For example, today's categorical aid program, which enables the aged poor to remain in their own homes, is certainly more humane than the nineteenth-century practice of forced institutionalization of helpless elderly people in almshouses. Furthermore, nineteenth-century indoor relief, and even some forms of outdoor relief (such as distributing free food or fuel instead of cash to the poor), were, indeed, ways of controlling the behavior of the needy.

I do not so much disagree with past explanations of the history of welfare as I approach the study of the evolution of welfare policy from a somewhat different perspective. I argue that a mixture of motives guided those who made and administered welfare programs. First, these individuals did exhibit genuine concern for the poor and were motivated by eleemosynary concerns. Secondly, the administrators also frequently worried about keeping a close watch on the poor, who might take unfair advantage of welfare programs, and about "reforming" those on the welfare rolls. Finally, welfare officials also traditionally tried to implement policies that were economical. They sought to save the taxpayer's money by not spend-

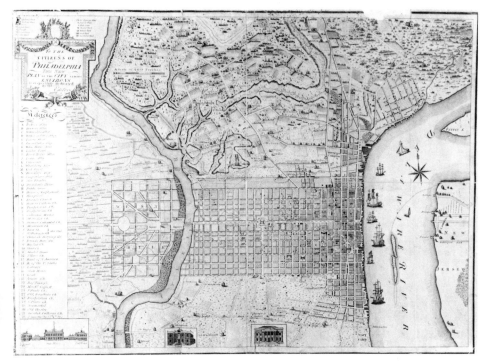

Philadelphia, 1802 (*Courtesy of The Historical Society of Pennsylvania*). The narrow, settled portion of the city and districts along the Delaware River is designated by darker tones.

ing extraordinary sums on supporting the poor.

At any given time, all three considerations affected welfare policy; no one consideration was ever totally absent. However, the relative importance of the three varied over time, depending on social, political, and most significantly, economic factors. Depressions, such as those that followed the Seven Years' War in the 1760s and the War of 1812, resulted in substantial alterations in relief programs and considerable emphasis on economy and social control in welfare-policy making.

In order to clarify the social, political, and economic milieu in which welfare change occurred in Philadelphia and the sort of people who were affected by that change, this study begins with a description of Philadelphia and its poor population between 1800 and 1854. There follows a discussion of how the growth of the city, political conflict within it, and the periodic economic crises that beset its population produced changes in welfare policy. The way in which humanitarian concerns were, to a large extent, replaced by considerations of economy and control are examined in relation to public outdoor relief to the poor in their own homes; institutional-

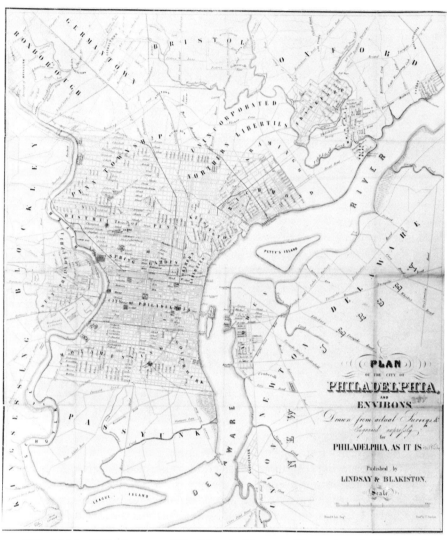

Philadelphia, 1852 (*Courtesy of The Historical Society of Pennsylvania*). The settled portions now include not only Philadelphia from the Delaware to the Schuylkill Rivers, but also nine districts north and south of the city.

ization, or indoor relief, in the almshouse; public and private programs to aid indigent children; and private-charity methods of assisting indigent adults. Throughout, those aided by Philadelphia's welfare authorities and the effects of changes in welfare policy on these people will be stressed. Finally, I examine the relevance of my findings to welfare issues today.

My study confirms that welfare history is cyclical and aid to the poor often contracts in response to predictable phenomena. Morever, Philadelphia's example indicates that the same sort of person sought public aid in the nineteenth century as applies for government assistance today. The indigent poor, past and present, also received comparable types of aid: currently popular relief measures, such as food stamps and AFDC, evolved from similar programs in the eighteenth and nineteenth centuries. Those who dispensed such relief have varied little over time: the profession of social work originated in the public-welfare system in the early nineteenth century. In the same era, the bureaucracy that characterizes our current welfare system began to develop. Perhaps this singular continuity in welfare history can not only help us to understand better the past, but also to plan sensibly for the future.

The City and Its Poor

Sailing up the Delaware River from the sea, a foreign visitor to Philadelphia in the early nineteenth century glimpsed a city that sprawled along the waterfront for several miles. The original city plan of 1683 determined the pattern of geographical expansion for Philadelphia by providing for settlement between the Delaware and Schuylkill Rivers on streets laid out in a neat grid pattern. The plan expected settlement to begin along both rivers, expand, and eventually result in one narrow, rectangular city between the rivers, extending from Vine Street in the north to Cedar or South Street in the south. However, when only the Delaware River proved deep enough for the navigation of large ships and the construction of wharves, settlers congregated near this river and ignored the Schuylkill. Instead of spreading westward, settlements first expanded north and south from the city along the Delaware into the neighboring districts of Northern Liberties and Southwark.[1] Thus, from the vantage point of the river, a visitor could see most of the inhabited parts of the Philadelphia area. By 1800, 61,559 people made their home in the city and districts, but this population was confined within such narrow limits that once a traveler disembarked, she or he could probably easily stroll the few square miles of streets where the majority of residents lived and worked.

Yet a visitor arriving in the 1820s would have found the western part of the city losing its rural aspect; a walk through populous sections of the city and districts, where over one hundred thousand people now lived, was no longer an easy morning's ramble. By the fourth and fifth decades of the century, a newcomer to the city would find homes and small shops lining many streets all the way to the Schuylkill. Districts adjacent to the city had also grown; by 1854, settlers had moved south into Moyamensing and north into Kensington, Spring Garden, Penn Township, and Richmond. At midcentury, with over 300,000 residents sprawled over so wide an area, Philadelphia was certainly no longer a "walking city."[2]

Throughout the nineteenth century, there was some residential segregation by class in Philadelphia. The most fashionable area in which to live was the commercial core of the city near the Delaware River. When public transportation was nonexistent, the most desirable and expensive area of town was inevitably the center, where most businesses were located. Still, this was not a segregated metropolis in the modern sense of the term. Between 1800 and 1854, a number of less affluent people also resided in the middle of town, many of them in crowded alleys between the larger thoroughfares where the wealthy had their homes.[3] Likewise, there were some well-to-do individuals who elected to live in the districts, especially those who owned businesses there or sought country homes, but generally members of the working class inhabited Southwark, Northern Liberties, and adjoining areas. Here, housing was usually cheaper than in the city but not always convenient to work places. Some district dwellers left home at six or seven in the morning to walk some distance into the city, where they usually labored till after dark and then again trekked out of the city and home. Still, others found living in the districts quite suitable for all their needs. Sailors, shipyard workers, and longshoremen often preferred to live in Southwark, adjacent to the docks; fishermen, in Kensington, close by the water; and industrial workers, in Northern Liberties, near shops and factories. Hand-loom weavers congregated with their kind in Moyamensing and Kensington.[4] Thus, there was a concentration of the well-to-do in Philadelphia proper and of the working class in the districts, but in all areas, there remained a much broader mixture of people from various backgrounds than exists today in neighborhoods of most large cities.

Diversity prevailed, and Philadelphia was not a unified community. Social variation was reenforced by the governmental structure of the metropolitan area. The city and districts remained discreet, distinct, self-governing units until 1854. Despite this formal governmental separation, there were some semiindependent committees or commissions, an inheritance from the colonial era, that functioned throughout the urban area.[5]

Controlling contagious diseases in the city and districts was the responsibility of members of the board of health. Relief for the indigent in Philadelphia and its neighboring communities was the task of the guardians of the poor, whom the councils in the city and commissioners in the districts appointed to office. Wisely, Philadelphia's metropolitan residents recognized that disease and poverty ignored narrow governmental boundaries and could best be handled by boards with jurisdiction over the entire urban area. Moreover, to curb both illness and indigence, it was often necessary to make large expenditures, and the tax bill proved less burdensome the more there were to share it.[6]

Still, the boards of health and the guardians of the poor were exceptional; they were the only unifying municipal units in the Philadelphia area. In most governmental matters, city and district residents were hopelessly divided; so, too, did they diverge politically. In the late eighteenth and early nineteenth centuries, affluent Philadelphians were inclined to support the Federalist Party, which, throughout the country, represented the commercial and professional classes. Albeit, in 1801, as Jefferson's party gained ascendency in most parts of the nation, political control of Philadelphia's city government passed from the Federalists to the president's followers, the Democratic-Republicans. This party, which pushed for more participation by citizens in government, drew most of its support from working-class voters in the districts, although the Democratic-Republicans had enough adherents in Philadelphia to enable them to control the city's government for most of the first decade of the century.[7]

But this political unity between the city and districts was short-lived. In the second and third decades of the century, while the Democratic-Republican Party retained control of Northern Liberties, Southwark, and Moyamensing, it lost its power in Philadelphia, where wealthy Federalists once more took charge.[8] In the late 1820s, Jacksonian enthusiasm finally dealt the death blow to the city's Federalist Party, but conservative Philadelphians sought another party to represent their interests, and they found it in the Whigs. This party won most elections in the city in the 1830s and 1840s, while the Democrats remained preeminent in the districts.[9]

By the nineteenth century, members of the Society of Friends no longer dominated Philadelphia's politics. Beginning in 1756 and continuing through 1774, Quakers withdrew from positions of political leadership in Philadelphia, yet they did not cease to serve their city; if anything, their dedication to philanthropy grew with the creation of the Pennsylvania Hospital, the Philadelphia Society for Alleviating the Miseries of Public Prisons, the Friends' Hospital for the Insane, and other charities. Philadelphia was also home to groups of Presbyterians, Episcopalians, German Lutherans, and Irish Catholics. Some members from these churches were, like the Quakers, actively involved in helping the city's least fortunate citizens.[10]

Most help was required during periods when Philadelphia's economy faltered. Early in the century, all major American cities depended greatly on foreign trade. From the 1790s through 1806, the value of American imports and exports escalated sharply, and American merchant vessels, many of which were constructed in Philadelphia, did a thriving business. The Embargo Act of 1807 cut off this lucrative foreign trade with Europe. The value of Philadelphia's exports dropped from $16 million in 1807 to $4 million in 1808. Ships rotted at the docks, and grass grew on the streets leading to the waterfront.[11] Increased investment in manufacturing somewhat offset the economic effects of the embargo and so, too, did a construction boom in the city, which may have provided employment for more than 8,000 men by 1808.[12] Probably some unemployed seamen, shipbuilders, ropemakers, and longshoremen found jobs in manufacturing and construction, but others may not have been able to make the transition to the new type of work. Many of those who did remain employed absorbed wage cuts, while, at the same time, between 1800 and 1815, the cost of living apparently increased fairly steadily.[13]

Just as serious was the depression that followed the War of 1812, which affected both pillars of the city's economy—commerce and manufacturing. After 1815, Britain and France denied American-owned ships, access to markets in the West Indies, markets which Americans had been able to penetrate in wartime. Meanwhile, the end of the war also brought a flood of British goods to the United States and checked the growth of America's infant industries, which had been protected from foreign competition by the war.[14] By 1817, Philadelphia's manufacturing enterprises were in trouble, and more economic problems loomed ahead. The country's banks, spurred on by the Philadelphia-based second Bank of the United States, pursued an inflationary policy and issued more and more notes. Finally in 1818 the Bank of the United States demanded payments in gold and silver and reduced its paper circulation. Other banks were forced to do the same and there followed the Panic of 1819. Facing severe competition from abroad and finding bank credit at home curtailed, businessmen laid off workers and unemployment grew. As a Philadelphia "scrivener" reported, "Distress is felt by all except brokers, usurers, tavern keepers, and office holders." By the early 1820s, there were at least 5,000, and possibly as many as 20,000, Philadelphians out of work.[15] Those who managed to cling to low-level, unskilled jobs at this time took wage cuts, just as had happened in the 1807 economic crisis.

Still, prices declined during the depression, and real wages steadily increased between 1815 and 1830.[16] Hence, those who managed to hold on to their jobs may not have suffered very much, but those who were laid off may have had more difficulty finding new situations than those unemployed during the embargo. Those who lost commerce-related jobs in the Panic of 1819 could not move easily into alternative positions in manufacturing, of which there were few. With both important sectors of the economy depressed, the unemployed in the early 1820s faced a greater dilemma than did those out of work during the embargo, since the latter at least had the option of seeking employment in the new manufacturing industries or the thriving construction field.

The third major economic crisis that troubled Philadelphia in the first fifty-four years of the nineteenth century began with the bank war of the 1830s. The Philadelphia-based Bank of the United States, which held federal government funds and a charter to operate until 1836, sought to have its charter renewed early in 1832. Although Congress passed a re-charter bill, President Andrew Jackson vetoed it, and after his reelection in 1832, Jackson ordered an end to depositing federal funds in the Bank of the

United States and transferred the funds to various state banks. A period of inflation ensued as the state banks issued much new currency. President Jackson attempted to end the inflationary actions of the banks by announcing that only specie would be accepted in payment for public lands. The resulting demand for hard money was so great that New York banks suspended specie payment in 1837, and so, too, did Philadelphia banks. The subsequent depression lasted into 1843. Because money was so scarce, wages, prices, and rents fell, stocks depreciated, and businesses cut production and laid off workers. In 1837, 5,000 people in the city were out of work, and by 1842, 4,000 remained jobless as the shipbuilding, construction, printing, and machine tool industries in the city continued to be depressed. Diarist Sidney George Fisher described the city in 1842:

> The streets seemed deserted, the largest houses are shut up and to rent, there is no business, there is no money, no confidence and little hope, property is sold every day by the sheriff at a fourth of the estimated value of a few years ago, nobody can pay debts, the miseries of poverty are felt by both rich and poor, everyone you see looks careworn and haggard....[17]

As in previous depressions, common laborers absorbed substantial wage cuts; so, too, did the city's many handloom weavers. Still, when wages decreased, prices followed suit. Many workers did not profit from this change, however, because employers paid them, not in cash, which was scarce, but in goods or store orders. Frequently, workers received goods they did not want or need.[18]

Various economic catastrophes troubled Philadelphians in the first half of the nineteenth century but so, too, did something seemingly more mundane—seasonal change. Philadelphia's harsh winters meant periodic unemployment for seamen, construction workers, and day laborers. When the Delaware River froze, as it frequently did in the early nineteenth century, seamen could find no berths and swelled the ranks of day laborers, who generally sought in vain for outdoor work in cold and snowy weather. Every winter, the almshouse population soared as hundreds were forced to take refuge there. Still, not all those in need could be accommodated in the poor asylum during severe winters. As members of the Northern Soup Society remarked in 1820, "It is well known that the provision which is made by law for the relief of the poor, liberal as it is, is not, by any means, commensurate with their wants, especially during the rigour of the winter season."[19]

Even in good times, laborers, who earned little, could rarely save enough to tide them over the long winter months of unemployment, and in slack times, when wages were low and unemployment high, cold winters led to acute suffering among thousands of Philadelphians. Their most pressing needs were food and fuel. The latter was especially hard to come by, since the cost of wood and coal escalated tremendously in the winter, and few poor laborers could afford to buy either. Some purchased a few cents worth of wood or coal at a time, others collected chips and shavings to burn in their home. Those who were really desperate pawned their clothes or bedding to buy food or fuel. These various expedients did not work for all, and some poor died of exposure. Critics charged that the true number of such deaths could not be ascertained, since coroners' juries "through regard for the honour of their respective neighborhoods" preferred to blame most deaths by exposure in the winter on "unknown causes" or "the visitation of God." [20]

Illness, like economic crises and bad winters, often led to unemployment and poverty. In the districts, where most of the poor lived, there were many health hazards. One observer of these areas in 1813 noted, "Ponds with stagnant water abound where dead animals are often thrown." Nearby, he found groups of ailing people crammed into small huts, six to ten in a room. The situation had not improved much by 1853 when a reporter for the *Evening Bulletin* described Moyamensing thusly:

> We saw men and women lying on the bare ground of cellars, suffering with fevers, and destitute of fire, food, drink or medicines. The poor wretches were covered with any bit of carpet or canvass they could procure. One man, who appeared to be dying with the prison fever, had no bed but the bare floor, no covering but a manilla coffee bag, and no fire, food, or attendance whatever. [21]

Workers who earned very little were usually unable to save much, and, therefore, when they or their children became ill, could not afford medical aid. Yellow fever epidemics that visited the city regularly in the summers of 1802, 1804, 1805, and 1806 especially complicated the lives of the poor. When all who could afford to had escaped the city, the poor were left behind with no jobs. Unable to flee, hundreds contracted the disease and died. [22]

Other fevers as well as smallpox recurred annually in the Philadelphia area. [23] Typhus struck in 1818, 1820, and 1847, and poor blacks were particularly subject to its ravages. [24] In 1832, cholera appeared and claimed its first victims among the residents of Moyamensing, which was, by most accounts, the poorest and dirtiest district in the metropolitan area. In 1849, when the disease reappeared, Moyamensing, Southwark, and Richmond, districts where most of the working poor resided, had the most unfavorable ratio of cholera cases to population of any community in the Philadelphia area. [25]

Philadelphians who suffered the most during economic, climatic, and medical crises in the early nineteenth century were the poor. At this time,

Americans classified such indigent people as either totally dependent or among the laboring poor. The dependent could not support themselves and relied completely on public or private charity. The laboring poor worked for a living but earned barely enough to survive.

Commonly, the dependent poor included those who were disabled or incompetent and lacked families to support them. Such people usually fell into one of three groups—children (either orphaned or bastard), the chronic or incurably afflicted, and the aged.

There were many impoverished children in Philadelphia from 1800 to 1854. Frequent yellow fever, smallpox, and cholera epidemics of the period left hundreds of youngsters without one or both parents. Many lived in extreme poverty. In 1805, a group of philanthropic Philadelphians discovered an "almost insane" woman, widowed by a recent epidemic, living alone with her two children, one of whom was "at breast" and the other suffering from smallpox. All three had virtually nothing to eat and were clad in the scantiest of rags.[26]

Bastard children were also a problem. When an unmarried servant woman became pregnant, she usually lost her job. She could seek free medical assistance at the lying-in ward of the almshouse, but if she later reentered domestic service, she would have difficulty supporting herself and a baby on the meager wages of a house servant. Day care was expensive, and few employers were willing to allow a servant to board her child in their home. No wonder so many women abandoned their babies in the streets or at the almshouse.[27] Even those who could support their children temporarily might be attracted by the idea of indenturing their offspring when they were of working age. Public- and private-welfare agencies made indenture contracts for poor children. Their masters, and not parents or welfare agencies, then cared for the youngsters until adulthood, when presumably they had acquired enough skills to support themselves.[28]

Other groups who often relied on welfare agencies for their very survival were the ill and the aged poor. Naturally, temporary illness did not make a person dependent for life; only chronic and incurable diseases, including insanity, resulted in complete dependency. Nineteenth-century Americans also included among the incurable those with severe handicaps, such as the blind, crippled, and mentally retarded.[29] Such individuals, as well as many among the aged, required considerable care and attention; however, if their family was impoverished, this care was not easily provided. The Fitzsimmons family is a case in point. Deserted by her husband, Mrs. Fitzsimmons was left with four children in her care. To support the family, her eldest son, James, went to work in a cotton factory, but there he lost his arm in an accident. Mother and children no longer had any source of income and because of their poverty could not properly care for the injured boy. Fortunately, James was admitted without charge to the Pennsylvania Hospital for treatment.[30]

The records of this hospital and other private and public charities can be used to formulate a rough estimate of how many children, ill, crippled, and aged people there were in Philadelphia between 1800 and 1854. The figures reveal that the absolute number of dependent poor increased over the years, but their proportion of the city's population did not alter too much. In 1800, the number receiving public and private assistance was 1,590, or $2\frac{1}{2}$ percent of the population; by 1810, it was 2,800, or 3 percent.[31] In 1820, the total had climbed to 5,836 and had reached the highest proportion of the population it would attain in fifty-four years—5 percent. By 1829, the number of dependent poor had again dropped to 5,400, or 3 percent of the population.[32] Later, the number increased again—to 4,421 in 1840 and 7,415 in the following decade. Notwithstanding, because of the remarkable growth of the city's total population during these years, the percentage of dependent poor remained close to 2 percent at this time.[33]

A word of caution about these figures is in order. They are aggregate figures drawn from annual reports, since records of the names of people aided by most private charities are not extant. Hence, there may be some overlap: the same people may have obtained aid from several charitable sources in a given year. On the other hand, the figures may also be an understatement, since they represent only the number of dependent poor that the city's welfare agencies chose to assist. There may well have been others in need whose application for assistance was rejected. Policy considerations as well as moral, racial, and ethnic prejudices may have precluded granting aid to some dependent poor (see chapter 6 for a fuller discussion of this issue).

While most of the dependent poor were quite helpless, the laboring poor were slightly better off. Most could and did work, although they held very low-paying jobs. Among male workers, those who pocketed the most meager wages in early nineteenth-century Philadelphia were seamen and day laborers. They generally earned about one dollar a day, and seamen's wage rates declined steadily until 1830 at least. Mariners were particularly hard hit by the Embargo of 1807, when thousands lost their jobs.[34] In the 1820s, Mathew Carey, Philadelphia publisher and concerned observer of the city's working class, demonstrated that laborers' wages were so low as barely to enable them and their family to survive. Carey estimated that a laborer earning 75¢ a day, working six days a week, who lost eight weeks of work due to illness and seasonal unemployment, could earn $198 a year, but the minimal cost of supporting himself, his wife, and two children was $198.64.[35]

In addition to unskilled laborers, certain groups of skilled workers also experienced need. For example, in the 1820s, handloom weavers, who turned out textiles for which Philadelphia was justly famous, earned only $5 a week, less than what an unskilled laborer made in good times and only slightly better than he earned during depression years. Weavers improved their economic position in the midforties, but by the end of the decade, the take-home pay of some was less than most had earned twenty-five years previously.[36]

The laboring poor were not only men holding low-paying jobs. A large number of women who were heads of families were included in that group, since, in the nineteenth century, there were few jobs open to women, and those jobs paid little. Some women worked as domestics and earned only $1.25 a week, considerably less than day laborers or seamen.[37] The only other socially acceptable work for women was sewing, and at least in the early nineteenth century, it paid more than domestic service. Nonetheless, even at this time, a seamstress earned only about as much in a week as a carpenter or mason in a day.[38] By the 1830s, seamstresses' wages were much lower; of course, low wages paid to men may have served to depress female wage rates also. Because male, unskilled laborers earned barely enough to support their families, their wives may have taken up sewing to supplement their husband's earnings. These married women helped produce a surplus of seamstresses, which, in turn, served to depress wages of all women who sewed.[39]

Certainly, by the 1820s the lot of the single female seamstress was a hard one, as Carey confirmed, although he may have exaggerated somewhat. He argued that a single woman working twelve to fifteen hours a day could make nine shirts a week and thus earn $1.125, or $58.50, a year. The minimal annual cost of her rent, clothes, fuel, candles, and food amounted to exactly the amount she earned, Carey calculated.[40]

Thus far, I have defined the laboring poor by occupation; the city's lowest paid workers—day laborers, seamen, domestics, and seamstresses—were often impoverished. But the laboring poor had a distinctive ethnic composition as well—a large number of them were blacks or recent immigrants. This is not surprising, since lack of skills and discrimination kept both groups in the lowest paying jobs.

Philadelphia had a sizable number of black inhabitants. For the first forty years of the century, they constituted between 8–9 percent of the city's population. Most of them were not in bondage, because the gradual abolition of slavery in Pennsylvania had begun in 1780.[41] Yet discrimination relegated most blacks to low-paying jobs and forced them to live in "lofts, garrets and cellars, in blind alleys and narrow courts, with no advantages of sewerage, gas, or water, and with not a fresh pure breath of air from one week to another." Since few schools admitted blacks and many whites refused to lend them money, blacks found it almost impossible to enter the professions or establish their own businesses. In 1820, one-third of the city's blacks were servants, and most of the remainder held poorly paid jobs as porters, wood sawyers, and coachmen.[42] Their lot did not improve much over the years and may, in fact, have worsened, especially in the 1840s. By then, 70 percent of all black males toiled in low-paying jobs as laborers, porters, waiters, seamen, and carters. When newly arrived Irish immigrants competed with blacks for somewhat higher paying semiskilled jobs, as they frequently did in the 1840s, the Irish usually

At Dock Street Wharf (*Courtesy of The Library Company of Philadelphia*). An early nineteenth-century street scene that portrays the kind of work available to day laborers at the commercial port of Philadelphia.

won and soon replaced blacks as hodcarriers, stevedores, and dockworkers. The total wealth of three out of every five black households in the 1840s was $60 or less. Most blacks lived in extreme poverty. In 1846, a reporter found a black father and his seven children huddled in a cellar in Moyamensing. Without bedding or blankets, the children kept warm only by burying themselves under a pile of ashes. Blacks were the victims of six race riots between 1829 and 1854, and they lost the right to vote in 1838, when Pennsylvania adopted a new constitution. Prejudice against blacks was strong, even among reformers who worked to better the lot of the city's poor. In 1832, the Union Benevolent Association charged that blacks begged food from the well-to-do, sold it to poor whites for 2¢ a plate, pocketed their profits, and headed for the nearest tavern, where they promptly got drunk. Perhaps because of the riots and the considerable prejudice against them, many blacks left the city; by 1850, they numbered less than 6 percent of the population.[43]

In contrast to blacks, immigrants constituted a growing proportion of Philadelphia's population between 1800 and 1854. Students of the subject estimate that about 6,000 immigrants entered the city annually from 1800 to 1806, when difficulties with Britain curtailed immigration until 1817.[44] Even early in the century, the Irish were the largest ethnic group in Philadelphia; they accounted for about 12 percent of the population in 1800.[45] Later, substantial numbers of them flocked to the city in two waves—the first between 1828 and 1833 and the second in the 1840s, during the great potato famine in Ireland. Subsequently, the proportion of Irish in the population rose to 17.6 percent in 1850, and in the same year, the total number of foreign-born in the city was 29 percent of the population.[46]

Quite a few new immigrants, especially the Irish, arrived with no money at all and simply camped on the wharves until they could find work. Most possessed few skills, so the jobs they eventually found paid little. Irish women frequently became domestics, while many Irish men worked as day laborers, often along the wharves or on the roads. Others took up shoe-making, tailoring, or weaving—all cottage industries in their homeland. Unfortunately, at these skilled crafts, Irish men earned little. Weaving is a good example: handloom weavers in most years between 1820 and 1854 were among the lowest paid workers in the city. J. O. O'Neal was one such Irish weaver. He migrated alone to the United States in 1832 and soon began to earn decent wages. He then sent for his wife and family, but not long after they arrived in 1835, his wages fell by one-third. He then earned only $3 a week working from five or six in the morning until nine or ten at night. He and his family lived in a one-room basement in Kensington, and all seven of them (husband, wife, and five children) slept in one bed. Another migrant, "J. B.," was even less fortunate; he, too, came alone from Ireland,

> was much depressed, but commenced weaving with alacrity, and worked almost night and day. As soon as he had earned ten dollars, he deposited them in the hands of a merchant towards paying the passage of his wife and children. He was almost immediately taken with ... fever ... and died in two weeks. Some persons came forward and had him decently buried.

His wife and children then arrived and soon found themselves in "the most destitute situation, *not having even a bed to lie on.*"[47]

Irish Catholics were also the targets of riots in the 1840s. A decade earlier, in prosperous times, immigrant workers, many of them Irish, and native Americans cooperated in the General Trades Union, which fought for a ten-hour day and higher wages. The union was fairly successful until the Panic of 1837 produced considerable unemployment and caused employers to ignore previous wage agreements. Many unemployed native Philadelphians blamed their plight on their former immigrant allies, who presumably retained their jobs, because they were willing to work for less. At the same time, native Americans also agreed with the city's "press and pulpit ... in attributing hard times to God's wrath visited upon people fallen from grace...."[48]

Consequently, native-American workers sought to regain the prosperity of the past with self-improvement programs, which included temperance crusades and support for free public education. The temperate, well-educated native worker was sure to be more successful in the marketplace than was the hard-drinking immigrant.

Regrettably, "the temperance and public education movements" put native Americans on "a collision course ... with ... Catholic immigrants." The conflict began when, as a part of their temperance crusade, native Americans tried to close many of the pubs where Irish men drank. Native Americans also insisted that a proper public school education include daily readings from the Protestant King James Bible. Catholics, who accepted only the Douay version of the Bible, objected strongly, and consequently, school officials excused Catholic children from Bible reading. Even so, many Protestants rejected this compromise and in 1844, met in an Irish neighborhood in Kensington to express their views. The meeting ended in rioting that lasted for three days. Thousands flocked to Kensington from all over the city and districts to join in the arson, looting, and killing. Shortly thereafter, another bloody riot erupted, this time in Southwark when natives objected to Catholics storing arms in one of their churches. After the militia fired into a crowd of rioters, citizens in Southwark fought lengthy street battles with the soldiers.[49]

Immigrant laborers suffered severely during these riots, but the plight of all laboring poor, immigrant and black, laborer and seamstress, was never easy. Even during the most peaceful and prosperous years, Philadelphia's poor suffered, and between 1800 and 1854, the economic crises, severe winter weather, and epidemics, which periodically befell the city, further aggravated their harsh lot. In periods of economic depression, male laborers absorbed wage cuts or lost their job entirely, as did female domestics and seamstresses. When numerous city homes were abandoned by their formerly affluent occupants, many domestics sought work in vain, and seamstresses suffered during depressions when the demand for handmade clothing diminished. In any year, those who earned little found it difficult to save enough to purchase fuel and warm clothes in the winter months. Savings proved even harder to accumulate for those who were incapacitated for any length of time by the diseases that frequently recurred in the Philadelphia area.

Yet most laboring poor experienced hardest times when the unfortunate combination of illness, inclement winter weather, and economic depression hit the city simultaneously. This series of events transpired in the early 1820s when typhus and yellow fever plagued Philadelphians in the depression years following the Panic of 1819. Also in 1821, the city endured its coldest January since 1780; both rivers were icebound. The poor were everywhere, wandering through the streets and begging for food and fuel.[50]

While the number of laboring poor in Philadelphia may have loomed particularly large in the early 1820s, throughout the first half of the nineteenth century, they constituted a significant proportion of the city's population. Of course, exact figures are difficult to obtain. City directories rarely included the poor, and most census takers did not bother to enumerate occupations. However, analyses by scholars provide a general idea of the proportion of laboring poor in Philadelphia at the beginning and middle of the nineteenth century. One historian found that in the late eighteenth century, between "one-quarter and one-third of the free population" paid the minimum amount of taxes. These were the city's poorest citizens—most of them laborers, mariners, journeymen cordwainers, and tailors.[51] As for later on, the percentage of unskilled laborers in the city who earned barely enough to make ends meet can be used as another rudimentary guide to the proportion of laboring poor in Philadelphia. Another scholar has estimated that 16 percent of Philadelphia's population consisted of unskilled workers in 1820 and the figure had risen to 23 percent by 1860. Thus, in the first half of the nineteenth century, the percentage of laboring poor in the city remained roughly one-quarter of the population.[52]

This analysis of geography, population, politics, and economy pertains to Philadelphia from 1800 to 1854, but much of it also applies to other nineteenth-century cities as well. New York, Boston, and Baltimore, like Philadelphia, grew in size rapidly, underwent some geographical concentration of their well-to-do and dispersion of their laboring classes, suffered through the same depressions, inclement winters, yellow fever and cholera epidemics.

The percentage of blacks in most cities, not just Philadelphia, declined before 1860, and the influx of immigrants in the 1840s drove blacks in most urban centers to the lowest level jobs. In addition, the religious and ethnic tensions that divided Philadelphians in the 1830s and 1840s also troubled New Yorkers. Like Philadelphia, New York began to develop into a manufacturing center by the 1820s.[53]

Of course, the history of Philadelphia and other U.S. cities in the last century diverged somewhat. Even before the construction of the Erie Canal, New York had supplanted Philadelphia as the chief commercial entrepot in the country, and Baltimore also rivaled Philadelphia in commercial trade. While all northeastern cities attracted immigrants in the 1830s and 1840s, Philadelphia was not a major port of entry, and fewer foreign-born settled in the Quaker city than in New York or Boston.[54] Because of the long-time influence of the Society of Friends in Philadelphia, the city was also exceptional in the number of its citizens concerned with philanthropy.

Yet whatever their differences, all American cities in the years between 1800 and 1854 contained dependent and working-poor people who frequently sought assistance from welfare agencies. As will be seen in the next chapter, the manner in which public-welfare systems in Philadelphia and other cities responded to the needs of the indigent changed substantially during these fifty-four years.

Evolution of the Public-Welfare System

Throughout the late eighteenth and early nineteenth centuries, the words and actions of urban-welfare administrators reveal their three primary concerns. The first was purely humanitarian; welfare officials exhibited genuine solicitude for the plight of the poor. Many welfare officials espoused the traditional Christian doctrine, popular in both England and America at this time, that the well-to-do were simply stewards of God's wealth. They had an obligation to use their wealth not simply for their own benefit but also to aid the poor.

A second concern of welfare officials was somewhat less benevolent: it was their commitment to control the actions of the poor. A rather moralistic attitude toward the needy appeared in England in the early eighteenth century when some reformers began to hold the poor accountable for their own condition. Supporters of this view advocated constructing public workhouses.[1] This attitude prevailed in America later in the century and stimulated reformers to build almshouses and houses of industry, where the activities of the poor could be monitored.

A third concern of welfare officials was thrift. They were anxious to placate taxpayers by caring for the indigent in the most economical fashion. Since no one wanted to spend an enormous sum of money on the poor, welfare officials searched for the most economical way of administering relief in and out of the almshouse.

These three motivations—the desire to treat the poor humanely, watch their actions closely, and do both as economically as possible—always influenced welfare decisions, but the relative importance of any one of these three factors varied depending on the economic, social, and political temper of the times. In Philadelphia, economic downturns in the 1760s in the aftermath of the Seven Years' War and in the 1820s following the War of 1812 most decisively affected welfare-policy formulation. These depressions caused public officials to emphasize thrift and social control: to reduce most relief programs and force those who most desperately required aid into the almshouse. In more prosperous times, especially in the early eighteenth and early nineteenth centuries, when Philadelphia was not yet a sprawling metropolis, its welfare authorities were more inclined to indulge their humanitarian sympathy for the poor by extending needed financial assistance to many of the impoverished in their own homes and by administering the almshouse in a fairly benevolent fashion.

From the beginning of American history, throughout the country, citizens customarily entrusted both the collection of taxes for the poor and the expenditure of this money to an appointive body. Those selected were local residents who generally served without pay for a year as overseers of the poor.[2] Twentieth-century Americans may find this system peculiar, because we have grown accustomed to more specialization—today's welfare administrators do not also help raise the money they spend. The overseers of the past did both; they were generalists, not specialists. They collected what was called a poor tax. Whereas today we pay for welfare from local, county, state, and most importantly, federal taxes, in the eighteenth and nineteenth centuries, there was a tax just for the poor. Our ancestors became immediately aware of the cost of the public-welfare program when they paid this tax.

Philadelphia's public-welfare system followed the usual American pattern. Overseers began to levy and collect the poor taxes at some time after 1700.[3] At first, the overseers simply granted small sums of money to the indigent. Later, in the 1720s, an economic slump led Philadelphians, and New Yorkers as well, to construct almshouses where they hoped to relieve larger numbers of poor more economically. However, by the time these early almshouses were completed, prosperity had returned, and so they housed few poor. This form of welfare became known as indoor relief. Assistance to the poor outside institutions, or outdoor relief, remained the most popular mode of poor relief in the first half of the eighteenth century.[4]

At this time, the traditional notion of stewardship of the poor apparently determined most of the actions of public-welfare officials. The Elizabethan Poor Law of 1601 had established the principle that local governments had an obligation to care for the poorest of their citizens. This notion was part of the cultural heritage English people brought to America, and it was soon enacted into law on this side of the Atlantic.[5] Those who administered local welfare programs were simply the stewards of the state; they had an obligation to spend poor-tax monies wisely while always exercising proper Christian concern for the needy. These local officials, or overseers of the poor, literally acted as stewards as they personally visited the homes of the poor and dispensed aid on a one-to-one basis.

In seventeenth- and early eighteenth-century America, the humanitarian concerns of rural and urban welfare officials meshed nicely with the social and economic realities of the times. Country towns and even cities were then relatively small both geographically and in number. It was perfectly feasible for poor relief officials to walk through most urban centers to carry out their role of steward to the poor. Such a role was all the simpler to execute in the absence of severe economic crises; there were simply very few indigent to assist.[6]

All this changed at the conclusion of the Seven Years' War. Once contracts to supply the war effort ceased and British soldiers and sailors departed, American merchants and tradesmen suffered. At the same time, war widows and their children, wounded soldiers and their families, swelled the urban-poor population. The resumption of Irish and German immigration to Philadelphia at the war's end compounded the city's labor surplus. In America's largest cities, the laboring poor suffered the most in the depression of the 1760s. They had a particularly hard time paying for food and fuel, both of which grew more costly. As more and more people became impoverished, so, too, inevitably did the poor-tax rate rise.[7]

In Philadelphia, dissatisfaction with this turn of events led a group of Quaker merchants to offer to replace public authorities and administer the city's welfare system. The offer was accepted in 1766, and the Quakers proceeded, with government sanction, to begin constructing a new and larger almshouse. In return for their financial assistance, the Quakers were granted authority to administer the new asylum as well as to determine the amount of the poor tax to be paid by city residents. Philadelphia's old overseers of the poor, most of whom were long-time city artisans but not members of the Society of Friends, now simply collected the poor tax.

The new relief system came into being partly because of benevolent concerns traditional among the city's Quakers. More importantly, the new system also became reality, because these same Quakers were influenced by the English public-workhouse movement in the early eighteenth century. Like many Englishmen before them, these Quaker merchants distrusted the poor and believed that poor taxes were increasing, because more citizens were loafing or begging instead of working steadily. Quakers named their new Philadelphia almshouse the Bettering House, thereby classifying the poor as errant and needing reform. Certainly of equal and perhaps slightly more importance to officials who inaugurated the post-1760 welfare program in Philadelphia was the desire to economize. The new Quaker poor relief administrators believed it would be cheaper to reduce sharply outdoor relief and force the majority of the city's poor to work to support themselves in the new Bettering House.

Eventually, this welfare reform failed in Philadelphia. Poor taxes did not decline as they had been expected to do. Instead, these levies remained high to pay off the Bettering House debt and keep this institution functioning properly. Proceeds from the sale of products made by the poor did not substantially defray the cost of their institutionalization. Apparently, needy inmates rebelled and refused to labor intensively in the poorhouse. In an economically depressed city, the needy could no longer accept the old argument that linked hard work and prosperity.

At the same time, the overseers of the poor, who because of their social origins remained closer to the average city taxpayer than the Quaker-merchant almshouse managers, refused to collect poor taxes from those who could not easily afford to pay. Overseers continued to insist on the value of outdoor relief, which the city's least affluent residents seemingly preferred over almshouse incarceration.

Disillusionment with the failure of the Quaker merchants' reform program led to its demise in 1788, when a purely public-welfare system was restored. Thereafter, the almshouse was the chief relief-giving agency in the city, but a more benevolent form of welfare—aid to people outside the poorhouse—was expanded. Because by now the city had passed through the economic travails of the pre– and post–Revolutionary War Era, different concerns came to the fore.[8] In a relatively prosperous, geographically circumscribed, and not overly large (in terms of population) city, welfare officials could again give freer reign to their humanitarian sympathies, as they administered both outdoor and indoor relief.

When Philadelphians reconstructed their welfare system in 1788, poor relief was one of the few governmental services provided by a single agency to people in both the city and neighboring districts. Officials, now known as guardians of the poor, were appointed to represent Philadelphia, Northern Liberties, and Southwark on a new public board of guardians. Later, in the first quarter of the nineteenth century, representatives from Spring Garden, Kensington, Moyamensing, Richmond, and Penn District, were added to this board.[9]

The changing political climate in the city in the early nineteenth century affected the board of guardians of the poor slightly. After 1788, justices of the peace in the city and districts supposedly chose welfare officials, but in actuality, each outgoing guardian suggested his own replacement.[10] After Jefferson's election to the presidency in 1800, leaders of the city's growing Democratic-Republican Party began to object to self-perpetuating governing bodies in Philadelphia like the guardians of the poor. It seemed undemocratic to allow welfare officials to choose their own successors (and less idealistically, to perpetuate Federalist control of public relief). Petitioners demanded that the state legislature change the laws, and in 1803, the Democratic-Republican-controlled state administration responded by reorganizing the board of guardians.[11] Henceforth, welfare officials no longer determined their successors, but rather, the chief governing bodies in Philadelphia and the districts selected the guardians of the poor.[12]

Elections were held biannually until 1828. Guardians served staggered one-year terms, with half of them appointed in the spring and half in the fall. Annually, the board reorganized and appointed from among its members a few almshouse managers who subsequently met separately and supervised the almshouse. The pattern continued of having almshouse managers each year set the amount of the poor tax that the rest of the board, now known not as overseers of the poor but as outdoor guardians, collected. In addition, the outdoor guardians, like the old overseers, furnished aid to the poor in their own homes.[13]

Between 1800 and the passage of the 1828 poor law, which substantially altered the Philadelphia public-welfare system, most guardians of the poor were well established businessmen and artisans. A minority of one-third were among the city's most substantial citizens, merchants, gentlemen, and professional people. The rest were comfortably well off but probably not rich. They included sea captains, editors, owners of small manufacturing and business enterprises, and craftsmen.[14] Only 17 percent of the guardians were members of the Society of Friends. Most of the others for whom religious affiliation could be ascertained belonged to the more established churches, Presbyterian or Episcopal. Evidently, Quaker-merchant control of the public-welfare system was an artifact largely of the years between 1767 and 1788. From 1800 to 1828, the median age of guardians for whom it can be determined (less than one-half) was the late thirties, indicating that most of them were probably established in their jobs and had time to devote to community work. Nevertheless, throughout this era, two-thirds of the guardians of the poor rendered their only public service when they agreed to act as welfare officials. Most of the remaining one-third engaged in other charitable activities; a very few served in some governmental capacity.[15] Finally, the majority of guardians served the regulation one-year term and no more. Only 16 percent stayed on the board for a longer period.

Apparently, most public-welfare officials in early nineteenth-century Philadelphia resembled their predecessors, the eighteenth-century overseers of the poor. In both groups well-established artisans and proprietors of small businesses predominated. Only a minority were members of the city's philanthropic or political elite. In New York, at this time, most welfare officials were also businessmen, although many more than in Philadelphia were involved in politics.[16] Philadelphia's public-welfare system was not controlled by politicians until after the 1828-poor-law change.

Nathan Trotter is a fairly typical welfare official of this era. He was a Quaker businessman, a metals wholesaler, who was not much interested in either private charity or politics. During his life, he donated little money to philanthropic endeavors and at his death, left his fortune to his family. His only "political" commitment was his service on four juries. When he was thirty and his business career was on the rise, he decided to do his civic duty and agreed to serve one term as a guardian of the poor.[17]

Early in the century, like Nathan Trotter, most men probably took the job of guardian of the poor when it was offered to them, because they felt a sense of community responsibility for the poor. Of course, a few may have become guardians, because they were unable to pay the fine levied on those who refused to serve.[18] Still, most guardians were of an age and economic position that probably left them time and the wherewithal to devote to civic service. Perhaps the guardians turned to public- rather than private-charity work, because the former was more accessible to them. Since most of the boards of the city's private charities were self-perpetuating, with the same people serving year after year, many upwardly mobile Philadelphians may have entered public-welfare service, because it was their one point of access to the city's philanthropic network. Notwithstanding, few found the job interesting and attractive enough to remain for long. After all, guardians received no pay, had to attend frequent meetings and serve on numerous committees. Of those few who stayed for more than one term, most were almshouse managers; probably, the job of manager was more prestigious than outdoor guardian. Also, a manager had the opportunity to obtain lucrative almshouse-supply contracts for his friends—no small advantage. Even so, with so few managerial posts available, most had to take the less attractive position of outdoor guardian.

The conflict that had developed from 1760 to 1788 between well-off Quaker managers of the almshouse and the less affluent overseers of the poor continued even after a purely public-welfare system was reinstituted in Philadelphia.[19] This conflict may have persisted because of social-class differences between these two sets of welfare officials. As in earlier years, between 1800 and 1828, almshouse managers were more likely than outdoor guardians to be members of the city's elite. Of equal importance in promoting strife was the inherent awkwardness of having two sets of officials administer semiautonomous parts (indoor and outdoor relief) of what was supposed to be a unified welfare system. Outdoor guardians often complained about how much the managers spent on almshouse repairs. In 1805, outdoor guardians presumably gained the upper hand when, at their request, the state legislature passed a law giving them final approval of all expenditures made for the poor. But disputes between the two boards persisted. They argued over the duties of employees who served both boards and even over small personal slights.[20]

Despite this conflict, records of their deliberations in the first twenty years of the nineteenth century reveal a remarkable congruity between almshouse managers and outdoor guardians. Like their eighteenth-century predecessors, both groups were anxious to economize. They never advocated lavish expenditures of public monies on the poor. Even so, for early nineteenth-century welfare officials in Philadelphia the need to practice thrift was no longer so significant as it had been during the economic depression that followed the Seven Years' War, when poor taxes were difficult to collect, nor was thrift as necessary as it would be again during the Panic of 1819, when hard times once more seriously impaired many residents' ability to pay their poor tax. Similarly, the desire to oversee carefully the activities of the poor continued to influence Philadelphia's welfare administrators between 1800 and 1820. Its clearest manifestation— the city's almshouse or Bettering House—remained open and functioning. Yet, again, social control of the poor was not so pressing a worry in more prosperous times, when there were apparently fewer lazy poor in need of close supervision in the poorhouse.

And the early years of the nineteenth century in Philadelphia, while not without some economic travail, were generally prosperous. In such an economic climate, in what was still a walkable city, guardians of the poor felt free again to emphasize their humanitarian concerns for the city's indigent. Between 1800 and 1820, both almshouse managers and outdoor guardians remained committed to the principle of stewardship of the poor. It was their job personally to attend to the poor, and in the process, they came to empathize with the needs of the indigent. The managers acted as stewards when, in committees of two, they visited the almshouse biweekly, inspected the apartments, conversed individually with the inmates, and responded to their requests. As for the outdoor guardians, each had a special section of the city or districts in which he lived and functioned as a steward by supplying relief to the poor. He visited the indigent in their homes, or they sought him in his. As the city grew, more guardians were added in order to enable each to serve as steward in a moderate sized geographical area. In 1800, there were twenty guardians; there were thirty in 1803 and fifty by 1820.[21]

In their role as stewards, the guardians of the poor became quite familiar with the needs of destitute Philadelphians. As the outdoor guardians tended the poor in their neighborhoods, the officials gained an appreciation for the particular difficulties faced by the needy, especially during frigid winters and summer months marked by epidemics. Every winter when the hardships of the poor grew acute, guardians distributed bread and clothing, sometimes handing out the bread themselves and occasionally entrusting the task to members of private female charities. When illness troubled the poor, guardians provided them with free medicine and medical care. When contagious diseases spread among the indigent, welfare officials either paid the board of health to care for the ill in the city hospital or rented separate buildings near the almshouse to accommodate them.[22] Such epidemics in the city nearly always necessitated larger welfare expenditures.[23]

Not only in Philadelphia but also in New York, welfare officials responded quickly to the needs of the poor during harsh winters and epidemics, perhaps because both were immediately recognizable problems of specific duration.[24] Furthermore, since disease did not respect class lines, it was in the best interests of welfare officials everywhere to hospitalize promptly the ill poor. Also, it may have been easier to extend aid in a sympathetic fashion in inclement weather and during epidemics, because fuel and medical aid were fairly inexpensive forms of assistance.

In view of this fact, it is instructive that between 1800 and 1820, the Philadelphia guardians of the poor always spent less on these relatively economical forms of assistance than on the more expensive weekly cash payments to the poor in their own homes. This form of assistance, called pensions, was particularly useful: regular cash aid could be used to pay rent and purchase food. Admittedly, these relief payments were small: in 1814–15, the average outdoor pension was 77¢ a week.[25] Such a welfare payment amounted to three-fifths of the regular weekly wage of the lowest paid female workers in Philadelphia and just 13 percent of that of the poorest male laborers.[26] Economy was always a concern. But outdoor pensions were a humane and useful way of dealing with poverty: they permitted the poor to remain in their own homes in their own neighborhoods and elect to buy what they needed themselves.

Philadelphia's welfare officials also demonstrated sympathy for the poor by extending special aid to them during the Embargo of 1807. In that year, the Philadelphia guardians augmented their expenditures and began to expand the almshouse factory, where, they set to work many of the jobless who sought refuge in the public institution. The initial success of these efforts is confirmed by the fact that in 1808, the Philadelphia Premium Society, an organization formed by city businessmen to stimulate manufacturing during the embargo, awarded the almshouse three prizes for its cotton manufacturing. Eventually overcrowding, a consequence of so many unemployed entering the almshouse in 1807 and thereafter, necessitated converting the factory into living quarters for inmates and curtailing work relief.[27] Somewhat similar developments occurred in New York, where the almshouse also became overcrowded. However, during the embargo crisis in New York, authorities also expanded work relief to unemployed men outside of the almshouse, something that Philadelphia's officials did not do.[28] In neither city were work-relief programs completely successful, but at least in both, welfare officials tried to respond in a creative and helpful way to the needs of the indigent during the first commercial crisis of the new century.

In addition, during another sort of crisis in the War of 1812, poor relief authorities in New York and Philadelphia increased disbursements for outdoor relief, much of which went to the wives and children of American servicemen who were away fighting.[29]

In the first two decades of the nineteenth century, the Philadelphia guardians of the poor may have generally preferred to act as benevolent stewards to the poor, yet economy was perpetually a concern, albeit less important than it had been from 1766 to 1788 or would be again after 1820. Rather naturally, welfare officials did not want to incur the wrath of taxpayers by spending money foolishly. Two examples of the guardians' frugality in this era include their commitment to indenturing poor children and their enforcement of the settlement laws. At this time, both programs were popular with welfare authorities throughout the country.[30]

One important reason for indenturing indigent children of working age was to save the cost of supporting them until adulthood with public poor-tax monies. Customarily, welfare officials paid the mothers or wet nurses of children who were public charges to care for the youngsters until they were between three and seven. At that time, the children were considered old enough to be transferred to the almshouse, where they signed indenture contracts with craftsmen. Each contract stipulated that an artisan care and provide training for a child in exchange for his or her labor for a given number of years. This system was economical, because wet nurses and institutional care, both of which required the expenditure of public funds, lasted for only a few short years. Once indentured, public-welfare officials ceased to be financially responsible for a child.

Although an economical mode of assistance, indenturing, at least in the early nineteenth century, was not necessarily harmful to children. It was certainly consistent with existing attitudes and practices among the working and artisan classes. Poor children were better off if they could learn a trade and ultimately become self-supporting. And since almost all children at this time began work at a tender age, it was only natural for the guardians to expect children in their care to do the same.

Besides indenturing, another example of the guardians' commitment to economy was the enforcement of the settlement laws. These laws, which almost all states, including Pennsylvania, implemented, provided that only genuine residents of a community could obtain poor relief there. The settlement laws were a natural accompaniment of a localized system of welfare. In every community, citizens required that the poor taxes they paid be spent not on aid to wandering beggars, but on assistance to fellow residents in need. Thus, settlement laws determined who was a genuine resident and stipulated that nonresidents who sought welfare be removed to their place of birth, where they could seek aid.[31] Although these laws often proved cruel, they remained in effect in many states until the U.S. Supreme Court ruled them unconstitutional in 1969.[32]

Pennsylvania's poor laws contained lengthy passages on how to ascertain who was "settled" and entitled to relief and who was not. Most people gained settlement and became eligible for public aid by owning or renting property in the city for a year. However, indentured servants who came directly from Europe to Philadelphia, became bonafide residents in just sixty days. A seaport town like Philadelphia could probably ill afford to ignore the needs of the hundreds of immigrants who landed yearly at its wharves. Thus, legislators did not make it overly difficult for the needy immigrant to qualify for poor relief. This may help explain the large number of foreign-born on the city's welfare rolls.[33]

At first, Philadelphia's guardians of the poor tried to enforce the settlement laws themselves, but few of the guardians relished carting back poor people to their last place of residence to collect from nearby towns the money Philadelphia had spent on the poor before their removal. So in 1806, guardians and almshouse managers agreed to hire an agent who would live in the almshouse, examine the poor, and remove nonresidents.

The agent later assumed the chore of collecting various monies due to the guardians. By 1818, two assistant agents performed these same tasks in the northern and southern districts, respectively. Later, guardians engaged a collector of monies due to the board and a bookkeeper. After 1819, all employees worked in a centrally located office rented by the guardians.[34]

At first glance, it appears that the appointment of the agent and his subordinates reflected a desire on the part of welfare officials to pass on to others their role of stewards to the poor; actually, this is not the case. The guardians entrusted only time-consuming, unpleasant chores, such as collecting debts and keeping account books, to their employees and reserved for themselves the task of ministering personally to the needs of impoverished Philadelphians. And while guardians did not violate the principle of stewardship, neither did they abandon their commitment to economy when they hired these employees.[35] Their salaries in 1814–15 amounted to one-tenth of 1 percent of the total amount spent on public welfare in the Philadelphia area.[36]

Although the guardians of the poor endeavored to be economical in many ways, they, along with welfare officials in other cities, relied greatly on the most costly form of relief—institutionalization in the almshouse.[37] From 1800 to 1820, Philadelphia's authorities usually spent the bulk of their funds on this asylum and relieved more indigent in it than were aided in their own homes (see appendixes 1 and 2). Actually, these actions are not so contradictory as they seem. Throughout the country, welfare officials felt that almshouses promoted economy, because they discouraged people from applying for relief. Many people may have, indeed, avoided seeking assistance if it meant leaving their home and taking up residence in a public asylum.

Almshouses fulfilled another vital function as well: they allowed officials to supervise the activities of the indigent. In poor asylums, the indigent could be made to work, and if not cûred of their propensity toward laziness, at least prevented from engaging in debauchery.[38] Thus, the reliance of Philadelphia's and other American welfare officials on the almshouse indicates the desire to exercise social control over the poor. Yet, Philadelphia's almshouse managers did not pursue this desire relentlessly. They spent a great deal of time personally ministering to inmates; they willingly permitted many to move freely in and out of the asylum and avoided introducing strictly institutional furniture or dress (see chapter 4 for a fuller examination of these issues). The very existence of the almshouse, the sizable amounts of money spent on it, and the large numbers accommodated in it are evidence of the desire to monitor the activities of paupers. Yet, the rather benevolent fashion in which welfare officials managed the asylum indicates that social control was not of overwhelming importance to them.

Neither was frugality the chief objective of the Philadelphia guardians of the poor between 1800 and 1816. Their pattern of expenditures in these years clearly reveals their empathy for the poor, especially when economic and other crises menaced the city. Philadelphia's officials increased their outlays for poor relief in ten of the first sixteen years of the century—most sharply during the epidemics of 1802 and 1804, the depression of 1807, and the war years of 1813–15. Poor-tax assessments rose in seven of the first sixteen years of the century, while the poor-tax rate also climbed. A city taxpayer contributed more to the support of the poor than to any other county service.[39]

Interestingly enough, between 1800 and 1816, there was no citizen objection to the high poor taxes. Philadelphians may not have been too concerned, because they anticipated the large levies to be temporary: extra monies were required for a few years to pay off debts incurred by the pre-1803 poverty board and to cope with recurring crises brought on by the weather, epidemics, the embargo, and the war.[40] Each of these vicissitudes, while serious, was of short duration. Moreover, the embargo effectively terminated immigration for some years and may have diminished the number of poor foreigners seeking assistance. In any case, the proportion of poor receiving welfare was not alarming: at 29 per 1000 in 1810, it was not much higher than it had been a quarter of a century before.[41] (See table 1.) Finally, even though the guardians frequently augmented expenditures from 1800–1816, after particularly large increases in disbursements in years marked by epidemics and depression, they cut poor relief. This happened in 1806–7 and again in 1810–12. Ultimately, the poor-tax rate, which had risen so sharply from 4¢ to 80¢ per $100 of assessed valuation between 1803 and 1808, dropped somewhat to 26¢ in 1811.[42]

For all these reasons, Philadelphians did not object early in the century about the cost of poor relief. In fact, the one major complaint lodged against the guardians in these early years of the century was not that they

Poor Relief in Philadelphia, 1800–1848[a]

Year	Population[b]	Poor Tax Rate[c] (¢)	Poor Taxes[d] ($)	Poor Tax/1000 ($)	Expenditures ($)	Expense/1000 ($)	Recipients[e]	Poor/1000	Expense/Recipient ($)
1800	61,559	(4)	50,000	819	47,212	773	1,390	22	33.96
1810	87,303	(26)	88,000	1,011	92,202	1,059	2,500	29	36.88
1820	108,809	—	140,000	1,296	95,010	879	5,237	48	18.14
1829	(156,025)	22	90,000	576	83,508	(535)	6,488	(42)	12.87
1841	(233,854)	—	(177,077)	(759)	120,035	(515)	(12,630)	(54)	(9.50)
1848	(327,872)	18	189,425	579	148,296	(453)	(28,512)	(87)	(5.20)

SOURCES: **Population:** George Rogers Taylor, "Comment on Population," in *Growth of the Seaport Cities, 1790–1825,* ed. David T. Gilchrist (Charlottesville: University Press of Virginia, 1967), p. 39; Sam Bass Warner, Jr., *The Private City, Philadelphia in Three Periods of Its Growth* (Philadelphia: University of Pennsylvania Press, 1968), p. 51. **Poor-Tax Rate:** PCA, Poor Tax Duplicates, 1803–11. For 1829, see PCA, MGP, 15 June 1829. For 1848, see PCA, MGP, 14 May 1849. **Poor-Taxes:** for 1800, see PCA, MAHM, 7 May 1809; for 1810, see PCA, MAHM, 26 February 1810; for 1820, see PCA, MAHM, 9 March 1820; for 1829, see PCA, MGP, 5 January 1829. See also PCA, MGP, 11 February 1839, *Pennsylvanian,* 27 January 1843, and *Auditors' Report of the Accounts of the Blockley Alms-House for the Year 1848* (Philadelphia, 1849). **Expenditures:** for 1800, see PCA, MAHM, 22 March 1801; for 1810, see *Poulson's,* 19 February 1812; for 1820, see *Poulson's,* 22 May 1822; for 1829, see *Philadelphia Gazette,* 12 January 1831; for 1841, see *Pennsylvanian,* 27 January 1843; for 1848, see *Auditors Report of the Accounts of Blockley, 1848.* **Recipients:** for 1800, see PCA, GP, Treasurer, General Ledger, 1789–1803 vol. and *Report of the Committee Appointed to Inquire into the Operation of the Poor Laws,* Read, January 29th, 1825, *Mr. Meredith, Chairman,* in *Hazard's Register,* 2:54; for 1810, see PCA, GP, Treasurer's "Weekly Entries," 1809–15 vol. and John Mease, *The Picture of Philadelphia* (Philadelphia, 1811; reprint ed., New York: Arno Press, 1970), p. 295; for 1820, see *Poulson's,* 29 May 1822 and PCA, MGP, 20 November 1821; for 1829, see *Philadelphia Gazette,* 12 January 1831 and *Hazard's Register,* 5:345 and PCA, MGP, 1829, passim ("visitors of the poor" reports); for 1841, see *Auditors Report of the Accounts of Blockley Alms-House for the Fiscal Year Ending May 17, 1841* (Philadelphia: Mifflin and Parry, 1841); for 1848, see *Auditors Report of the Accounts of Blockley, 1848.*

[a]This table from Gary Nash, "Poverty and Poor Relief in Pre-Revolutionary Philadelphia," *William and Mary Quarterly* 33 (January 1976): 9, enables readers to compare Nash's data on the eighteenth century with mine on the nineteenth. All estimates are in parentheses.

[b]The 1841 and 1848 figures assume a linear relationship between the 1840 and 1850 population figures.

[c]The earliest nineteenth-century records are for 1803, which indicate the rate was then 4¢, and I have estimated that it was the same in 1800. The 1810 rate is an estimation based on the assumption that it was identical to the 1811 rate.

[d]The 1841 figure is an estimate based on the assumption there is a linear relationship between the 1839–40 and 1842–43 poor-tax assessments.

[e]These figures include both those housed in the almshouse and after 1820, in the children's asylum and those who received outdoor relief. The institutional admission figures may be somewhat inflated, because some people may have been admitted more than once in a year. As for the outdoor-relief figures, before 1841, they include only those who received regular weekly pensions from the guardians of the poor, although not many received any other form of relief in these years. The 1841 and 1848 figures include all those who received wood relief (by then the major form of outdoor aid). Some people received pensions and some medical aid in these years, but I have assumed that such indigent also received wood. Thus, these figures are estimates.

had done too much, but that they had done too little to cope with distress. During the coldest months of 1805, well-to-do Philadelphians formed committees to collect funds for the impoverished and proposed to the state legislature revamping the public-welfare system in such a way that more work in and out of the almshouse could be provided for the poor, so they could remain self-sufficient in winter as well as summer.[43]

Although never written into law, the 1805 proposal did lead to some changes in the public-welfare system.[44] Nineteen members of the 1805 citizens' collection and distribution committees became outdoor guardians or almshouse managers in the next five years. At their urging, welfare officials began a program to enlarge almshouse manufacturing in 1805 and 1806 and expanded this program even further during the embargo crisis, which began in 1807. Welfare officials also initiated a new program, which remained in effect for the next two decades, of employing women at spinning in their own home.[45]

By the 1820s, the prosperous era that had so largely conditioned the sympathetic response of welfare officials to the poor was over. The serious economic depression that followed the War of 1812 occasioned a shift in the balance of concerns of the Philadelphia guardians of the poor. They began to exhibit more interest in economy and less empathy for the needy. Nonetheless, most guardians retained a philanthropic commitment to aiding the indigent and continued to visit and assist the poor in their homes or in the almshouse and to extend cash aid and medical assistance. Likewise, in the 1820s, the guardians did not abjure their goal of controlling the activities of the indigent: they persisted with institutionalization and close supervision of the poor in the almshouse. Yet humanitarianism and social control, while important, were not nearly so vital to the guardians in the 1820s as thrift. The economic problems posed by the Panic of 1819 necessitated a greater interest in money-saving schemes. Also, first the depression after the War of 1812, then, in later years, social and political disputes in the city and districts provoked many Philadelphians to demand cutbacks in welfare. This public pressure, which culminated in the 1828 poor-law reform, likewise affected the guardians and throughout the decade, kept them committed to economy in poor relief administration.

Public concern about the increase in welfare recipients and poor taxes, accompaniments to the post-War-of-1812 depression, first found expression in 1817. Philadelphia's elite then launched an investigation of poverty in the city. Citizens convened a public meeting and appointed some of their members to study the causes of pauperism. This inquiry led to the formation of the Pennsylvania Society for the Promotion of Public Economy, and its library committee, composed principally of wealthy Philadelphians, including philanthropist Roberts Vaux, completed and published a study on indigence. In this report, the library committee listed many reasons for destitution, including low wages paid to women, increased immigration of poor foreigners, and unemployment occasioned by the depressed state of manufacturing, cold winters, and illness. But the committee argued that the major cause of pauperism was a moral failing—intemperance.[46] Suddenly, instead of empathy for the poor who were unemployed due to the economic travails of the postwar era, their propensity to drink was used to explain their impoverishment. This attitude marks a major change from the prewar era.

Not only in Philadelphia did citizens examine the poor and find them morally wanting: in Boston, New York, and Baltimore, investigations of pauperism in the depression years between 1817–20, were also launched and they, too, revealed intemperance to be a major cause of unemployment and rapidly increasing welfare rolls.[47]

Pauperism was the word used frequently in all these cities. To nineteenth-century Americans, paupers were the unworthy poor, those who preferred to rely on public and private relief rather than work. Thus, pauperism was the dependence on welfare of intemperate, lazy, and frequently promiscuous individuals. Such paupers were quite distinct from the worthy poor, who drank sparingly and labored willingly, but who, through no fault of their own, became impoverished due to illness or unemployment. The worthy poor rarely asked for charity, and if they received aid, made good use of it. Unlike paupers, the worthy poor never became dependent on welfare. In 1817, in all eastern cities, the first concern of reformers was pauperism. They did not ignore the worthy poor, but they clearly considered them to be of secondary importance. Individual moral weakness engendered most destitution: people were poor because they were too lazy or intemperate to keep a regular job. This emphasis on immorality among the indigent reflects a growing distrust of them.

During these same years in England, there was also considerable concern about pauperism, where, as in America, a postwar depression resulted in unemployment and a swiftly climbing poverty rate. In 1817, a Select Committee of the House of Commons studied pauperism and found, as had Americans, that the indigent were responsible for their own condition. Englishmen also contended that since the poor grew dependent on public relief, the welfare system actually promoted pauperism and therefore should probably be abolished.[48]

Philadelphia's guardians of the poor did not go so far as to eliminate welfare in the post-War-of-1812 years, but they certainly curtailed it. In 1819, when unemployment was on the rise and more people were seeking public assistance, the guardians called a meeting with city and district officials to ascertain how best to employ the poor during the "depressed state of domestic manufactures." However, officials formulated no work-relief projects at this meeting. Instead, outdoor guardians tried to reduce welfare rolls by limiting those eligible for monetary assistance to the very old, very young, handicapped, and ill. The guardians also sharply reduced the amount paid these people. The guardians completed their economy drive by cutting the salaries of their employees. Meanwhile, almshouse managers discharged all inmates who appeared in some way capable of supporting themselves. The most immediate concern of welfare officials during the depression was not how best to aid the poor, but how to reduce the cost of welfare.[49]

In stressing thrift, guardians acted partly out of necessity. The postwar depression not only left thousands jobless and in need of relief; it also so reduced the income of many others that they found it exceedingly burdensome to pay their taxes. Guardians worried that they could not collect tax monies from everyone and thus were determined to keep poor taxes high— higher than all other taxes assessed for county services. From 1817–25, levies for Philadelphia's needy were greater than they had been at any time earlier in the century (see appendix 1). Although the actual tax rate is not known, the poor tax per thousand Philadelphians in 1820 was 28 percent higher than in 1810 (see table 1). Just as guardians had expected, many Philadelphians turned collectors away; by the end of 1822–23, welfare officials had in their coffers just $40,000 of the $100,000 levied. The tax situation did not improve in 1823 and 1824. Guardians borrowed money regularly to meet expenses and as early as 1820, sought to balance their budget by cutting the amount spent on each relief recipient to about half of what it had been in 1810.[50] Meanwhile, immigrants, no longer impeded by the war, flocked to the city and swelled the ranks of the unemployed. More people applied for public relief than ever before; in 1820, forty-eight people in every thousand, more than double the figure of ten years ago, were on the public-welfare rolls (see table 1).

After the War of 1812, not only in Pennsylvania, but throughout the northeastern United States, there were huge increases in the number of poor. In the early 1820s, state legislators in Pennsylvania, New York, Massachusetts, and New Hampshire initiated investigations into poverty. Although the Pennsylvania study, conducted in 1821, did not motivate legislators to act, inquiries made in other states proved more productive. When these investigations concluded that the needy themselves were to blame for the increase in pauperism, state officials endorsed the construction of poorhouses with farms attached. Presumably, the establishment of work-oriented institutions as the only dispensers of relief would discourage the lazy poor from becoming dependent on the public-welfare system.[51]

The English Parliament also undertook several investigations in the 1820s of various aspects of poverty, but they led to no alterations in the laws. At the same time, the writings of Thomas Malthus, Thomas

Chalmers, and others stimulated interest in the complete abolition of the poor laws, but the harshness of this view provoked many to reject it by the end of the decade.[52] Nevertheless, the theory that relief payments that supplemented the earnings of low-paid laborers should be eliminated grew more popular. Such payments, inaugurated in Speenhamland in 1795, probably became more widespread during the Napoleonic Wars; recipients were largely underemployed men. The only counterpart to these payments in Philadelphia and other U.S. cities were cash pensions that may also have supplemented wages but were largely given to women. In nineteenth-century America, men were rarely granted outdoor cash aid (see chapter 3). Because those who benefited from this aid were so different, allowances supplementing wages in England and cash pensions in America were not identical. Even so, the substitute for allowances adopted by many English localities in the 1820s—namely, the workhouse as the only bestower of relief for the able-bodied—became a popular welfare panacea in America also.[53] As we have seen, by 1825, legislators in several states advocated erecting new poorhouses, and three years later, Pennsylvania lawmakers did the same.

In these three years, Philadelphia's economy revived. As one citizen observed in 1825, in the last six months, "the city has been healthy, labour abundant, and distress has vanished from our city and suburbs." This return to prosperity did not lessen many residents' hostility toward the poor and the welfare system; one resident remarked, "Those who are incapable of any kind of labour must of course be provided for, but the number of such is very small."[54] This harsh attitude toward the poor, originally provoked by the Panic of 1819, intensified through the 1820s, because of sharp social and political conflicts between residents in the city of Philadelphia proper and those in the adjacent districts. Both areas were, of course, parts of a unified poor relief system. Philadelphians resented the fact that because the total wealth of the city was greater than that of the districts, city dwellers paid the largest proportion of poor taxes, yet relief rolls bulged with indigent from the outlying areas. Such was not always the case. From 1800 to 1819, more residents from Philadelphia than the districts received both aid in the almshouse and outdoor relief. In contrast, between 1820 and 1828, while the majority of almshouse inmates continued to hail from Philadelphia, indigents from the districts dominated outdoor-relief rolls.

The turning point was 1820, because in that year, due to the population spreading farther from the city into distant districts, more guardians from these outlying areas were appointed. District guardians expressed sympathy for their needy neighbors by expanding outdoor aid to them. This turn of events angered Philadelphians, as did the fact that after 1820, city representatives were, for the first time, outnumbered by district representatives on the board of guardians. The conflict had a political component as well: the Democratic-Republican-controlled governments in the districts appointed their representatives, while councils dominated by Federalists chose the city's guardians.[55] Angered by the costliness of outdoor cash aid given largely to the poor in the districts by Democratic-Republican welfare officials, Philadelphians, many of whom, if not avowed Federalists, were at least political conservatives, initiated the poor-law-reform movement in the late 1820s to reduce public welfare. District leaders fought poor-law reform but lost.

In 1825, the case of conservative Philadelphians against the welfare system was made by a wealthy Federalist lawyer and legislator from the city, William M. Meredith, when he presented a report on Philadelphia's poor relief program to the state legislature. In most ways, Meredith's report was simply a recapitulation of many of the arguments against public welfare leveled by English people in previous years. Like them, Meredith insisted that the effect of all poor laws was to increase the number of poor "and to destroy or diminish the virtue and industry of the labouring classes." This unfortunate trend had developed, because public relief inevitably went to many undeserving applicants whom welfare officials never bothered to investigate, because they were giving away other people's money and not their own. According to Meredith, as long as public welfare was available, the poor, most of whom were intemperate, would obtain it and so avoid work. Meredith also argued that private-welfare rolls went up in conjunction with public ones. Nonetheless, he was probably not familiar with attempts by various English localities in the 1820s to make the workhouse the center of the welfare system. Instead, Meredith argued that institutionalizing the poor would not solve the poverty problem. If almshouses were at all comfortable, the poor would flock to them and relief costs would soar. Further, Meredith contended, such institutions were not self-supporting, because the idle poor could not be forced to work.

Although it would appear from Meredith's report that he like many English people in the early 1820s, wanted to terminate all poor relief, the American did not openly urge abolition. Rather, he proposed three economy measures. First, he suggested that the settlement laws be repealed, because they were too costly to enforce, and second, that there be no more increase in poor-tax rates. Finally, he wanted elected representatives directly chosen by the voters in the city and districts, and not by the guardians of the poor, to set these rates. Since in 1820 the population of Philadelphia was greater than that of all the districts combined, Meredith may well have expected representatives chosen by the whole urban area to be more anxious than the district-dominated board of guardians to please Philadelphia taxpayers by keeping levies small.[56]

Meredith put the Philadelphia guardians of the poor on the defensive.

They objected to his suggestions for change, and several of them wrote to the newspapers, albeit anonymously, defending the amounts they had spent on the poor in previous years and insisting that they had practiced thrift. The guardians had indeed tried to curb expenditures during the Panic of 1819 and thereafter, but Meredith's proposal to set a limit on poor-tax rates was too much of an economy measure for them. Acting as personal stewards to the poor, most guardians still sympathized with the needy. Therefore, the board appointed its own committee on poor-law revision and successfully combated an effort by a Meredith-inspired state legislature to prevent all escalation of poor taxes as well as all borrowing by the guardians.[57] Yet, eventually Philadelphia's representatives on the board of guardians convinced others of the enormous public interest in poor-law revision and suggested that the board try to influence the course of change itself. In 1827, the board appointed a committee of four guardians, all conservative, wealthy Philadelphians, which was chaired by Robert Earp, a friend of Meredith's, to investigate welfare programs in other cities and recommend improvements in the Philadelphia plan.

The committee concluded that the welfare systems of all the cities studied, including New York, Boston, and Baltimore, were superior to Philadelphia's. Not surprisingly, these Philadelphians found the worst abuses in their system "in administration of relief, *other than in the Alms House*" (my italics). They decried outdoor cash relief to the poor, which, of course, by now went largely to families in the districts, and sought to minimize this form of aid and alternatively emphasize outdoor relief in kind and institutionalization. Chairman Earp once confided to Meredith that he, Earp, thought the Southwark commissioners appointed guardians "to answer the political purposes of designing politicians." Perhaps with an eye to regaining control of the board of guardians from politicians in the districts, Earp and his fellow Philadelphians on the committee suggested that the board be revamped with fewer members serving longer terms. The committee also repeated the arguments of many of the earlier critics of public welfare. For example, the committee expressed alarm at the number of poor immigrants in the city in the postwar era "who never have *nor never will* contribute one cent to the benefit of this community, and who have in many instances been public paupers in their own country." To raise funds for immigrant aid, the committee suggested that a head tax on all incoming ship passengers, similar to the one in New York, be assessed in Philadelphia. In addition, guardians voiced the oft-repeated argument that individuals became dependent because of drink and the concern that such people were not properly punished by the present relief system. Therefore, the committee suggested that in the future the intemperate poor be made to work in the almshouse to repay the cost of their care.[58]

The 1827 study differed from Meredith's in that it contained more concrete suggestions for change and lauded rather than criticized alms-house care. The report impressed many city residents, including Carey, who wrote a series of articles publicizing it. He went farther than the guardians, however, and proposed the complete abolition of outdoor relief. At Carey's suggestion, citizens convened a town meeting in July 1827, at which time they appointed a committee made up of a majority of wealthy Philadelphians and a minority of district representatives to draft an indictment of the poor relief system and a series of suggestions for its improvement.[59] The committee's report was adopted and sent to the legislature in the form of a petition or memorial.

The memorialists, like almost all reformers since 1817, worried about immigration and hence endorsed the guardians' suggestion that a head tax be levied, with the income therefrom used to help defray the cost of public welfare in Philadelphia. Yet, immigration was not the chief concern of these reformers of 1827–28. They were more interested in eliminating outdoor relief and augmenting the influence of Philadelphians on the board of the guardians of the poor.

Like all the Philadelphia reformers before them who resented so much outdoor cash relief being dispensed in the districts, the memorialists criticized outdoor aid and proposed eliminating it except for temporary relief in kind as soon as a new larger almshouse could be constructed. In common with reformers elsewhere in the United States and England in the 1820s, these Philadelphians put their faith in the poorhouse, which they expected would both reduce relief expenditures and punish the lazy and intemperate.

As for the board of guardians itself, the memorialists proposed that the number of guardians be reduced to twelve—six from the city and six from the districts. In this way, Philadelphians would regain power on the board—power they had lost in 1820. To stabilize this new arrangement, each guardian would serve for not one but three years. This smaller group of guardians would concentrate on administration (activity befitting the high social status of those whom conservative Philadelphia welfare reformers hoped to have on the board) and leave the chore of dealing with needy individuals to employees. To unify and consolidate the power of these new guardians, the memorialists suggested that the old, separate board of almshouse managers be eliminated. As for the excessive financial power of the old board, first noted by Meredith, the memorialists proposed to reduce it by having the amount of the poor tax determined not by the guardians, but by a board of twelve directors chosen from among the city councilmen and district commissioners.[60]

By pressing for a reduction in the size of the board of guardians, Philadelphians may have been seeking largely to enhance their own influence, but regardless of their motivation, this reform was probably necessary, given the social reality of urban Philadelphia in the 1820s. The growth of the city had required the appointment of more members to the board of guardians, so that by 1820, there were fifty of them, and each outdoor guardian in 1823 and 1825 attended to an average of 126 pensioners. It would have been an Herculean task for any official, working part-time on relief, as most did, to become intimately acquainted with the needs of over one hundred destitute people. Earlier, in 1814–15, when both the city itself and the welfare board were smaller, each outdoor guardian attended to forty-one pensioners on the average, a much more manageable number.[61] The increasing size of the city had made the old relief system based on stewardship difficult to maintain. Moreover, a large welfare board of constantly changing members was chaotic. It seemed preferable to transform the guardians from almsgivers to administrators and create a new bureaucracy to handle aid to the poor.

Philadelphia's representatives in the state legislature drafted a bill incorporating all of the suggestions in the memorial adopted by the town meeting—suggestions that were clearly more to the benefit of the city than the districts. This bill also lengthened the time it took an immigrant servant to gain residency (and entitlement to poor relief) from sixty days to six months, reduced the amount each citizen could be taxed to support the poor, and created a special commission to erect a new almshouse.[62] Not surprisingly, district representatives in the legislature fought the bill. They particularly objected to the provision terminating outdoor relief but failed to have it stricken from the legislation. In addition, one district unsuccessfully sought to obtain more representation on the board of guardians and another tried but failed to separate itself from the poor district entirely.[63]

There are several parallels, and some notable distinctions, between the ways in which Philadelphia's welfare system was revamped in 1828 and similar efforts to alter poor relief in both England and other American cities in the 1820s and 1830s. At this time, institutionalization of the poor in almshouses became the most accepted mode of relief in the United States and Britain. Yet, Philadelphians, in abolishing outdoor cash aid in 1828, took a far more drastic step than other reformers at home and abroad. Bostonians and New Yorkers continued to supply some cash relief and so, too, did the English. In New York, a welfare bureaucracy appeared even before it did in Philadelphia. By 1808, New York's almshouse commissioners had assumed largely supervisory roles. They relied on employees to dispense relief to city residents. Philadelphians created and operated their own welfare bureaucracy only after 1828, and so, too, did the British; their poor-law reform of 1832–34 also required people be hired to minister to the needy while welfare officials became exclusively administrators.[64]

When the 1828 poor law went into effect, Philadelphia's councils immediately appointed some of the city's most prominent citizens to the board of guardians. Public welfare had become so much a cause célèbre that Thomas P. Cope and Mathew L. Bevan, wealthy merchants and philanthropists, were willing to relinquish membership on the illustrious board of managers of the Pennsylvania Hospital and serve instead as guardians of the poor. While the Philadelphians appointed were notable for their philanthropic commitment, almost all the district representatives were politicians, including John Keefe, later president of the Southwark Commissioners, William Binder, long-time Northern Liberties Commissioner, and Dr. Jesse R. Burden, whose career is typical of many guardians of this era.

Burden was a fellow doctor and political confidant of Joel B. Sutherland, who began to build a Democratic political machine in Southwark and Moyamensing in the 1820s. Sutherland first served in the state legislature and then went to Congress in 1826, at which point Burden took his place in the state house. About the same time, the Southwark Commissioners, many of them Sutherland's political cronies, appointed Burden as guardian of the poor, a job he held for nine years (three terms). Burden was a politician working his way up the ranks of Sutherland's southside Democratic machine, and being a guardian of the poor was just one way of serving his party.[65]

The pattern of governmental and charitable activities of Burden and his fellow guardians of the poor, from 1829 to 1854, was quite dissimilar from that of their predecessors. Earlier, only one-third of the guardians performed any kind of community service beyond serving as a public-welfare official, but two-thirds of the guardians from 1829–54 engaged in some other type of governmental or charitable work. Three-fifths of these men were, like Burden, government officials. Most hailed from the districts, which, contrary to the expectations of 1828 reformers, gained more representatives on the board, so that they outnumbered Philadelphia's guardians of the poor by 1844. The districts simply grew in population faster than the city and hence demanded and obtained more power on the welfare board. It is also interesting that 37 percent of the guardians of the later era, like Burden, remained in office for more than one term, even though terms were longer after passage of the 1828 poor law. From 1800 to 1828, only 16 percent of the welfare officials served more than a single one-year term.

In other ways, guardians of the 1829–54 era were not unlike earlier welfare officials in Philadelphia. Occupationally, they were much the same: one-third were well-to-do merchants, bankers, brokers, and doctors, while the rest were grocers, druggists, artisans, tradesmen, and proprieters of small businesses. About the same proportion of guardians after 1828 as before were members of the Society of Friends.[66]

Yet, what is most distinctive about the guardians appointed after 1828 is that so many were low-level politicians. Like Burden, they held elective office or were serving political apprenticeships before winning nomination to higher posts. Appointment to the position of guardian of the poor was both a reward and a method of rendering further political service. The position was a reward, because even though guardians received no salaries, they enjoyed a number of privileges, such as access to their own carriage and frequent dinners at public expense. Baskets of vegetables from the almshouse farm and innumerable supplies from the institution's store-rooms were also available to them free of charge. Those who served as treasurer of the board had the opportunity of using taxpayers' money for speculative purposes and enhancing their personal fortune. This practice worked to the detriment of Treasurer John Hemphill, who, during the depression of 1837–42, built several buildings with poor-tax funds and then found that he could not sell them. When auditors checked his accounts for 1841–42, they found only $60 of the $32,000 that was supposed to be there. Of course, not everyone could be treasurer and gain access to tax monies, but quite a few guardians could and did serve on committees that pur-chased supplies for the almshouse.[67] Such service allowed committee members to obtain kickbacks and grant favors to friends. Seemingly, the financial attractions of service in public welfare were considerable enough to persuade many welfare officials to serve several terms on the Philadel-phia board of guardians. In 1853, critics published convincing evidence that two longtime board members had benefited financially from several almshouse supply contracts, but their fellow guardians exonerated both from any wrongdoing. Abuse of the position of welfare official eventually earned the board of guardians the unflattering appellation of the board of buzzards in the 1850s.[68]

These politicians who oversaw the city's post-1828 public-welfare pro-gram were much less interested than their predecessors had been in creating and maintaining humanitarian programs to aid the city's indigent. Of course, the guardians were not altogether uncharitable. After 1828, as well as before, Philadelphia's welfare officials demonstrated sympathy for those impoverished by disease: they continued to extend free medication and medical care to the needy.[69] Officials also supplied food and fuel to the hungry and cold during the winter months. Beginning in 1828, the new guardians handed out more groceries, coal, and medicine to the poor than had their predecessors. By the 1840s, fuel aid became predominant: guardians then supplied more people with wood and coal than with any other forms of public aid (see appendix 2). In this way, guardians reversed the priorities of welfare officials in an earlier era, who seemingly assisted most poor in the almshouse and a fewer number with cash pensions. Of course, after 1828, guardians never doubted the efficacy of the almshouse, but it accommodated only the lazy and the helpless; there were many more laboring poor in the city. To those, who earned little and were often out of work in the winter, fuel was a very useful form of assistance. Cash aid would have been even more helpful, but after 1828, guardians gave very little monetary relief even when they were legally empowered to do so. (Only between 1835 and 1840 did state law forbid granting cash pensions in Philadelphia.) Guardians argued that pensions were both costly and "pauperizing": they encouraged the indigent to become dependent on welfare indefinitely. In contrast, receiving an occasional load of wood was not likely to make someone permanently dependent on welfare. Just as important, fuel aid was relatively inexpensive: officials purchased large lots of wood at low prices in the summer and kept it for winter distribution.[70] Other forms of relief in kind, such as medicine and food, were also among the cheapest forms of public assistance. Thus, providing free wood, medication, and groceries to large numbers of poor people between 1828 and 1854 is evidence of both the guardians' humanitarianism and their dedication to economy.

The refusal of Philadelphia's guardians of the poor after 1828 to increase poor relief in economically depressed years, while further proof of the guardians increasing belief in thrift, is also confirmation of some decline in sympathy for the needy. During the Panic of 1837, neither in Philadelphia nor in New York did welfare officials bother to expand aid to the indigent. When the panic began, Philadelphia's guardians were legally unable to grant cash aid, probably the most useful form of assistance in a depression, since it helped those out of work pay their rent and buy food and fuel. In 1840, before the depression was over, the state legislature empowered the guardians again to grant pensions, but they chose to give very few; between 1840–43, welfare officials assisted on the average less than 200 people a year with cash relief (see appendix 2). Although the guardians augmented expenditures in 1837–38, they spent less during the rest of the depression years and did not much expand almshouse admissions either (see appendixes 1 and 2). In 1841, the poor-tax assessment per thousand Philadelphians was about $759, greater than it had been in 1829 but less than in the depression year of 1820 (see table 1). The only special assistance guardians gave the city's poor in these difficult years was free soup and wood, both of which were intended as much to help the indigent cope with cold winters as survive the depression.[71]

Guardians not only responded minimally to the needs of the poor in the depression following the Panic of 1837, they also supplied little in the way of special assistance to the thousands of immigrant poor who flocked to the city in the late 1840s. Welfare officials spent more in the second half of the decade than they had in the first, and they also admitted more people to the almshouse, a large portion of whom were foreign-born, most of them Irish (see appendixes 1 and 2 and chapter 4). However, the increase in absolute numbers admitted is deceiving; the fraction of the total city population in the almshouse was roughly the same in 1850 that it had been ten years before. In addition, guardians did not attempt to aid those Irish made homeless by the 1844 riots. In 1834, welfare officials opened the almshouse to blacks whose homes had been destroyed in rioting that year, but not to immigrants who were burned out ten years later.[72]

Not only did the guardians commitment to frugality prevent them from extending special aid to poor immigrants in the 1840s or to the unemployed during the depression in 1837–43; it also justified continuation of an old economy program—the enforcement of settlement laws. Another traditional relief measure, indenturing poor children was, by the 1840s, no longer so economical as it once had been, hence, guardians, in the interest of frugality, deemphasized this program.[73]

Among welfare officials between 1828–54, the need to economize became more predominant, as did the desire to exert more social control over the poor. Even before the 1828 law required guardians to do so, they sent most recipients of cash relief to the almshouse. Presumably, the asylum would better punish and possibly reform the lazy poor than would outdoor pensions, which allowed the destitute altogether too much independence. Of course, complete reliance on the almshouse was an economy measure as well: only the most desperately poor would relinquish freedom to enter the institution. As it turned out, when officials suspended *all* outdoor cash aid in 1835, no former pensioner elected to enter the new poorhouse. For the next five years "the iron and heartless provision" that sent all poor to the almshouse "remained uncontested." Not until a depression swelled the ranks of the poor, did the state legislature in 1840 re-institute cash relief in Philadelphia, but even then, guardians deliberately chose to grant such aid to very few poor.[74] Cash aid and institutional care were the two most substantial forms of public relief, and in stressing the latter and almost totally ignoring the former, post-1828 guardians indicated a commitment, stronger than their predecessors', to closely supervising the activities of the most destitute public charges.

The explanation for Philadelphia welfare officials' diminishing empathy for the poor and growing emphasis on thrift and social control is simple. Thanks to the 1828-poor-law reform, guardians became administrators instead of almsgivers; employees of the guardians, including the agent and the visitors of the poor, rather than guardians themselves, were the officials to whom the indigent applied for aid. While the practice of stewardship had previously stimulated compassion for the needy, its absence caused welfare officials in the 1830s and thereafter to lose interest in the real-life concerns of the city's poor.

The position of agent was not a new one. Ever since 1806, guardians had employed someone to handle settlement cases and supervise the care of illegitimate children. After 1828, the agent retained these former duties and also took on the additional tasks of managing the guardians' office in the city and collecting the head tax on immigrants, authorized by the new poor law. If the agent needed any assistance in executing these duties, he sought it from the visitors of the poor.[75]

These visitors of the poor, who earned $400–$500 a year, were among the first paid social workers in America, and it is instructive that they were public- and not private-charity officials. Historians have generally assumed that the social work profession had its origins in the volunteer friendly visitors used by charity organization societies in various cities in the United States and England in the late nineteenth century. The same historians acknowledge that while the friendly visitors had some predecessors, they were all in such private charities as the Association for Improving the Condition of the Poor in New York in the 1840s and Joseph Tuckerman's ministry to the poor in Boston in the 1820s. Public welfare has generally been considered a backwater where few innovations took place and social workers did not make many inroads until the twentieth century. In actuality, as early as 1808 in New York people were employed to visit the poor and deliver aid to them. These workers, along with Philadelphia's visitors of the poor in the 1830s and thereafter, were much closer to contemporary social workers than the volunteer visitors used by private charities in the nineteenth century. Like modern social workers but unlike volunteer charitable workers, New York and Philadelphia visitors were paid to deal personally with the poor and to dispense relief.[76]

Yet, in one way, the Philadelphia system was not so modern. In the nineteenth century, the position of visitor of the poor grew increasingly political. A proposal first made in 1839, and finally written into law in 1851, permitted each guardian to choose the visitor in his section of the city or districts.[77] Since so many guardians were politicians, they may have sought this change so that they could appoint political allies to dispense outdoor relief to voters in their areas. In any case, as political appointees, the visitors were probably less professional than later social workers would be.

Visitors were, however, efficient: they worked full-time and kept better records than guardians had under the old system.[78] On the other hand, the new program had many of the disadvantages of any bureaucracy. While a poor applicant still had to present character references, she or he no longer applied for aid directly to a guardian, who might grant or deny it on the spot. Now, the indigent sought assistance from the visitors, who investigated applications, then gave the results of their inquiries to guardians, who then determined whether or not to extend poor relief.[79] These new administrative procedures made the operation of the public-welfare system more impersonal and contributed to the declining emphasis on humanitarianism within the system.

After 1828, as the new welfare bureaucracy made the poor virtually faceless to Philadelphia's guardians of the poor, their inclination to provide much aid to the needy declined. Thus, the welfare bureaucracy stimulated an economical spirit that was perfectly in tune with the import of the 1828 poor law. In conformity to this law, guardians reduced the number of poor entitled to the most substantial forms of relief—admission to the alms-house and cash aid. Although in 1800, twenty-two out of every thousand in Philadelphia received such public assistance, by 1840 just thirteen per thousand obtained this aid and by 1850, fourteen per thousand. Yet, even as they curbed the most expensive forms of welfare, guardians expanded the cheaper sort: they gave medical and fuel aid to thousands. Therefore, the proportion receiving some form of welfare, no matter how small, leaped to fifty-four per thousand in 1841 and eighty-seven per thousand in 1848 (see table 1).

While guardians in the 1830s and 1840s annually passed out relief to thousands more than had obtained it earlier in the century, Philadelphians rarely objected, because their poor taxes remained nominal. The pattern of welfare expenditures only partly explains these low taxes. Interestingly enough, guardians spent more total dollars on the average in the 1830s and 1840s than their predecessors from 1800 to 1829.[80] Yet the city's population grew at a faster rate than the welfare budget, so that poor relief expenses per thousand city dwellers were actually less in 1841 and 1848 than they had been earlier (see table 1). At the same time, the poor-tax rate declined from 50¢ in 1838 to 18¢ per $100 of assessed valuation ten years later. These rates were considerably lower than the 62¢–90¢ per $100 paid by Philadelphians between 1804 and 1808.[81] Taxes remained low after 1828, partly because in relation to the total population, welfare expenditures were less than before the poor-law reform. Equally important is the fact that the assessed value of property in the city and districts increased enormously near midcentury. In 1849, property values were fourteen times what they had been in 1805 and double those of ten years before.[82] With an expanding tax base, welfare officials could leave the tax rate unchanged, or even lower it, and still obtain adequate revenues.

Herein lies the explanation of why the 1828-poor-law reform succeeded, whereas the comparable late eighteenth-century welfare reform did not. Those who sought change in both eras tried to curb the cost of public welfare and the number receiving it, but only the 1828 reformers were able to accomplish part of this goal. They managed to keep taxes low, because the city's tax base expanded in the midnineteenth century, while it remained nearly static in the late eighteenth century.[83]

Between the late eighteenth and the middle of the nineteenth century, three considerations—the desire to treat the poor benevolently, the interest in managing their behavior carefully, and the need to be provident in spending poor-tax monies—always influenced the behavior of Philadelphia's welfare officials. At any given time, these considerations were, however, tempered by the social, political, and economic climate of the city.

The social change that most affected the city's welfare system was the growth of Philadelphia in both population and area. By the 1820s, this growth made personally attending to, or stewardship of, the poor extremely difficult and necessitated creating a welfare bureaucracy complete with paid visitors of the poor. The appearance of these embryonic social workers placed a barrier of officialdom between the needy and the public administrators charged with assisting them and virtually eliminated the personal contact that had previously promoted sympathy for the poor.

Political conflict also affected the city's welfare system, particularly in the 1820s. At that time, anger of conservative Federalist Philadelphians over the high poor-tax rates they paid to a welfare system controlled by Democratic-Republican representatives from the districts, who dispensed cash aid to large numbers of poor outside the city proper, led to a change in the poor law in 1828 and a consequent emphasis on both thrift (eliminating outdoor pensions) and social control (constructing a new almshouse).

Finally, economic downturns triggered the most decisive changes in the city's welfare system. In the eighteenth century, the depression following the Seven Years' War led officials to emphasize thrift and social control over the poor by reducing outdoor relief and forcing most needy people into the almshouse. The persistence of this institution throughout the nineteenth century reflected the continuing importance of social control, although the manner in which officials administered this asylum from 1800 to 1828 revealed a strong humanitarian concern for the indigent. At the same time, this philanthropic spirit was also reflected in the expansion of outdoor cash aid to the poor. The failure of poor-law reform in the 1760s, combined with returning prosperity in the 1780s and 1790s, promoted an increased emphasis on humanitarianism. Frequent social contact between welfare officials and the poor they aided also stimulated a sense of stewardship at the beginning of the nineteenth century.

With the Panic of 1819 and the resultant expansion in both the number of poor and the amount of taxes assessed for their benefit, anger over the public welfare system and distrust of the needy who depended on it resurfaced. Once again, officials found it expedient to stress thrift and social control and deemphasize humanitarianism. At the same time, both the growth of the city, which made personal stewardship by public-welfare officials virtually obsolete, and political demands to end outdoor cash aid, reduced charitable concern for the poor and inclined welfare authorities toward frugality. Their commitment to thrift did not diminish significantly throughout the rest of the years until 1854. Another depression between 1837 and 1843 once more provoked welfare officials to hold down both expenditures and almshouse admissions.

Later economic crises in both the nineteenth and twentieth centuries also resulted in efforts to economize and control the poor more closely. In the depression years of the 1870s, Philadelphia's welfare officials, along with those in Brooklyn and in New York City, suspended outdoor cash aid and required the needy to enter the almshouse. Most recently, economic problems posed by inflation in the 1980s have prompted conservative Repub-

Scene in St. Mary Street (*Courtesy of The Library Company of Philadelphia*). Street life among the poor in nineteenth-century Philadelphia: black and white, male and female, old and young.

lican political leaders to reduce spending on social welfare programs for the needy. Thus during both the eighteenth- and nineteenth-century economic crises discussed in this chapter and in the 1980s, a desire to lower taxes promoted retrenchment of welfare programs.[84]

Outdoor Relief: Public Assistance to the Poor in Their Own Homes

From the last half of the eighteenth century to the present, the form of public assistance most likely to come under attack and be curtailed is aid provided to the poor in their own community and home. In the past, this form of welfare was called outdoor relief, or aid to the indigent outside of the almshouse. Under this rubric, fell a plethora of relief programs, including regular cash subsidies or pensions, work relief, free medical assistance, and relief in kind (clothes, food, and wood). Although all forms of outdoor aid have been at one time or another criticized, the most unpopular has been cash aid. Principally during economic downturns, such as those in the 1760s and 1820s, it was castigated for promoting both fraud and pauperism. Its critics conveniently ignored the virtual helplessness of its recipients—women and children. By the 1840s in Philadelphia, cash aid was so discredited and so entangled in bureaucratic red tape that it was rarely granted. Instead, medical and fuel aid came increasingly into vogue. They permitted officials to be, at one and the same time, frugal (these forms of aid were relatively cheap) and philanthropic (thousands could receive an occasional visit from a physician or be given a load of wood). Yet, medical and fuel aid also permitted officials a measure of social control over the poor, since these forms of aid could not be abused in the way cash relief could.

Before the 1828 poor law, indigent Philadelphians applied for all forms of outdoor relief to the guardians of the poor, who, in their respective neighborhoods, acted as stewards of the impoverished. A poor person who desired public aid could approach a guardian directly in his home. (The names and addresses of welfare officials were published periodically in newspapers and city directories.) If the guardian denied assistance, the indigent applicant could appear before a regular meeting of the board to appeal the decision. By 1805, many of the poor made their initial requests for aid to the entire board. This procedure may have seemed simpler, because outdoor guardians changed so frequently, but the time and place of their meetings did not. Some guardians probably preferred this system, too, because they found it comforting to have the advice of colleagues when determining who was worthy of aid and who was not.[1] In any case, guardians had personal contact with the poor—they saw and spoke to the indigent in their districts and at their meetings.

Of course, officials did not give aid indiscriminately; they only assisted those who specifically requested relief and willingly answered questions about their personal worth. It worked to the advantage of the destitute individual if she or he presented a letter of recommendation from some substantial citizen. For example, in 1800, when Rose, a black woman, applied to Abraham Garrigues, a guardian of the poor, for aid, she gave him a letter from her former employer, William Savery. Savery acknowledged that Rose had worked for his family and was now poor and needed wood. She was sober and "Industrious, but is grown old and can get no Employ suitable for her."[2] Such letters of recommendation allowed guardians to dispense aid as they were legally supposed to do: to legitimate Philadelphia residents who were in need. No matter how conscientious a guardian might be, it was difficult for him to know personally all the poor in his district. He had to question them and he had to rely on recommendations from fellow citizens.[3] Such procedures, though cumbersome, kept welfare officials in direct contact with the poor and enabled them to understand and perhaps sympathize with the problems of impoverished Philadelphians.

Nevertheless, in this system, possibilities for fraud were considerable. For example, early in the century, some unscrupulous guardians devised a scheme for obtaining kickbacks from grocers whom they commissioned to furnish poor pensioners with food. A dishonest welfare official might apply to the board's treasurer for $25 to give his pensioners, make a deal with a grocer to supply them with provisions for $15, and pocket the balance. To guard against this type of fraud, the board of guardians eventually ruled that outdoor-relief recipients be paid in cash.[4]

However, some guardians also capitalized on the traditional, haphazard record-keeping methods of the board to cheat the poor out of welfare payments. Prior to the 1820s, although public officials took an occasional census of pensioners, no official roster was kept of those on outdoor relief.[5] Apparently, guardians informally passed on pension lists to their successors. Therefore, a guardian might draw money for his outdoor pensioners from the treasurer and keep it for himself or give it to his friends. No one would be the wiser unless one of his poor clients complained. This defect, among others, led reformers in the early 1820s to brand the welfare system inefficient. Guardians responded by appointing from among their regular members standing committees of three in adjoining districts to examine together pensioners in their areas and enter on permanent registers the names of those entitled to regular outdoor relief. Thenceforward, when a guardian submitted bills to the treasurer, board rules stipulated that he include the names of the poor he had paid. Presumably, the treasurer accepted a guardian's bills only if they tallied with the permanent list of outdoor pensioners. Although this system was an improvement over casually transferring pauper rolls from one guardian to another, it did not completely prevent fraud. Guardians could lie about whom they paid, and treasurers could ignore the rules and reimburse guardians whether or not they submitted correct lists. Nevertheless, just one-tenth of 1 percent of the guardians who served between 1800 and 1828 had charges of fraud leveled against them.[6] Although there may have been cases of undetected wrongdoing, in all probability, most welfare officials tried to serve the poor honestly.

Yet, censure of welfare officials for negligence and, in some cases, dishonesty, helped discredit Philadelphia's entire poor relief system in the 1820s and produced a much harsher system after 1828, one where outdoor relief was extremely difficult to obtain. This is not an unusual pattern. Periodically, even in recent years, either welfare recipients or welfare officials or both have been charged with fraudulent manipulation of the system. Such charges discredit welfare in general, justify cutbacks in public aid, and discourage many needy people who are entitled to assistance from applying for it. (Few want to be identified as cheating "reliefers.")[7]

In Philadelphia, the new 1828 poor law was designed to prevent once and for all any wrongful manipulation of cash relief. The new visitors of the poor kept careful records of all the beneficiaries of outdoor cash aid.[8] The indigent secured pensions only after a visitor of the poor had thoroughly investigated them and endorsed their applications to a committee of the board of guardians, the committee reported favorably to the board, and the board gave its sanction for aid. Even those who simply requested a load of wood had to be investigated by a visitor and approved by the guardian of the district.[9] These new procedures probably reduced opportunities for unprincipled welfare officials to profit from the outdoor-relief program, but these procedures also made it much more inconvenient for the indigent to procure any type of outdoor aid.[10] Many may have been dissuaded from applying for aid at all, given the lengthy bureaucratic red tape they had to endure before receiving assistance. And if many who were entitled to relief did not apply for it, then the chief objective of the 1828 reformers would be realized—to reduce the cost of public welfare and save the taxpayers money.

Before 1828, of all the forms of outdoor relief furnished to the poor, cash aid was the most important; more dollars were spent on cash aid, and probably more people received it than any other type of outdoor assistance. The amount of these cash awards varied over the years. In 1814–15, guardians usually paid an indigent mother 25¢ a week for herself and each of her children and assigned aged and disabled persons 50¢–$1.00 a week. The average weekly pension was 77¢. Later, during the Panic of 1819, when money was scarce, guardians decided to limit pensions of 25¢ a week to children only and to pay the aged and disabled just 50¢–75¢ a week. By 1822–23, the average pension was only 63¢ a week, and in 1826, it was 55¢. Such amounts were much lower than the weekly wages earned by the lowest paid male and female laborers in the city—wages that were often insufficient for normal expenses. Outdoor-relief payments in other nineteenth-century cities as well as in many urban areas in the eighteenth century were also extremely small; they probably did not cover the cost of adequate food.[11]

The occasional censuses of cash pensioners made by Philadelphia's welfare officials reveal that the typical recipient was a woman who was head of her household. From 1811 through 1829, 86–91 percent of those on outdoor-relief rolls were women, although women then constituted just over half of the city's population. Women composed a smaller proportion of the almshouse population, roughly one-third in most years (see chapter 4), yet because of their predominance on outdoor-relief rolls, they comprised the majority of public-relief recipients. Perhaps guardians felt more sympathy for impoverished women who, no matter how hard they worked, generally earned less than the lowest paid male laborers. Probably for this reason, guardians gave women the most attractive form of public assistance (even if it were small in amount), aid in their own home, and accorded men the least attractive kind—institutional care.

Of the women on Philadelphia's outdoor-relief rolls, an 1814–15 census reveals that roughly two-thirds were single, ill, disabled, and/or aged. They included Catherine Long, who was aged and lame and lived alone as well as Sarah Strand and Sabre Smith, one of whom was rheumatic and the other consumptive; both were without families. The remaining one-third of the women on the relief rolls were mothers (most of them widows), each of whom had several children to support. Among such mothers were Mary Kinney, a widow with breast cancer and four young children to care for, and Mary Price, whose husband had gone to sea and left her alone with their two youngsters. The average size of all female-headed households on outdoor relief in 1814–15 was 2.09.

Clearly, there are significant similarities between public-pension lists in early nineteenth-century Philadelphia and public-welfare rolls today. Presently, in our major government-sponsored relief program, AFDC, four-fifths of the recipients are women. In early nineteenth-century Philadelphia, the proportion of women on the outdoor-relief rolls was roughly the same. In both centuries, the pattern was to keep men off the rolls and thereby force them to take jobs, no matter how low paying. It is also interesting that in neither era were the families on welfare particularly large. Actually, the average size of families on welfare today, which is 3.3 people, is about the same size as families not on welfare.

However, in the last century, not only were families on outdoor relief in Philadelphia smaller than families on AFDC today, they were also smaller than the typical midnineteenth-century household, which contained 5.55 people. One explanation for this difference is that there were more single people on the rolls in the past than today. Single people, as well as many mothers who were widowed or deserted by their husbands, may have sought welfare precisely because they did not have large families to rely on in times of need. Further, all these women probably consciously limited the number of children they bore, not only out of economic necessity, but also because illegitimacy was then so much more frowned on than it is today.

Not only were welfare families smaller in the nineteenth century than today, but the racial composition of the relief rolls also differed in the two eras. Since 1948, the percentage of blacks on welfare has been much larger than their proportion of the nation's population, but in Philadelphia in the early nineteenth century, the reverse was true. Between 1811 and 1829, just 1–4 percent of the pensioners were black, yet blacks constituted 8–9 percent of the city's population. There are several reasons why blacks secured little welfare relief. Since so many of them were live-in servants, they may not have needed welfare money for rent or fuel. Those who did require assistance lived in areas of the city that white outdoor guardians may well have avoided. Generally, when guardians did encounter needy blacks, they were sent to the almshouse rather than supplied with outdoor aid, perhaps because of the then prevalent belief that blacks were especially improvident and unlikely to spend cash pensions wisely.

More immigrants than blacks obtained outdoor relief in Philadelphia. The foreign-born constituted over one-third of those on pensions, yet their proportion of the city's total population was probably less than 25 percent between 1800 and 1830. Since immigrants often arrived with little money and were generally relegated to the lowest paying jobs, it is not surprising to find so many of them on welfare. Apparently, discrimination against blacks in granting outdoor relief did not extend to the foreign-born.[12]

Not only did guardians of the poor elect to award cash aid chiefly to white people, many of whom were foreign-born, these officials also gave preference to indigent women and men with some age- or health-related disability. This pattern became more pronounced over the years. As figure 1 demonstrates, the proportion of both the ill and the aged on the cash-pension rolls rose dramatically between 1814 and 1829. Perhaps guardians responded to criticism leveled at outdoor relief in the 1820s by limiting cash aid to the most feeble among the poor. Probably even these ailing and aged poor on pensions had some family or friends to care for them, and some of the poor may also have been able to work occasionally. Carey noted that poor women paid their rent with outdoor-relief money they collected from the guardians of the poor and used their own earnings to pay for food and clothing. As guardians themselves observed in 1823, they sent "the sick ... lunatic, and ... infirm" directly to the almshouse but granted weekly pensions to others who, with a little help, could earn a "bare subsistence for themselves and their children." [13]

Even though not completely incapacitated, most of those who accepted public cash relief in nineteenth-century cities were probably among the most desperately poor. Only such people would have found the scant pension payments attractive. Most men and women probably preferred to labor if they were physically able at the lowest paying jobs rather than subsist on a meager pension or submit to the regimen of the almshouse. Thus, public welfare may have maintained the pool of those willing to work for the lowest wages and consequently served the needs of the business community. Businessmen could therefore expect to keep their costs down by paying their workers little if the public-relief system discouraged people from going on welfare and thus made them available to private industry at the cheapest rates. [14]

In Philadelphia, cash aid came under severe attack for the first time in the 1760s. Conveniently ignoring the unemployment and poverty caused by the depression that followed the Seven Years' War, critics charged that cash pensions were in large part responsible for swelling relief rolls, promoting laziness and dependence on welfare. Accordingly, cash aid was severely curtailed, and most poor were required to enter the almshouse. The failure of this poor relief reform to reduce poor-tax rates and the return of prosperity led to a resumption and expansion of cash pensions after 1788. Even so, in most years between 1800 and 1828, far fewer people received outdoor cash aid than were admitted to the almshouse (see appendix 2). Most likely because they allowed the poor discretion in expenditure, pensions remained somewhat suspect.

Then in the 1820s during another postwar depression, cash aid once again came under attack. Critics charged that pensioners spent public funds on "riot and intoxication" and outdoor cash aid served "to pamper the most detestible and destructive of vices." [15] Reformers were determined to save the taxpayers' money by preventing the lazy, able-bodied poor from profiting from this welfare program. Actually, there were few such people on the pension lists, but reformers conveniently ignored the fact that cash aid went primarily to destitute women and children, the aged, and the ill. Politically powerless, these people could not interfere with the passage of the 1828 poor law, which provided for pensions to be replaced with relief in kind once the new almshouse opened.

In turn, the men who drafted and enacted this poor-law change may well

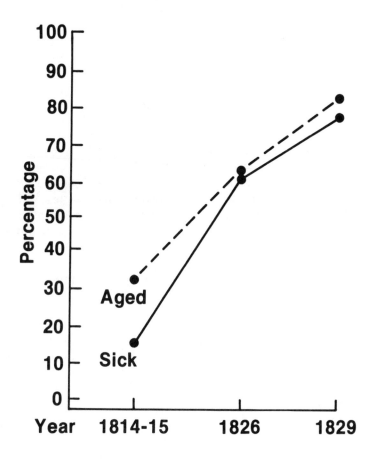

**Figure 1
Proportion of Sick and Aged
Receiving Cash Relief,
Philadelphia, 1814-1829**

SOURCES: PCA, GP, Register of Relief Recipients, 1814–15; PCA, MGP, 30 August 1826; *Hazard's Register*, 6:266.

have known that they were economizing on aid to the group least likely to thwart reform. To forestall any possible criticism of the program for terminating aid to helpless women, male reformers focused on a small group of women (between 4–20 percent of those on the outdoor-relief rolls between 1814 and 1826) who, they said, were very undeserving of aid— mothers of bastard children. Critics claimed that these women were insolent, demanded relief "as a right," and were not properly thankful for it.[16] By vociferously objecting to aid to such immoral people, reformers erroneously implied that most women on outdoor relief were fallen women who used public monies to support their illegitimate offspring. The critics' argument was that since outdoor cash aid fostered vice, it should be eliminated and all public aid dispensed through the almshouse.

Actually, even before the new almshouse opened in 1835, guardians of the poor sharply reduced the number of people receiving cash pensions and expanded relief in kind.[17] Carey, who had previously pressed for an end to outdoor relief, was one of the first to see how damaging to the poor the reduction and eventual elimination of pensions were. Soon, he began urging legislators to alter the 1828 law to permit guardians to continue dispensing pensions indefinitely. He thought it unjust to force respectable poor people out of their home and into the almshouse. A law incorporating Carey's suggestion was introduced in the state legislature in 1829 but was defeated after welfare officials campaigned against it.[18]

When the new almshouse opened in 1835, guardians promptly announced that "no relief other than temporary shall be granted to the out door poor and said relief [shall] be confined entirely to fuel, provisions, clothing, medicine, and medical attendance. . . ." No one who had previously accepted cash aid elected to enter the new almshouse. Instead, former pensioners, most of them women and children, went into the streets to beg.[19]

Such examples of destitution, as well as others occasioned by the depression that began in 1837, prompted many Philadelphians to ask the state legislature to reinstitute outdoor cash relief. Guardians of the poor opposed this suggestion. They argued that there were only two kinds of poverty—that produced by disease and that brought about by inability to find work at wages sufficient to support a family. Guardians contended that they could do something about the former but nothing about the latter. Relying on the theories of those who had reformed the poor law in England in 1832–34, Philadelphia's officials asserted that if they aided the laboring poor, they might "mitigate present suffering" but in the end do more harm than good, since the relief they dispensed might depress wages even more. Guardians apparently assumed that outdoor cash aid would go largely to male wage earners, as it may have at one time in England, although that had never been the case in Philadelphia. Cash assistance to women, children, the ill, and the aged, such as Philadelphia's guardians of the poor had provided before 1828, would hardly depress laborers' earnings to the extent that allowances supporting wages did in England. Nevertheless, with this argument, guardians successfully forestalled change for a few years, but by 1839, they acknowledged that amending the poor laws was inevitable and sought merely to influence the form of revision. The legislature accepted their suggestions and in 1840 authorized the reinstatement of cash relief for six-month periods. Thenceforth, a poor person could secure a pension, good for six months and thereafter renewable, once the visitors of the poor and a majority of the guardians approved her or his application for relief.[20]

Even after the 1840-poor-law revision, guardians awarded pensions for just two-to-four-, rather than six-month periods, and then to very few indigent; generally fewer than two hundred people a year obtained them (see appendix 2). Most pensioners collected $1.00 every two weeks. Such payments were actually somewhat less than the average weekly amount granted in the 1820s, which was even then quite meager. Hence, when resumed in the 1840s, outdoor cash relief still served the same labor-regulating function it had in the years before 1828. Low benefit levels compelled all but the most destitute to accept any work they could find. Additionally, recipients of the few small cash awards officials made after the legislature revamped the poor law were generally women, primarily widows, the same people who had received most of the pensions before 1828.[21]

Between 1828 and 1854, indigent women received less of the most substantial types of public aid than men. Cash aid and institutionalization were the most comprehensive forms of poor relief, since the first allowed a person to subsist at home and the second provided full room and board in the poorhouse. Very few women (or men, for that matter) obtained cash aid after 1828, and the female proportion of the almshouse population actually declined at the same time (see figure 2). Of course, women may have been the recipients of other types of public assistance, such as medical and fuel relief. There are no extant records of who obtained medical aid, and only two censuses of recipients of fuel relief, made between 1831–33, exist. These tallies indicate that women did, indeed, obtain 80–90 percent of the fuel distributed by public officials in those years. In the year 1831–32, of all those receiving some form of public aid (cash, institutionalization, fuel), over 60 percent were women, but of those receiving the most costly and useful types of public assistance, cash relief and almshouse care, only 39 percent were women.[22] Possibly, guardians extended the most comprehensive forms of aid to more men than women, because there were a number of charities in the city ready and able to assist indigent women but virtually no private-welfare programs available to men (see chapters 4, 6).

Figure 2
Proportion of Adult Men and Women Receiving Cash Pensions and Almshouse Assistance, Philadelphia, 1811-1850

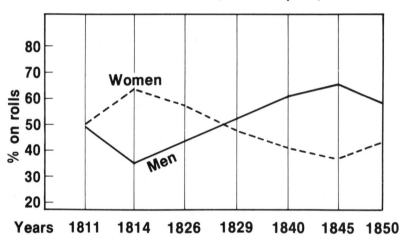

SOURCES: Almshouse-admission figures from *Poulson's*, 19 November 1812, 19 October 1815; *Philadelphia Gazette*, 7 November 1826, 19 January 1830; *Auditors' Reports of the Accounts of the Blockley Alms-House for the Fiscal Years Ending May 17, 1841, May 18, 1846, May 19, 1851* (Philadelphia: Mifflin and Parry, 1841, Daily Sun, 1846, O.I. Search, 1852). Outdoor-relief figures: PCA, Alms House Admission Book, 1811–14; PCA, Register of Relief Recipients, 1814–15; PCA, MGP, 30 August 1826, and 1840, 1845, 1850 passim (reports of the visitors of the poor); *Hazard's Register*, 6:266.

It is also tempting to speculate that the politically minded guardians of the post-1828 era may actually have preferred to succor needy men rather than women in the poorhouse, since the former were potential voters and the latter were not.

Besides cash pensions—there were three other forms of outdoor aid provided to Philadelphia's poor: work relief, medical assistance, and relief in kind. Beginning in 1806 and continuing for the next twenty years, guardians annually employed several hundred women to spin flax and wool, which was then woven into cloth by almshouse inmates. This program proceeded satisfactorily as long as there was adequate demand in the city for cheap textiles manufactured in the almshouse. Such demand existed when European-made cloth was virtually unavailable from the time of the Embargo of 1807 to the end of the War of 1812. Later, in the postwar era, when textiles could again be imported from abroad, the demand for inexpensive almshouse "sheeting" diminished. As a result, welfare officials discharged many women whom they had previously employed to do home spinning and in 1826, terminated this work-relief project altogether.[23]

At this time in Philadelphia, women alone profited from noninstitutional public work relief. Welfare officials may have awarded jobs exclusively to indigent women, because their spinning tied in so nicely with the almshouse production of cloth and perhaps also because women's job opportunities were much more limited than men's. Public work relief may likewise have gone largely to women in order to force more men into the labor market. In addition, by the 1820s with cloth manufacturing, in which low-paid female workers were much in demand, fast on the way to becoming a major industry in Philadelphia, ending public work relief to women may have forced some of them into the large textile mills. Of course, those with young children could not afford to leave their homes to work in mills, so eliminating public payments for the spinning these women did at home worked a particular hardship on them.

Somewhat more significant than work relief both in terms of total expenditures and number of beneficiaries was another form of outdoor aid—medical assistance. This aid took two forms—hospitalization in special facilities during epidemics, as described in chapter 2, and home care (including drugs and medical attendants) for the poor suffering from noncontagious diseases.

Early in the century, physicians employed in the almshouse, which was essentially a hospital, accepted the task of visiting the homes of the afflicted poor referred to them by guardians. In 1806, when physicians complained that it had become overly burdensome to travel all over the city and districts to minister to the maladies of the poor, the board of guardians assigned each doctor to a specific geographical area. A few years later, guardians became annoyed at the high cost of medicine prescribed by public physicians for the ailing poor outside the almshouse. To save money, welfare officials agreed to pay $200 a year for medical aid to the privately run Philadelphia Dispensary, which had been founded in 1786 to provide free medical care for the worthy poor. For a year, the dispensary sent doctors and medicine to the homes of public-relief recipients, but in 1811, guardians terminated the contract, because it was an inconvenience. Guardians may have found their money treated as a donation and used to help all the poor who could secure recommendations, whether or not they had been referred by public officials. After this, guardians concluded an agreement with almshouse doctors to reassign districts to them and pay them for attending the poor therein. Still later, public officials arranged with selected area druggists to supply the indigent with medicine.[24]

Eventually in 1815, guardians ceased to employ almshouse physicians to succor the outdoor poor and instead hired special doctors for this purpose. Guardians continued this practice through 1854. Each outdoor physician had a particular portion of the city or districts where he attended the poor. Doctors assisted regular pensioners as well as any poor person who applied to them for medical care. Guardians continued to employ apothecaries in various parts of the city and districts to prepare and distribute to the poor medicines prescribed by public physicians.[25]

Public medical aid to the poverty-stricken was a popular and successful program for a variety of reasons. It especially appealed to guardians of the poor, because they sympathized with the ill who were impoverished through no fault of their own. Welfare officials were also quite willing to extend needed medical aid, because it was relatively inexpensive: they paid physicians only about 1/6¢ a house call. The economical nature of medical relief became increasingly relevant after 1828, when thriftiness in welfare administration was the chief objective of guardians of the poor in Philadelphia. Perhaps partly for this reason, they began for the first time in the 1840s to publicize the number of poor annually granted outdoor medical aid (see appendix 2). Public medical assistance also flourished because doctors supported it. These physicians, like their colleagues who rendered service to dispensaries during this era, willingly accepted low wages in order to gain useful clinical experience among the poor. Also, public medical relief, like private dispensary care, worked well, because both supplied the poor with free drugs, which, along with bleeding and cupping (services delivered by public and dispensary doctors) were the standard therapeutics of the time.[26]

The last type of outdoor relief, which by midcentury was most in vogue, was relief in kind, or the allocation of free clothes, food, and fuel, to the indigent. Only occasionally did guardians supply warm clothing to the destitute in winter, but regularly every January and February, guardians handed out about one thousand loaves of bread to the needy. By the 1830s, visitors began to distribute a few free groceries as well as orders to local soup houses. The board of guardians made such orders possible by contributing annually during the depression years between 1837 and 1844 to various privately run soup houses. Managers of these agencies agreed to use donations from public-welfare officials to pay for soup furnished to the poor who had orders signed by a visitor or guardian.[27]

Although clothes and food were useful forms of relief in kind, guardians never considered them so important to the poor as free fuel. In fact, when welfare officials delineated items in their relief budgets, wood was significant enough to be listed separately, but clothes and food were grouped together with other items in the general category of outdoor relief. These budgets reveal that between 1807–18, guardians devoted between 5–13 percent of their outdoor-relief funds to purchasing wood and coal, but by the 1820s, the proportion had dropped to 1 percent or less. Welfare reformers, angered by the diminishing value of relief in kind, wrote into the 1828 poor law the requirement that such aid in food, fuel, or clothes become the prevailing form of outdoor relief once the new almshouse opened. From that time forward through 1854, fuel was the largest single type of outdoor aid granted. Purchases of wood accounted for between 50–60 percent of the money spent by welfare officials on outdoor aid to the poor. Expenditures for medicine, food, and after 1840, cash aid made up the remainder of outdoor-relief budgets between 1835 and 1854.[28]

Like medical aid, fuel relief had the advantage of being inexpensive. In the 1840s, it cost guardians less than $2.60 each winter to supply a poor family with wood. (In contrast, a cash pension of 50¢ a week cost welfare officials $26.00 a year per recipient.)[29] Because medical and fuel aid were inexpensive, guardians could afford to extend them to many thousands and thereby confirm their own benevolence yet never jeopardize their reputation as frugal public servants.

Relief in kind (clothes, food, and fuel) had the same attractiveness for nineteenth-century Americans as food stamps and fuel-tax credits have today. The principal advantage of such relief is that it permits a greater measure of control over the poor than does cash aid. The poor may waste welfare money on foolishness or, worst of all, liquor, so that, poor relief may actually promote rather than alleviate poverty. On the other hand, assistance in the form of such necessities as fuel and food can presumably be used only to alleviate need. In all likelihood, the nineteenth-century reliance on fuel aid and the twentieth-century faith in food stamps simply reflect the peculiar combination of sympathy for, and distrust of, the poor that has so long been present in the United States.

The forms, functions, and recipients of outdoor relief altered considerably when Philadelphia's public-welfare system itself underwent revision in the first half of the nineteenth century. As a welfare bureaucracy replaced the old system based on stewardship, the indigent found that they could no longer make a simple, personal appeal to one official to obtain public aid. Relief-granting procedures grew increasingly complex when visitors of the poor and guardians of the poor had to evaluate all applicants. Customarily, guardians had provided most of the city's helpless poor with small weekly pensions. When economic concerns became predominant after the 1828-poor-law change, cash relief was virtually eliminated, and wood relief replaced it as the single most important form of outdoor relief. Welfare officials argued that cash aid was expensive and "pauperizing" while fuel aid was cheap and unlikely to increase dependency. One effect of the triumph of relief in kind was to increase to many thousands the number receiving small amounts of public assistance (such as a half cord of wood annually) and to reduce to several hundreds the number who obtained the most substantial form of outdoor aid—cash awards. After 1828, the most helpless of the poor, especially women and children, were not altogether denied public aid; they simply obtained less of it.

Philadelphia Almshouse, 1799 (*Courtesy of The Historical Society of Pennsylvania*).
Officials collecting runaway hogs in front of the Bettering House on Spruce Street.

The Almshouse: Home to the Homeless, Hospital, and Factory

Between 1800 and 1854, the same concerns motivated those who governed the Philadelphia Almshouse and those who administered outdoor relief in the city. Almshouse managers, like outdoor guardians, displayed regard for the plight of the indigent as well as the desire to regulate their behavior and spend a minimal amount on their maintenance. Similar considerations governed indoor relief: by the 1830s and 1840s, both the tendency to regiment the lives of the poor and to economize on their care took precedence over philanthropic notions. Of course, because the almshouse was an institution, social control was always of paramount importance, but benevolent programs for the city's institutionalized poor were never absent; they merely diminished in number. Between 1800 and the 1828-poor-law change, administrative practices in the city's almshouse, or Bettering House, were decidedly more benign than the institutional routine in the new Blockley Almshouse, which from 1835 through the rest of the century was Philadelphia's asylum for the poor. This change in regimen is a direct result of the poor-law-reform movement in the 1820s, which emphasized both social control over the poor in a restrictive setting and thrift, which could be realized by discouraging the poor from applying for welfare at all. The erection of a forbidding poorhouse in Blockley Township, west of Philadelphia, and the elimination of outdoor cash aid were intended to provide this necessary discouragement and thus, ultimately, prove economical.

Records of both almshouses, retained by Philadelphia, make it possible to determine to what extent the goals of social control and economy were actually realized in the day-to-day operation of public poorhouses. These records also reveal some characteristics of almshouse inmates and how they were affected by both benevolent and harsh institutional practices.

Institutionalization of the city's poor began in 1732 when Philadelphia constructed its first almshouse. By the late eighteenth century, most large eastern cities had expanded their poorhouses at least once, and Philadelphia was no exception. In 1767, officials constructed a second almshouse, known as the Bettering House, on a square bounded by Spruce and Pine and Tenth and Eleventh streets, in what was then the country. Like its counterparts elsewhere, the Bettering House consisted of a large fenced-in compound in the midst of which stood two sizable brick edifices encircled by many smaller outbuildings. In Philadelphia, according to the original plan, one building, called the house of employment, was to accommodate the working poor, while the other, known as the almshouse, sheltered the helpless. But officials soon abandoned this plan, probably because so few of the inmates proved capable of laboring in the house of employment. By 1800, poor women were lodged in one building, indigent men in the other, and in 1814–15, the managers supervised the construction of a center building to connect the two. Adjacent to the men's and women's sections of the institution stood smaller buildings, including a wash house, smoke house, apothecary shop, and "dead house." As was characteristic of poorhouses in other cities, hogs rooted around these buildings. (Officials captured hogs that frequently ran loose at that time and deposited them at the local almshouse. If not claimed by their owners, inmates slaughtered the hogs and prepared and consumed the meat.) Cows were also kept at the Philadelphia Almshouse for milk, and they, too, contributed to the barnyard atmosphere around the asylum.[1]

Inside the institution, most wards were reserved for the ill, because the Philadelphia Almshouse, along with other public poor asylums, was principally a hospital. Between 1804 and 1807, two-thirds of Philadelphia's almshouse inmates lived in hospital wards; in 1812–13, of all poor admitted to the institution, three-quarters were ill; and between 1829 and 1834, in a sample of new admittants, 85 percent required medical attention. Most were sent to medical or incurable wards rather than surgical wards, which probably indicates that inmates suffered from chronic ailments, such as rheumatism, or were handicapped in some way.[2]

In addition to wards for the ailing poor, on the women's side of the Bettering House, there were three large apartments for those able to labor, and in the cellar, several smaller rooms for vagrants. On the men's side of the almshouse, adjacent to wards for the ill, there were at first two, and by the 1820s three large wards for indigent men capable of labor. On the men's side, there was also a cellar for vagrants and cells for both male and female lunatics.[3]

From 1800 to 1828, administration of all these wards came under the aegis of the managers of the Philadelphia Almshouse, who generally exercised their authority in a benevolent fashion. They demonstrated personal concern for the needs and comforts of inmates by twice weekly walking through the wards, conversing with the poor, attending to their various problems, and writing up leaves of absence or discharges on the spot.[4] Managers were especially attentive to unmarried pregnant women in the lying-in ward and aged men and women in the married ward.

While midwives and doctors attended most respectable and financially secure women in their home during pregnancy and labor, poor women could not afford such care. The Pennsylvania Hospital welcomed only indigent, married pregnant women and sent the unmarried to the almshouse. There, managers appointed special doctors and midwives to attend to the women during labor and delivery and had them served hearty and nutritious food. Later, after her discharge, an unwed mother often received weekly payments from the outdoor guardians to support her child.[5] This money was intended to sustain her until she and/or her child could find work. In all probability, this combination of indoor and outdoor relief was quite useful to poor mothers. As for older "respectable" married couples who were in need, managers of the Bettering House refused to "punish" them by consigning them to separate men's and women's wards but, instead, assigned aged husbands and wives to the married ward. They, like residents in the lying-in ward, were given dietary privileges: such costly items as tea and sugar were theirs for the asking. Aged paupers also enjoyed the right to leave and reenter the institution freely. Thus, Mr. and Mrs. George Lighthouse, long-time residents of the married ward, customarily left each summer to visit their grown children in the country.[6]

The Lighthouses may have been somewhat unusual, because they were permitted to leave the almshouse for such a long period, but early in the century, managers were not opposed to letting almost any inmate leave the asylum temporarily, especially on Sundays for recreation or amusement. Another sign of the managers' sympathetic attitude toward the poor was the willingness to permit inmates to keep small articles of furniture in the wards, a practice that gave the asylum a somewhat homelike appearance. Managers also permitted considerable diversity in dress. The poor customarily wore clothes they had brought from home, although officials obligingly replaced tattered garments. Never, however, did officials issue uniforms to inmates. While those in the lying-in and married wards ate especially well, the food served other inmates was certainly adequate. Though starches were the largest staple, almshouse fare also included daily helpings of meat and vegetables. Fresh fruits were, on the contrary, a rarity. By the 1820s, managers began to use diet as a form of punishment when, in response to frequent criticisms of the almshouse by poor-law reformers, officials introduced a strict daily regimen of rye coffee, bread, and mush for all healthy poor people and venereal patients. Yet, when managers discovered that there were few such people in the asylum, they relented and allowed even the "unworthy poor" occasional servings of meat and vegetables.[7]

This tendency to compromise, to try to act in the best interests of the

poor by providing them with a nourishing diet, attending to them personally, willingly granting them leaves, permitting them to keep their own
clothes and personal items, and extending to certain groups of the poor,
such as indigent pregnant women and aged married couples, special care,
all reflect the charitable vision of Philadelphia's almshouse managers
between 1800 and 1828. Apparently in contradiction to this sympathetic
attitude toward the poor are three examples of uncaring treatment of
the indigent. The first involves the unwillingness of the Philadelphia
Almshouse managers to classify inmates rigorously; the second, denial of
the poor's right to privacy; and the third, refusal to provide for mentally
deranged patients in a humane fashion. In actuality, none of these practices
was a deliberate effort to harass inmates but rather care typical of the times.

In the first instance, classification of inmates in Philadelphia's Bettering
House was always rather haphazard. For example, a moderately deranged
patient might be assigned to the cells or almost any other ward in the house.
In 1807, there were a few deranged patients in the women's upward
incurable, incurable, flax (for women capable of labor), sick, and venereal
wards and in the nursery as well as in the men's sick and convalescent wards
and the long garret (a dormitory on the top floor of the almshouse).
Furthermore, scattered throughout the house were old and sickly people,
such as sixty-eight-year-old Mary Lloyd in the flax ward, seventy-year-old
Eleanor Boyd in the sick ward, seventy-five-year-old Jane Moore in the
incurable ward, sixty-three-year-old Michael Foy in the men's surgical
ward, seventy-year-old Andrew McBride in the long garret, and sixty-
eight-year-old Elizabeth Parker in charge of nursery 2. Of course, raving
lunatics, severely ill people, pregnant women, aged married couples, and
orphaned children were routinely assigned, respectively, to the cells, the
medical, lying-in, and married wards and the nurseries. Nonetheless, these
were the only moderately specialized wards in the almshouse. In all others
diversity prevailed. Thus, in most of the institution, inmates ranged in age
from twenty to eighty years, and the newest entrant might have her or his
bed next to someone who had been there the longest. In 1807, ailing, thirty-
one-year-old Elizabeth Thompson, who had been at the Bettering house
less than a week, lived in the flax ward with forty-nine-year-old Jane
Crawford, who, because she was "weak and unable to support herself,"
had been in the asylum for seven years; and infirm, eighty-year-old Molly
Swaggerton, who had been an inmate for twenty to thirty years. At night,
those with unrelated maladies slept next to one another. In the men's
surgical ward in 1807, fifty-six-year-old Paul Jones, a sailor from the West
Indies with a wooden leg, slept next to Mingo Carey, a blind cooper ten
years his junior; Andrew Williams, a fifty-year-old ship's carpenter suffering from venereal disease; and Tom McGee, a nine-year-old boy, who was
apparently in good health. This situation caused critics to complain that

the almshouse was "a school of vice" where the "virtuous and the vicious" were lumped together.[8]

Inmate classification was absent in other early nineteenth-century alms-houses as well, because separating the poor, the criminal, and the insane was new at this time.[9] Houses of refuge for adolescents, mental hospitals for the insane poor, and most orphanages for the very young were unheard of in American cities or towns until the second quarter of the nineteenth century. Earlier, welfare officials in Philadelphia and elsewhere had little inclination to segregate inmates in any rigorous fashion. New arrivals were simply assigned to whatever beds were currently vacant on the men's or women's side of the almshouse.

A second sign of apparently unsympathetic treatment of almshouse inmates is the disinclination of welfare officials in Philadelphia and other cities as well to accord the poor much privacy. In all almshouses, paupers ate together at large tables in institutional dining halls. Attendants wedged the beds close to one another, and between two to six people occupied each. In Philadelphia, when the poor worshipped together in one of the largest wards on Sunday, they were often joined by curious visitors who afterward wandered through the poorhouse staring at the inmates. While exercising in the courtyard of the Philadelphia Almshouse, the poor were objects of scrutiny by passersby who peered through the broken fence. As one re-called, "How often have I peeped through a knot-hole in the old white-washed fence to see the living curiosity of those days—an 'idiot with a horse's head.'"[10]

Today, such a lack of privacy seems unpleasant, but it was not unusual in the nineteenth century, where even in the best inns and hotels, travelers often shared rooms and ate together at long tables. In all probability, welfare officials' lack of concern for privacy reflected no special disregard for the rights of the poor but rather common practice at the time.

A third and final indication of presumably inhumane care is the treat-ment accorded the insane in the Philadelphia Almshouse. From the late eighteenth century to 1803, public-welfare officials paid the Pennsylvania Hospital to care for all indigent lunatics. Always concerned about economy, managers eventually decided that this arrangement was too expensive and removed the lunatic poor to cells in the almshouse basement. Even though they were lined with wood boards, these cells remained cold and damp, and their windows opened onto the courtyard, which served as an exercise yard for healthy inmates, who often paused to tease and taunt the mentally deranged inside. In the 1820s, when there were sometimes not enough well, able-bodied poor in the almshouse to work the tread wheel that drove machinery in the factory, officials put lunatics on the wheel in their stead.[11]

Cruel as this treatment may appear to us, it was not unusual in this era. In the early nineteenth century at the Pennsylvania Hospital, which has been given credit for pioneering humane care for the insane, most cells were damp and unhealthy and below ground level. Managers of these institutions were not intentionally cruel; they simply did not know what to do with the violently insane, and since such people appeared to have few feelings, they received the most unfeeling care. Even so, almshouse managers removed harmless deranged people from cells and lodged them in the more comfortable upstairs wards. And those too violent to be placed anywhere but in cells were entrusted to caretakers, who displayed "leniency and kindness." [12]

While lack of concern for classification, inmate privacy, and the comforts of the insane were examples of unintentional severity on the part of the Philadelphia Almshouse managers, they, and other poorhouse directors as well, spent a good deal of time deliberately devising schemes to control the activites of the needy in their charge. Even in the years prior to the 1828-poor-law change, when welfare officials were frequently benevolent toward the poor, such benevolence was exercised within a restrictive setting. The Philadelphia Bettering House, along with other asylums for the poor, was originally erected to serve as an instrument of control, and that remained its purpose throughout its history. And although social control proved difficult to institute, it continued to be the foremost goal of Philadelphia's almshouse managers.

This goal was obvious to even the most casual visitor who gazed at the high fence that surrounded and enclosed the city's poorhouse. The fence was intended to keep paupers in rather than visitors out. Similarly, other nineteenth-century urban almshouses were walled in and their inmates presumably isolated from temptations. Inside the Philadelphia Almshouse and all others, inmates were segregated by sex. Managers even divided the courtyard of the Philadelphia Almshouse into men's and women's compounds after officials discovered that fraternization between the sexes in a single open yard occasionally led to sexual intimacy. [13] Administrators also introduced racial segregation into both the Philadelphia and Baltimore Almshouses, but not until the 1820s. Although there had been a significant minority of blacks in the Philadelphia asylum earlier, only after the War of 1812, when a depression led to a sharp escalation in the number of jobless seeking welfare, did many Philadelphians begin to scrutinize carefully the city's poor population and single out needy blacks as especially requiring control. In 1820 for the first time, Philadelphia's guardians argued that blacks were "indolent, improvident, and extremely prolific" and thus moved them to special almshouse wards where their behavior could better be managed. [14]

Fences and sexually and racially segregated wards were not the only methods used to restrain inmates. Managers also imposed restrictions on paupers, requiring them to obey strict rules that were posted in the wards of all poorhouses. These rules required the needy to show respect "to their superiors or governors" and behave "in an orderly, sober, and submissive manner." In Philadelphia, inmates who failed to obey their betters or refused to work, could be confined in cells with lunatics for one week and forced to subsist on only bread and water. The steward and matron meted out lesser punishments to inmates who begged (they were put in cells for forty-eight hours) and to those who were not in bed when the lights went out at night (they lost two meals the following day).[15]

One group of poor whom Philadelphia's officials singled out as being especially in need of control were venereal patients, many of whom were confirmed prostitutes. To punish and reform such women, in 1808, managers opened an account for each, charging her with the cost of her care and requiring her to work in the asylum to repay such costs before being discharged. This plan never worked well. A number of venereal patients escaped rather than endure forced labor. Nor were the managers ever able to punish transgressors by indenturing them as servants after they left the institution. Few respectable citizens were willing to employ in their home these women who exhibited "lewdness and drunkenness and other evil practices."[16]

The failure of managers to punish effectively and limit the freedom of venereal patients is just one sign of their inability to successfully regulate the activities of inmates. While social control was the chief purpose of all poorhouses, in early nineteenth-century Philadelphia, and probably in other cities as well, it was never fully achieved. Part of the reason why welfare officials were unable to control closely inmate behavior was that officials relied on paupers to keep the asylum functioning. There were, of course, people hired to direct all almshouses, but in Philadelphia, as elsewhere, they were few in number. Customarily, a steward was employed to take overall charge of each asylum, although he was most directly responsible for the men's section, and a matron was employed to run the women's side of most poorhouses. In Philadelphia, other employees included an agent (who handled removing nonresident poor for both outdoor guardians and almshouse managers), several clerks, an apothecary, a gatekeeper, and a factory foreman. While these employees performed important supervisory functions, in Philadelphia, as well as in other almshouses, inmates themselves kept the institution running: they did the cooking, baking, butchering, painting, gardening, washing, watched the cells, and nursed the ill. In return for their services, inmates received small grants of money or clothes and extra provisions.[17] Almshouse employees directed the inmates' labor, but the steward, matron and others, being in a distinct minority, probably had to be cautious about how they exerted their authority. Between 1807 and 1826, there was approximately one employee for every seventy-five inmates in Philadelphia.[18] In such an environment, the poor may well have enjoyed considerable freedom. Almshouses may have been designed as places where welfare authorities could restrain the poor, but with the ratio of poorhouse officials to inmates so low, it is unlikely that a truly firm control over the poor could be exercised.

Other evidence of laxity in the Philadelphia Almshouse's administration between 1800 and 1828 are the ease of escape and the availability of alcohol. While inmates were presumably incarcerated until the managers chose to release them, in actuality it was quite simple for paupers to leave at their pleasure by scaling the almshouse fence, which was often in disrepair. Once free, some inmates pawned goods stolen from the institution and used the money to obtain liquor, which they carried back to friends in the asylum. The consumption of liquor in almshouses was a sore point with welfare officials. Since poverty itself was commonly deemed a result of excessive drinking, it was natural that poor relief officials would not want to allow inmates access to alcohol. In theory, tobacco, snuff, and liquor were all forbidden to inmates, but in reality, all were easily obtainable. For example, almshouse employees rewarded those who performed hard labor in the institutions with sizable liquor allowances. Further, since alcohol was an important ingredient in medicines during this era, officials stored spirits in almshouse hospitals. In Philadelphia, physicians sometimes left the keys to the liquor cabinet lying around, and healthy paupers made use of them. Occasionally, inmates also found their way into a Philadelphia Almshouse meeting room, where managers kept a variety of liquors for their own use. Even if it were possible to make the asylum's liquor inaccessible to all but the ill, owners of the grogshops that lined Spruce Street opposite the Philadelphia poorhouse were more than willing to cater to the needy and thereby served "to increase the irregularities in the House."[19]

In all probability, the ever-present need to economize on almshouse administration inhibited managers from employing many people either to operate or supervise the institution. Instead, officials relied heavily on inmate laborers who had to be rewarded in some way—often with alcohol. The managers' commitment to thrift also precluded spending money to repair the fence, thereby making escapes possible. Evidently, adherence to one goal—economy—prevented welfare officials from completely achieving another—social control.

Yet, ironically, even though managers adopted many money-saving schemes, economical administration of the Philadelphia Almshouse proved to be an elusive goal. Before passage of the 1828 poor law, not only did welfare officials have trouble monitoring closely behavior of almshouse inmates, managers were also unable to balance the institution's accounts. By retaining few full-time paid employees and skimping on almshouse repairs, managers saved some money, but not much. They felt the most sensible way to economize and make the institution partially self-supporting was to sell at a profit goods manufactured by inmates. Unfortunately, almshouse manufacturing proved remunerative only when there were a large number of able-bodied poor in the asylum and at the same time, economic conditions in the city were conducive to selling items manufactured by inmates, a combination of events that occurred all too rarely.

During the early years of the nineteenth century, the major "manufacturing" enterprise in the Philadelphia Almshouse was picking oakum or untwisting and picking apart old ropes to obtain oakum, a calking for the seams of ships. This was not particularly profitable. In 1805, after citizens on an ad hoc winter-relief committee demanded more work for the poor, managers initiated a program to expand manufacturing. They set poor women living in and out of the almshouse to work spinning thread and hired a few weavers to help inmates complete the manufacture of sheeting and toweling. Output rose, but not until 1808 did the almshouse factory begin to expand rapidly as both the labor supply and the demand for cheap textiles escalated. Because of the embargo, many people formerly employed in commerce lost their jobs and took refuge in the almshouse. There was an average of 190 people a week working in the factory in 1808, in contrast to the 140 employed weekly the year before. The demand for almshouse products increased at the same time, because the embargo made it difficult for Americans to obtain these products from England. The value of goods made in the almshouse more than doubled between 1805 and 1808, and while managers sent a portion of these items to the almshouse supply closets, they sold well over half to city residents.[20]

Still, the success of the poorhouse factory was short-lived. As the institution grew more and more crowded due to the influx of unemployed, welfare officials found it necessary to move beds into the factory in place of the looms. As a result, the total worth of goods produced in the factory declined, although managers were still able to sell most of the goods. The ready market for almshouse-made products, combined with the large number of poor in need of employment, indicated the need for a larger factory and almshouse. Hence, almshouse managers, along with many other concerned citizens, in 1809, petitioned the legislature for authority to construct a more spacious almshouse in the country, where inmates could labor not only in a cotton factory but also on a farm and in a flour mill. After discussing the petitions at several sessions, in 1811, legislators, concerned about economy and afraid that moving the almshouse to the country would be quite costly, voted against it. Undeterred by this rebuff, managers were determined to enlarge the old almshouse, and completion of the new building in 1815 finally enabled them to reopen the factory.[21]

Unfortunately, the market for almshouse-made sheeting and toweling was not then very promising. Philadelphians evidently preferred to purchase higher quality British-made textiles, which were in plentiful supply after the war ended in 1815, or American-made items woven by laborers under the "putting-out" system or in one of the city's privately owned cotton factories. Almshouse-made goods were never top quality, since inmates required to perform unpaid labor were not the most industrious or careful workers. From 1816 through 1835, the annual income from the sale of goods produced in the almshouse dwindled from over one thousand to less than $200. Responding to these financial setbacks, managers discharged women who had previously done spinning in their homes but were reluctant to shut down the factory when the almshouse was crowded with people made jobless by the Panic of 1819.

Welfare officials had always been willing to find work for the unemployed during a depression, but in this instance, Philadelphia's officials did not extend themselves overly much on behalf of those out of work. Almshouse managers simply kept the factory open and ordered items made there to be used in the institution itself.[22] Of course, the factory had always been supply source for the almshouse, but it now became almost exclusively that.

Philadelphia's unsatisfactory experience with almshouse manufacturing in the early nineteenth century was not altogether unexpected, and could have been foreseen by astute welfare officials. Earlier, in Boston in the 1750s and in New York and Philadelphia as well as in the 1760s, poor relief adminstrators had overseen the manufacture of large quantities of low-quality cloth. Officials had hoped to sell the material made by the poor in almshouses and thereby turn a profit for their asylums. In both cities, these experiments failed, because the institutions produced only low-quality cloth with the labor of ailing and disabled inmates. The more able-bodied poor, accustomed to home manufacture, avoided labor in any factory. At this time, buyers inevitably rejected almshouse goods in favor of better made merchandise from abroad. By the nineteenth century, when urban factories were somewhat more common, the poor were less averse to them, yet because almshouse inmates were still forced to work without pay, they were resentful and careless. Poor houses continued to market cloth of low quality which, consumers purchased only when no other was available to them. Nevertheless, officials in Boston and Philadelphia, as well as elsewhere in the country, still tried to make money from almshouse factories. Of course, in Philadelphia, they were successful for a time, but only due to extraordinary conditions during the embargo and the War of 1812. The success of the Philadelphia Almshouse factory during these economic crises apparently deluded its managers into believing that they would always be able to sell textiles woven by the poor.

By 1823 in Philadelphia, almshouse managers realized that they could not make a profit from products made in the asylum, so they seized on a new, practical reason for keeping the factory open: it could be made unpleasant enough to deter the poor from seeking indoor relief. Following the example of New York's public-welfare officials, managers sold the horses previously used to drive the cotton and woolen machines and erected two tread wheels in their stead. Laboring on these wheels became a punishment for lazy inmates as well as venereal patients who had been discharged from hospital wards. When such unworthy poor were in short supply, lunatics worked the wheels instead. Even though the almshouse manufacturing committee found the tread wheels inefficient and recommended replacing them with steam-driven machinery, the majority of public-welfare officials disagreed. They insisted that the wheels remain in operation to discourage the poor from seeking asylum.[23]

No one considered the factory to be a job-training center. At best, early in the century, the almshouse factory prepared a few men to be weavers, a very low-paying occupation, and some women to be spinners, a job that was fast becoming outmoded. At worst, labor on the tread wheel in the 1820s was no sort of job preparation at all. The idea that welfare money should be spent on training that would equip the poor with the skills necessary to become self-sufficient and no longer dependent on public relief was largely a conception of twentieth-century reformers. In the nineteenth century, in almshouses, as well as prisons and juvenile reformatories, inmates worked not to learn new, useful skills but to earn dollars for the institution. Of course, labor was also a means of controlling prisoners, juvenile delinquents, and the poor: the busier they were, the less likely they were to upset institutional regimen. In addition, labor could be used as a punishment, and it might even be loosely viewed as being a reform measure. Since crime, delinquency, and poverty were often blamed on laziness, officials argued that labor in institutions taught inmates work habits that would later be useful. Nevertheless, the main purpose of institutional labor programs was to save the taxpayers' money. In the case of the Philadelphia Almshouse factory, it saved dollars for a time by providing welfare officials with a source of income that they used to defray a fraction of total almshouse expenses. When this income declined, almshouse managers expected the factory's tread wheel to continue to promote economy by discouraging applications for institutional relief. In this expectation, they were disappointed, for the average yearly admission of paupers to the almshouse between 1823 and 1834, when the wheel was in operation, rose to 3,636. Earlier, from 1815 to 1822, when the postwar depression was at its height, average yearly almshouse admission was just 3,309.[24] Except in the most extraordinary circumstances, the poorhouse factory, with or without the tread wheel, did not prove very economical.

Although managers were generally unable to earn money through manufacturing, they were able to promote economy in one important division of the almshouse—the hospital. Here, they used a medical program that was inexpensive, practical, widely accepted in other hospitals of the day, and in tune with the needs and interests of members of the medical profession.

In Philadelphia and elsewhere, rather than pay doctors to minister to ailing almshouse inmates, welfare officials opened their door to well-established city doctors who used the institution as a training clinic for their fee-paying pupils. In this era when medicine was learned largely through apprenticeship, experienced physicians and surgeons with many apprentices needed a population of ill people on whom they and their students could practice, and ailing poor patients in the almshouse served this purpose nicely. Therefore, eminent Philadelphia doctors willingly accepted positions as attending physicians and surgeons in the almshouse. On a rotating basis, they visited the institution twice weekly with their medical-student apprentices, whom they instructed while making the rounds. The Pennsylvania Hospital operated in the same fashion, and there doctors initiated the practice of delivering clinical lectures to fee-paying pupils in 1766; by 1803, the Philadelphia Almshouse doctors did likewise. Patients with particularly interesting illnesses were thereafter removed to the clinical wards for study. Since attending physicians and surgeons were not at the almshouse around the clock, at the Philadelphia poorhouse and other hospitals for the needy as well, officials retained medical students who were fairly advanced in their training to do most routine medical work. In Philadelphia, such a program was economical, because the medical students paid for the privilege of living and boarding in the almshouse for one year while they learned medicine by carrying out the orders of the attending physicians and surgeons. Although managers selected the interns (or "students," as they were called), after 1825, officials allowed the attending physicians and surgeons to check credentials of applicants and recommend the best candidates.[25]

While this program allowed the poor access to the very best medical talent of the day, it also made them objects of study and left them, for a good part of the time, in the care of inexperienced student doctors, who often disrupted the asylum's routine. Sometimes they gave the poor access to the medicine cabinet, and the medical students themselves brought liquor into the asylum to enliven their parties. Distressed by these practices, almshouse managers temporarily ignored the need to economize and from 1823 to 1826, paid two young graduate doctors to preserve order among the student interns. Once order was restored, managers recalled their commitment to thrift, and the graduate doctors departed. When they did, the students reverted to their old ways, quarreled with other almshouse employees, and on several occasions, threw wine glasses and meat at the steward's dining table.

As for nurses, to save money, almshouse managers in Philadelphia and elsewhere customarily employed inmates to attend to the ill. The nurses were no more decorous nor experienced than the student interns. Doctors complained that the nurses appropriated for themselves the laudanum, ether, and malt liquors prescribed for patients. In 1804, a nurse in the men's medical ward, James Maloney, while drunk with liquor intended for his patients, administered the wrong medication to John Moore, an ailing barber, and Moore subsequently died. Maloney's female assistant in the ward, Elizabeth Donnelly, was also frequently drunk and commonly sold to friends outside the almshouse coffee she should have served her patients.[26]

While using paupers as nurses and student doctors may not have been in the best interests of poor patients, it was economical, as was retaining unpaid attending physicians and surgeons. Although not ideal, this mode of hospital administration was normal in nineteenth-century America, and it did save the taxpayers' money. In contrast, the Philadelphia Almshouse's factory in most years proved to be far less money saving. Thus, between 1800 and 1828, Philadelphia's almshouse managers were only partly successful in promoting one of their chief objectives—thrift. They were even less successful accomplishing their other main goal—careful regulation of the lives of needy inmates. Of course, almshouse administrators alleviated considerable suffering and made the lives of many poor more comfortable, but such humanitarian objectives were always of secondary importance. Close direction of inmate activities and an economical mode of administration were the officials' central concerns, but they were unable to achieve either fully.

After passage of the 1828 poor law, which mandated construction of the new almshouse in Blockley, Philadelphia's welfare officials grew even more obsessed with social control and economy, while their commitment to kind and benevolent treatment of paupers diminished. The changing nature of the officials' interests is indicated by the structure and appearance as well as the mode of operation of the new poorhouse.

This almshouse was situated on the west bank of the Schuylkill River, outside the city, on a 180-acre farm. Four buildings, connected by walls, formed a square that covered and enclosed ten acres. Beyond these walls, on the rest of the property, were forty acres of meadow and 130 of farmland. Visitors to this large complex usually approached it from the river and thus entered the easternmost building, which was the men's almshouse. In the central section of this three-story structure were offices of the guardians and almshouse employees; living quarters for the steward; the men's dining hall, which seated 500; and eight attic rooms, where visitors observed aged men devotedly reading the Bible. On each floor in the two wings of this building were five wards for incurables as well as others for men physically able to work.

Directly opposite and west of the male almshouse facility across the enclosed square was an identical building for women. Here were wards for healthy but impoverished women alongside wards for convalescents, the incurably ill, the lame, and the idiotic.[27]

The central section of the northernmost building at Blockley was originally a house of employment, or factory. On the lower floors were a grist mill, cotton and woolen spinning jennies, and on the topmost floor, quarters for male paupers who labored downstairs. The steam engine that drove the machinery never worked very well, and in 1845, guardians shut it down and sold all the equipment in the factory. Two years later, they converted most of the nearly empty building into a hospital, and in 1849, they freed more space for patients by moving the few remaining factory workers to a new, small house on the almshouse grounds. While guardians changed the central section of the north building in the 1840s, they left its two wings generally untouched. In the east wing was the children's asylum and in the west was the old women's asylum.[28]

The last major building of the four that together made up the almshouse was on the south edge of the enclosed square. The three-story central section of this building was originally the hospital. Here also were the apothecary's shop, the medical library, and a surgery-lecture hall that seated 300. The two wings of this building housed the insane, with males on the east side and females on the west. When guardians moved patients to the vacant factory in 1847, the entire southern building became an insane asylum. In the square formed by the four almshouse buildings were other smaller structures. There was a washhouse topped by a steeple, a bell, and a four-sided clock; closeby was a storehouse for food, clothing, and other supplies.[29]

Interestingly, the general layout of the new almshouse, with its fenced-in compound dominated by large buildings containing separate men's and women's divisions, a hospital, and a factory, was not unlike the old Bettering House. The same pattern held true in other cities. Both the exterior and interior arrangements of almshouses constructed between 1772 and 1816 in Baltimore and New York resembled Philadelphia's Bettering House, and when officials in these cities opened new poorhouses in 1823 (Baltimore) and 1848 (New York), these structures were much like their predecessors. Innovative design in almshouses was a rarity. Nonetheless, nineteenth-century urban poor asylums were distinctive in that they were larger and more isolated from cities than the institutions they replaced. All were imposing buildings intended to inspire awe and by their very appearance, frighten new inmates into submission as well as discourage would-be paupers from becoming dependent on public charity.

Philadelphia Almshouse, 1838 (*Courtesy of The Historical Society of Pennsylvania*). Built in 1835 in Blockley Township west of Philadelphia, this institution is much larger and more forbidding than the Bettering House.

In addition, designers of new nineteenth-century almshouses situated them well outside cities. While Philadelphia and Baltimore relocated their almshouses on country farms, New York moved its poorhouse to an island. In all three cases, the intent was to remove paupers from the temptations of urban life.[30] In Philadelphia, no longer could paupers simply scale the almshouse fence and walk across Spruce Street to a bar. Instead, escapees from the new Blockley Almshouse found themselves in the midst of farmland, across a river and several miles from the heart of the city. Hence, even though new almshouses in nineteenth-century cities were traditional in design, by their very size and location, they reflected a greater commitment to social control.

The desire to isolate and closely monitor the behavior of the poor replaced much of the former humanitarian concern for them. Among public officials, the charitable impulse, although never altogether absent, nonetheless diminished in intensity after passage of the 1828 poor law. Thereafter, welfare authorities no longer attended personally to the needs of the poor. A committee of the board of guardians rather than a separate group of almshouse managers supervised the Bettering House from 1828 to 1834 and subsequently, the Blockley Almshouse. Although officials visited the asylum regularly, they devoted most of their time to supervisory chores and sought less contact with individual inmates than had the pre-1828 almshouse managers.[31] With the opening of Blockley, guardians demonstrated no special compassion for aged married couples forced by poverty to enter the public asylum. Officials refused to establish a separate married ward, comparable to the one in the old Bettering House, although they generally assigned elderly paupers to special wards for the aged in the men's and women's divisions of the almshouse. Officials did maintain a lying-in ward for unmarried, pregnant women at Blockley, but once having delivered, mothers with their infants were turned out of the asylum and expected to fare as best they could on their own. The abolition of outdoor cash relief, timed to coincide with the opening of Blockley, precluded the possibility of these women receiving, as they had previously, financial aid outside the institution until they had become self-sufficient.

There were other signs of diminishing sympathy for the needy at Blockley as well. Inmates in the new almshouse were forbidden to keep small personal belongings, including articles of furniture, in the wards, and they were no longer permitted to wear their own clothes. Once admitted, all donned the pauper's uniform, which consisted of thin blue trousers and shirt for the men. Temporary leaves from the poorhouse, which had in the past been passed our fairly readily by the Bettering House managers, became almost unobtainable at Blockley. Paupers applied to the steward or matron, who awarded a small number of passes to men and women in alternate months. If a pass were secured, an inmate was permitted to leave just once a month. When a pauper left or returned, she or he had to submit to a search: guardians were determined to prevent the poor from stealing and selling the asylum's property and using the proceeds to buy liquor for themselves and fellow inmates. Perhaps guardians also restricted leaves because of community pressure. The *Public Ledger* reported that almshouse inmates on leave often terrorized residents in West Philadelphia. One drove a teacher and her pupils into the street and stayed in the school until forcibly removed; another entered a house and "mistreated" its female occupant until neighbors had subdued him.[32]

While welfare officials who administered Blockley abandoned many of the more benevolent practices of their predecessors who had managed the old Bettering House, they continued one less satisfactory habit—that of assigning newly admitted paupers to any available bed. Classifying the inmate population at Blockley remained fairly inconsistent. Of course, early in the century, by failing to separate rigorously patients of different ages with different ailments, managers were only following common institutional practice. However, by 1835 when Blockley opened, specialized asylums were more common; orphanages, houses of refuge, and mental hospitals had been or were being constructed throughout the country. These asylums popularized the notion that different types of poor should be assisted in different settings. Philadelphia's guardians of the poor recognized this new trend, for they divided the institution into men's and women's divisions, hospital, insane asylum, and factory; yet, they continued to permit a composite group of inmates to inhabit most wards. Thus, drunks and vagrants often shared cells with the insane. In 1837, in the black women's surgical and venereal wards, there were several women suffering from rheumatism, one of whom was aged, while the other was deaf and dumb. These women ranged in age from thirteen to eighty. In the black women's medical ward were patients from thirteen to forty-three years old, including two alcoholics and one labeled only "weak." Even in the black nursery, there were three elderly women and one alcoholic. Although these examples are drawn from the one extant census taken at Blockley before 1854, which was made up only of blacks, there is no reason to suppose that whites were classified any more carefully within the institution.[33]

While a generous, forbearing attitude toward the poor may have been somewhat out of vogue at Blockley, it did not altogether disappear. The diet of inmates improved as attendants frequently served fresh fruit and vegetables raised on the Blockley farm. Of course, the farm was primarily intended to be a money-making venture, but some produce harvested from its fields also ended up on dining tables in the almshouse. As a result, the nutritional value of meals served the poor at Blockley was enhanced. Welfare officials also dispensed with the factory's tread wheel at the new almshouse, partly to increase production efficiency, but their decision had the added advantage of freeing inmates from punitory labor on this device. Another change introduced by guardians, which unlike improvements in diet and the abolition of the tread wheel seems to have been motivated purely by the desire to improve living conditions for the poor, was the provision for more privacy. Guardians arranged wards so that in the center of each there was common space, with partitions around the outside forming a series of tiny three-sided rooms; and in each of these cubicles was an inmate's bed. This new arrangement allowed the poor more privacy at Blockley than at the old Bettering House.[34]

Empathy for the needy is most evident in the administration of the hospital at Blockley. Accommodating ailing paupers remained the chief function of the new as well as the old almshouse. Among a sample of those who were admitted to Blockley between 1835 and 1850, three-quarters were ill, and as in earlier years, most entered medical rather than surgical wards. Like their counterparts in the old almshouse, the majority of the patients at Blockley probably suffered from chronic complaints. Officials showed concern for the ill poor by improving medical facilities at Blockley. One innovation was the introduction of receiving wards where attendants bathed new patients and gave them clean gowns. Physicians in these wards examined all new entrants and assigned each to a bed in one of the hospital's many divisions. In the new almshouse hospital, just as in the old, patients were segregated by sex and color, but there were many more wards for patients at Blockley than in the old Bettering House. Physicians assigned white men to medical, surgical, eye, or venereal wards, while black men entered either a medical or surgical/venereal ward. Doctors placed women in either black or white medical, surgical, venereal, obstetric, or nursery wards. Of course, classification of patients in these wards was not always consistent, but in all of them, the ill poor enjoyed more privacy than in the old Bettering House. At Blockley for the first time, every ill pauper had her or his own bed, at the head of which was a sign inscribed with its occupant's age, date of admission, and ailment. [35]

While more attention to the patient's cleanliness, comfort, and privacy reflect the guardians' humanitarian concern for the ill poor, this concern is even more evident in the innovations instituted in caring for the insane at Blockley. These innovations were the direct result of community pressure, yet the fact that Philadelphia's welfare officials yielded so willingly to this pressure reveals their solicitude for the mentally deranged.

By the time Blockley opened in 1835, many American reformers had initiated a new regimen for treating the insane, called "moral treatment"—a synonym for personal, humane care. Proponents of moral treatment eschewed physical restraints, emphasized close attention by trained medical personnel to the different needs of patients suffering from various types of mental aberrations, and stressed the importance of regular work and recreation for patients with disordered, confused minds. By the 1840s, several mental hospitals, including two in the Philadelphia area, the Friends Asylum and the Pennsylvania Hospital for the Insane, practiced moral treatment. It was probably inevitable in this era that a large hospital like Blockley, where custodial care had at first been the norm, should come under attack. Guardians did not ignore their critics. Officials agreed that "the moral Treatment of the Insane is all important for the restoration of Reason," and they were determined not to "walk ... behind the enlightened and philanthropic of our day and generation." As a result of the guardians' commitment "to give comfort and succour, to the sick and the suffering—the idiot and the manic" improving the lunatic asylum at Blockley became one of their major concerns. [36]

When Blockley first opened, the insane moved into the two wings of the hospital building. Here, the most violent slept in cells, while others had beds in one of the six large ward rooms. Fortunately, no one slept below ground as they had in the old almshouse, because guardians had decided that cellars were too damp and unhealthy for patients.[37]

While the insane were somewhat separated at night, they were not during the day. In 1844, reformer Dorothea Dix observed in a women's day room a number of patients rolling on the floor and screaming, others sitting quietly, a fiddler playing in one corner, and in another, a young girl strapped into a "tranquilizing chair." Dix also found a male patient in the other wing tied to such a chair with a heavy leather cape over his shoulders and from a container above his head, melting ice dripped on his hair and face. Dix and others questioned the value of such physical restraint, and they also objected strongly to the lack of classification at Blockley, where the violently insane mixed freely with newly admitted patients in the day rooms and exercise yards. Critics argued that lack of classification precluded cure—new patients soon fell into the same patterns of behavior as the old—which, in turn, led to the insane poor being supported indefinitely at public expense.

Not only was classification absent, so, too, were trained attendants. In the early 1840s, paupers working as nurses, supervised by two male attendants, one for each sex, staffed the lunatic asylum. Frequently, male nurses cared for female patients. In addition, attending physicians and resident student doctors were often too busy to visit the insane several times a week as they were supposed to do.

When they did come, they noticed that minimal comforts were provided for the insane. Stoves warmed only the halls and day rooms, so that temperatures frequently dropped below freezing in the cells. In February 1849, a patient was found wrapped in her bed clothes under her bed in a cell where the temperature was below 18 degrees. In the same month, a towel froze in the hands of a nurse as she bathed a delicate female patient. Furthermore, inmates had little opportunity for exercise or recreation and engaged in very little useful labor. When doctors permitted male patients outdoors, attendants crowded them all into a tiny paved yard enclosed by high walls. The only labor insane patients ever performed was to pump water occasionally for the poorhouse. Critics argued that moral treatment was impossible in the absence of recreational and work facilities.[38]

Guardians responded to their critics and instituted a variety of improvements in the lunatic asylum between 1845 and 1854. They attempted to classify patients better by separating them by color and type of mental aberration. Guardians also opened a convalescent lunatic ward and applied to the legislature for funds to construct a separate building for noisy female lunatics. The legislature complied, and in 1848, guardians moved the loudest and most violent female patients to the lodge. Despite these improvements, classification at Blockley was never as carefully attended to as in other mental hospitals during the era. Until 1849, guardians persisted in placing alcoholics in the lunatic asylum. Officials also regularly used it as a place of punishment, and thus there were always some inmates in the cells whose only mental problem was that they had not obeyed almshouse rules.[39]

In addition to changes in classification procedures, guardians also improved medical care in the lunatic asylum by replacing the two male superintendents with women and by ruling that only female nurses could attend to female patients. Guardians also hired another resident student physician for the asylum and encouraged the chief resident physician to learn more about the proper care of the insane by paying his way to conventions of the Association of Medical Superintendents in Charge of Lunatic Asylums. Still, guardians stopped short of doing all that their critics suggested. Officials could never altogether ignore their commitment to economy and so retained paupers as nurses in the lunatic asylum despite what guardians acknowledged were the objections of "all enlightened people." Financial constraints also prevented guardians from appointing a full-time medical superintendent to oversee care for the insane—an administrative arrangement adopted in other private and state mental hospitals of the day.

Not only did guardians act, albeit not with total effectiveness, to improve classification and medical care at Blockley, they also tried to improve physical facilities and recreational activities. The most important change they made was expanding the lunatic asylum to include the whole south building. Officials also installed a better heating system in the women's wing and introduced some recreational activities, including a ballroom dance in 1845, as well as religious services and classes. Guardians also put books and musical instruments in most wards and assigned mentally deranged inmates to light gardening around the institution. Welfare officials had come to believe that "pleasant employment, constant occupation, and exercise in the open air, are most efficient in breaking up the train of morbid ideas" in the insane.[40]

Improving hospital facilities for the insane and other patients, changing the diet, abolishing the tread wheel, and installing single beds in semi-secluded alcoves reveal a certain benevolence on the part of Blockley's administrators. Yet, while they sometimes displayed a benign attitude toward the poor, these same administrators more frequently sought to impose tight restrictions on inmates' behavior. Welfare officials expected these restrictions to make Blockley such an unappealing place that few would choose to take refuge there. Thus, social control would promote economy.

The main purpose of Blockley, to goad the poor to work and thereby remain self-sufficient, as already noted, was reflected in the very size and location of the institution. Huge imposing buildings situated well away from the city proper were intended to frighten the poor into doing all they could to avoid incarceration. Further, the regimen inside the asylum was also designed to be discouraging. Requiring all inmates, even the most worthy aged married couples, to live in sexually segregated wards and wear uniforms; and permitting inmates to leave the asylum only rarely are all signs of guardians' efforts to impose social control.

There are other signs as well. For example, inmate movement was strictly limited, not only to the outside, but also within the poorhouse. Walls, pierced only by an occasional gate, enclosed each building at Blockley, and the needy had to apply for passes in order to walk from one division of the asylum to another. Andrew Caffrey, an itinerant bookseller who took refuge in the almshouse one winter, recalled how he left his ward about midnight one night to go downstairs for a glass of water. He was apprehended by watchman Brown who forcibly returned and strapped Caffrey to his bed, where he remained until a doctor released him the next day.

Caffrey's experience also calls attention to another aspect of life at Blockley—severity of punishments. Guardians were determined to keep inmates under control by imposing strict penalties for even the most minor infringement of the rules. Thus, in 1846, officials sent Emeline Campbell to the cells with her hands tied behind her back for "destroying alms house property." She could not be released until she apologized to the steward, matron, and nurse. Guardians stated that if Campbell violated an alms-house rule again, she would be incarcerated in the cells and her "hair cut close to her head."[41]

Even though guardians tried to control inmates in Blockley, they were not altogether successful. Just as social control had been incomplete in the old Bettering House, so was it only partially realized in Blockley. The failure of those who administered both the new and the old Philadelphia almshouses to govern strictly inmate conduct is explained in part by reliance on the labor of the poor. At Blockley, inmates continued, with only minimal supervision, to perform most of the daily tasks required to keep the institution running smoothly, including washing, baking, and nursing.[42] Of course, there were more employees at Blockley than there had been at the old almshouse. In the new asylum, as in the old, there was a steward who directed the entire institution but especially the men's alms-house, and an agent who interviewed paupers when they first arrived; recorded pertinent information about them, including their place of settlement; removed nonresidents; and took weekly censuses in all wards. In addition, there were two matrons, rather than one as before, who managed the women's almshouse and children's asylum, respectively; and many more subordinate employees at Blockley, including several gatekeepers, a clerk, a storekeeper, a superintendent of the factory, a bookkeeper, a farmer, an apothecary; and after 1845, a chief resident physician. Yet even though there were more salaried personnel at Blockley, there were more inmates as well, and the ratio of employees to inmates was about the same as at the old almshouse. In 1839, there was one employee for every seventy-three inmates, and the ratio had risen to one for every eighty-seven by 1848.[43] With so many employees required to supervize so many poor people, close management of inmate behavior was problematical.

The poor enjoyed considerable independence at Blockley; they even formed organizations and tried to influence welfare officials. In 1839, guardians applauded the efforts of approximately eighty religious-minded inmates who preached temperance in the asylum. It may have been this same group that in 1846 requested and obtained from guardians better facilities for Sunday worship. If this inmate organization existed (and of course guardians recognized it, because its goals conformed to theirs), others may have also.

Aside from organized group activity, there was plenty of the unorganized variety on the wards as well. Brawling and fighting were by no means uncommon, and the house committee spent a great deal of time disciplining contentious inmates. The poor brought the ethnic tensions in the city in the 1840s into the almshouse. For example, Robert Lewis, an Irish Catholic, repeatedly attacked fellow inmate James Platt, an Englishman, after Platt read aloud to a blind inmate from a book Lewis found religiously offensive. As a consequence of the attacks, Platt died.[44] Inmates were not the only ones who disrupted the wards: visitors also caused commotion when they flocked in, sat on the beds, and handed out fruit to patients—a practice much frowned on by the doctors. Eventually, guardians restricted visitors to one day per week to minimize the disorder they provoked.

Inmates and others who peddled articles in the institution created another type of disturbance. There must have been some medium of exchange within the almshouse, although it may not have been money, because paupers presumably handed over all they had to the agent when he admitted them. Nevertheless, inmates managed to sell one another pins, needles, thread, and other small personal articles, and gatekeepers peddled drugs, fruits, and candy. Liquor, too, was available for purchase. Inmate Caffrey reported that the bookkeeper regularly visited the wards and sold "wine and spirits" to all who cared to buy.[45]

Just as closely monitoring inmates was an objective never entirely achieved at Blockley, economical management of this institution was also not fully attained. Of course, economically administering public welfare was of even more importance to Philadelphia's officials after the 1828-

poor-law reform than before, and they made heroic attempts to practice thrift at Blockley. Nonetheless, they were only partially successful in their efforts.

From the beginning, employing paupers at Blockley was viewed as a money-saving venture. The institution was located on a farm in order to provide work for inmates and income from the sale of fruits and vegetables for welfare officials. The farm did prove profitable: every year from 1835 to 1854, the sale of farm products generated some income to offset institutional expenses. In fact, the farm not only yielded items for sale, but plenty of produce for house consumption as well.

In marked contrast to the farm, the factory at Blockley was not successful. Ignoring the example of previous almshouse factories in Philadelphia and elsewhere, the 1828-poor-law reformers expected the factory at Blockley to produce items for both sale and use in the institution. To augment productivity and presumably sales, Blockley's administrators abandoned the punitive but inefficient tread wheel and instead installed in their house of employment a steam engine to drive the grist mill, stocking loom, and weaving machines. Here, when the institution first opened, male paupers labored to produce flour, clothes, sheets, and carpets as well as shoes, furniture, tinware, ropes, and buckets.

From 1835 to 1837, welfare officials happily reported success: they were able to market a small fraction of the items manufactured at Blockley. But their pleasure was short-lived. Factory productivity diminished as the steam engine broke down periodically, perhaps due to the carelessness of inmates who had no great fondness for performing unpaid labor in the poorhouse. When the steam engine was functioning, inmates produced flour "fit only for hogs," which was virtually unsaleable. Inmates also turned out textiles of poor quality that were not particularly competitive with cloth woven by free laborers in Philadelphia, which by the 1830s was the largest textile manufacturing center in the United States. Still, the low price of almshouse-made cloth made it somewhat attractive to buyers until the depression of 1837–43, when the price of all cloth manufactured in the city dropped, and consumers who bought any at all naturally preferred goods of higher quality produced by free laborers. Between 1837 and 1849, guardians recorded no profit at all for the Blockley factory.[46] Accordingly, in 1845, guardians sold most of the factory machinery, shut down the house of employment, and converted most of it into a hospital. Nevertheless, some manufacturing for almshouse use continued. Every year from 1844 to 1854, about fifty inmates labored in the institution as shoemakers, tailors, weavers, and carpenters. Still, at this time, probably no more than 250 men out of an inmate population of over 1,500 ever worked on items for asylum use.[47]

In Philadelphia, in most years between 1800–1854, the sale of goods made in almshouses did not significantly reduce the expense of institutional relief. Even so, Blockley officials, like the managers of the old almshouse, were determined to continue some manufacturing to discourage "lazy, intemperate vagrants and paupers" from flocking to the poorhouse. Guardians wanted to show the needy "that it is quite as easy to work in mechanic shops in the City and Liberties and enjoy their liberty as it is to be confined within these walls and be compeled [sic] to work in our Factory." Thus work programs were used like other features of asylum regimen—as a means of dissuading the poor from entering the almshouse for "trifling and insufficient reasons."[48] Presumably, forced labor at Blockley would prove economical by deterring applicants.

To make it quite clear to the poor that public welfare was not free, beginning in 1835, guardians initiated an accounting system similar to that used in other nineteenth-century almshouses. They opened accounts for inmates, charged them for the cost of room and board and credited them for labor performed in the institution. Supposedly, an inmate could not be released until the account balanced. By 1850, guardians were crediting each inmate $2.50 for every week worked and charging $1.00 a week for room and board.[49] At this rate, a former patient had to work three weeks in order to pay for a month spent in the hospital.

This work program was difficult to administer, but it, along with other unpleasant aspects of Blockley, seemingly did discourage paupers from seeking entrance. From 1835 to 1854, average yearly admissions to the almshouse were 3,773, whereas they had been 3,501 from 1815 to 1834, an increase of 8 percent.[50] Yet between 1820 and 1850, the population of the city and districts rose two and a half times. That is, in 1820, there were thirty-six people per thousand in Philadelphia's population in the Bettering House, and by 1850, there were only fourteen per thousand in Blockley. Thus the strict work program in the new poorhouse helped promote economy by lowering the admission rate.

The Philadelphia guardians of the poor practiced another type of economy in the almshouse hospital. Like the managers of the old almshouse before them, Blockley officials endeavored to save money on some aspects of hospital administration. Of course, on occasion, their humanitarian commitments resulted in increased medical expenditures, as in the case of improving of facilities for the insane, establishing a receiving ward, and providing single beds in partitioned wards for inmates. Nevertheless, there were many other ways in which guardians tried to exercise thrift in hospital management. For example, they continued to rely, as had managers of the old almshouse, on the cheapest nursing staff possible—pauper inmates. Since such nurses remained in the almshouse "against their will," compelled to work off the cost of their care, they were poor attendants and, guardians acknowledged, immune to both "praise and punishment."[51]

When the new almshouse first opened, adherence to the principle of frugality also led guardians to reinstitute the method of medical care used at the Bettering House. Thus, welfare officials retained prominent Philadelphia physicians, surgeons, and accoucheurs (obstetricians), many of them instructors at one of the local medical schools, to attend to patients at Blockley on a rotating basis. Occasionally, they all met together as a board and advised guardians on medical matters. These eminent doctors willingly served without pay in order to use the almshouse hospital as a training center for their medical students. At Blockley, as in the old almshouse, young medical graduates, who paid for room and board and the right to practice at the hospital, provided most of the routine care patients required. The students were not too closely supervised by attending physicians, and these young men were quick to take umbrage at the smallest slight and evidently just as quick to escape hospital routine for a day or two of "gunning or fishing or boating."

Although this economical system of hospital administration had satisfied welfare officials for many decades, in 1845, guardians of the poor abandoned it, not in order to save money, but because of a disagreement with resident medical students. They had resigned en masse after a minor dispute with the steward, and when the board of physicians appeared to take the part of the students, guardians angrily decided to alter the entire system of medical care at the hospital by replacing the medical board with one full-time, salaried chief resident physician. To assist him, officials appointed a physician, a surgeon, and an accoucheur, each of whom received a consulting fee. Six resident medical students, who paid room and board, completed the new medical staff.[52]

While the new program was instituted for emotional rather than economical reasons, it did not prove very costly: salaries for the chief resident physician and consulting doctors amounted to just $2100 a year, or about 2 percent of the almshouse's net expenditures in 1846. The new program also meshed nicely with the guardians' desire to improve medical care for the poor at Blockley. Now patients saw an experienced physician almost daily and were no longer objects of study in the lecture hall, which welfare officials closed when they dismissed medical school instructors from the hospital staff. To justify terminating clinical instruction, guardians argued, "There are rights possessed even by the recipients of public charity which should be guarded, and feelings which should be respected."[53]

The new medical program was undoubtedly an improvement over the old for both patients and guardians of the poor, who appreciated the firm manner in which the chief resident physician ran the hospital.[54] Student doctors were less appreciative. Long accustomed to going their own way, they opposed the new system and staged walkouts in both 1847 and 1848. Older doctors in the city also objected to the new administration, because it prevented them from using the Philadelphia Hospital for their medical school classes and to instruct their personal pupils.[55] Still, the new scheme of medical administration at Blockley was not abolished. Although it proved somewhat more costly than the old, the guardians' decision to retain paupers as nurses and fee-paying medical students held down hospital expenditures.

So far, the history of Philadelphia's almshouses has been told largely from the perspective of welfare officials who administered them. But what of the needy who at one time or another took up residence in these poorhouses? Who were they, why did they come, and how long did they stay? Their stories illuminate the history of part of the city's population that until recently has been largely ignored by scholars. The experience of these needy people also reveals to what extent two concerns of Philadelphia's welfare officials—humanitarianism and social control—affected the city's poor.

An admission list from the old almshouse in 1812–13 and a sample of 600 people admitted to both this asylum and Blockley between 1828 and 1850 allow us to compare the types of indigent people who entered the city's two poorhouses.[56] In general, those admitted to both asylums were much alike, but the few differences between those who entered early and those who came later in the century illustrate how the declining interest in benevolent institutional practices and the growing commitment to strict poorhouse administration affected the city's poor.

One difference regards inmate readmission. In 1812–13, almost one-half of those residing in the Bettering House had been in the asylum before, yet from 1828 through 1850, the number of inmates who had previously lived in a Philadelphia almshouse dropped to one-third. In addition, one-half of these returnees had been in the poorhouse just once before. The large number of former inmates in poorhouse wards in 1812–13 is in part explained by the willingness of almshouse managers at this time to admit "old customers" like Barney Ripton, an out-of-work shoemaker; Peter Jaurdan, an alcoholic; and Sara Kain, a sickly woman whose husband had deserted her and returned to Ireland.

The benevolent attitude toward the poor, characteristic of welfare officials between 1800 and 1820, is shown by their willingness to admit even the most "hardened" paupers, like Mary Sherry, "an old and well known customer," and William West, who reentered the asylum just four days after having been discharged.[57] Those who found it next to impossible to remain self-sufficient and who, when periodically down on their luck, wanted to take advantage of free room and board at the almshouse, were not turned away. Of course, these poor people may have also been more inclined to seek readmission, because early in the century at the Philadelphia Almshouse, rules were not enforced too strictly and welfare officials were willing to permit inmates a good deal of freedom.

All this changed as a result of the poor-law-reform debate in the 1820s. Benevolent concern for the poor was in large part replaced by criticism of them. This change is reflected in the diminishing number of poor who entered the asylum more than once. Of course, the severity of institutional regimen may have discouraged many poor from reapplying. In addition, Philadelphia's welfare officials, who, like other concerned citizens in America and Britain at this time, increasingly blamed the poor for their poverty, were probably less inclined to admit former customers than officials earlier in the century.

A second difference between those who entered Philadelphia's almshouses before and after 1828 concerns the proportion of indigent inmates who absconded; that is, people who were not formally discharged but deliberately chose to flee the asylum. The escape rate rose over the years from a low 3 percent in 1812–13 to 12 percent in 1828–34 to 25 percent when Blockley was the city's almshouse between 1835 and 1850.[58] Even though before the 1820s, escape over or through the dilapidated Bettering House fence was relatively easy, very few inmates absconded, probably because they had little reason to do so. Official discharges were not hard to come by, and the regimen within the old poorhouse was not severe enough to make many want to leave. In contrast, after the 1828-poor-law reform, welfare officials tightened control over the Bettering House, and the more restrictive routine they imposed probably helps account for the higher escape rate between 1828 and 1834. Yet not until Blockley opened did the proportion of paupers eloping rise to one-quarter, presumably because the regimen in this almshouse was the most restrictive. Even though security was tighter at Blockley, the requirement that the poor work off the cost of their care may have provoked many to flee rather than endure forced labor.

Among the variables studied, the one that best accounts for flight from both Philadelphia poorhouses in the nineteenth century was the number of admissions. The type of people most likely to escape were those who had been in the institution before. Fully 90 percent of those who fled in 1812–13 and two-thirds of those who absconded later in the century were paupers who had been institutionalized previously. Presumably, they had learned their way around the buildings and discovered that they could come and go at will.

The only other group with an extraordinarily high propensity to flee the institution were venereal patients; this was especially true after 1828. Earlier, in 1812–13, only 7 percent of those who escaped from the almshouse suffered from venereal disease, but by 1828–50, the proportion had risen to 52 percent.[59] Welfare officials always disapproved of venereal patients. Early in the century, almshouse managers punished such patients with a restricted diet and attempted to indenture them when discharged, but managers did not consistently enforce dietary rules, and the indenturing program never functioned as expected. Venereal patients, therefore, were probably not treated too differently from other patients. They were certainly no more likely to abscond than healthy, normal, or even deranged patients. By the 1820s and thereafter, welfare officials acted on their moral judgment of venereal patients more consistently. These patients were treated more callously: first, they were put on the tread wheel and later forced to labor long hours in the factory or elsewhere in the institution to pay for the cost of room and board and medical care.[60] It is no wonder that between 1828 and 1850, venereal patients preferred to escape as soon as they were well enough rather than endure unpleasant treatment until guardians deemed them worthy of receiving an official discharge.

A third and final difference between indigent inmates admitted to Philadelphia's almshouses early and late in this century pertains to the likelihood of dying while institutionalized. At the old Bettering House, from 1828 to 1834, the death rate was 18.7 percent; it declined slightly to 15 percent when Blockley first opened from 1835 to 1842, but between 1843 and 1850, after the new almshouse had been in operation for a few years, the proportion who died in its wards diminished to 7 percent. The larger percentage of people dying in the old Bettering House in its last years may be attributed in part to the cholera epidemic in 1832, which ravaged a good part of the pauper population. In addition, medical facilities at this institution were never too good, and the practice of placing several patients, often with unrelated illnesses, in the same beds probably facilitated the spread of infection, which, in turn, may have led to the eventual death of many inmates.[61] Interestingly, in the first seven years Blockley was open, the death rate did not much diminish. Apparently, the benevolent intent of guardians to improve hospital facilities by providing cleaner, more private accommodations for the poor did not at first affect the number who died in the new institution. However, from 1842 to 1850, despite another outbreak of cholera in the city and almshouse in 1849, the death rate at Blockley did drop sharply.[62] In these years, conceivably improvements made by guardians in the insane asylum, enlarging the hospital, and changing the medical administration all contributed to reduce the percentage of inmates who died in the new almshouse.

While the death, escape, and readmission rates for Philadelphia's almshouse inmates varied over time, in many other important ways the poor who knocked at the gates of the old almshouse early in the century were no different from those who crossed the river to enter Blockley later on. In both almshouses, the average age of entrants was between thirty-two and thirty-eight. In the Baltimore Almshouse at midcentury, a little over half of the inmates were also in their twenties or thirties. Interestingly, neither the

Philadelphia poorhouse nor its Baltimore counterpart was primarily a refuge for the very young, who constituted just 10–15 percent of the inmate population in both asylums. (For an explanation of this phenomenon, see chapter 5.) Likewise, neither almshouse was predominantly a home for the aged, although older people made up a much larger proportion of the population in the Philadelphia and Baltimore Almshouses than they did in the country at large. Between 1830 and 1850, only 4 percent of Americans were over forty-five; yet in the same years, 17–18 percent of Baltimore and Philadelphia poorhouse inmates were over fifty.[63] Nevertheless, it was largely men and women in the middle years of their lives probably lacking the physical stamina of youth, but not yet incapacitated by old age who filled the almshouse wards. Such inmates included people like Marmaduke Lackey, a thirty-four-year-old ship joiner who took up residence in the Philadelphia Almshouse for a few months in 1830 when a sore leg prevented him from practicing his craft; and Jane Wood, an Irish woman who, when her husband could not support her and their two children, took the youngsters to Blockley, where all three lived for a few months in 1850.[64]

Although their plight was serious, gradually over the years between 1800 and 1854, more men like Lackey and fewer women like Wood found refuge in Philadelphia's almshouses. In 1800, 38 percent and by 1854, 59 percent of poorhouse inhabitants in the city were male. This increase came at the expense of women and especially children, who were admitted in much fewer numbers between 1830 and 1854 than before (see figure 3). This same sort of change occurred in other cities, although at a different rate. Thus, not until the 1840s were there more men than women in New York's Almshouse.[65]

The relatively large number of men in Philadelphia's public poor asylums is explained by the fact that city officials routinely denied men outdoor cash aid, so that the only substantial form of public assistance available was institutionalization. Leaving one's home and family to reside in a poorhouse was probably not a very appealing proposition to most, and the very unattractiveness of this option may have discouraged many men from applying for public welfare. This, of course, was what welfare officials intended. They expected men to work to support their families and anticipated that the threat of the almshouse would encourage them to do just that.

Between 1800 and 1854 in Philadelphia, even as men began to constitute the bulk of almshouse inmates, they always composed a minority of all public-relief recipients. Because women and their children received such a disproportionately large share of outdoor assistance, in the form of both cash and later, wood relief, they made up well over half of the entries on the public-welfare rolls. Yet between 1828 and 1854, when cash pensions were infrequently granted, institutional care remained the only truly substantial

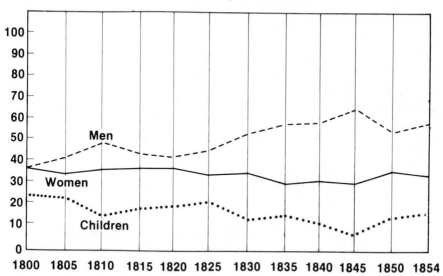

Figure 3
Proportion of Men, Women and Children in Philadelphia Almshouse, 1800-1854

SOURCES: PCA, GP, Treasurer, General Ledger, 1789–1803, 1820–30, vols. and PCA, Treasurers' "Weekly Entries," 1803–9, 1809–15 vols.; *Poulson's*, 19 November 1816, 22 May 1822; *Philadelphia Gazette*, 7 November 1826; *The Pennsylvanian*, 7 December 1837; *Auditors Reports of the Accounts of the Blockley Almshouse for the Fiscal Years Ending May 17, 1841, May 18, 1846, May 19, 1851, May 19, 1854* (Philadelphia: Mifflin and Parry, 1841, Daily Sun, 1846, O.I. Search, 1852, Crissy and Markley, 1854); *Statement of the Accounts of the Guardians of the Poor, July 3–Dec. 31, 1854* (Philadelphia, Crissy and Markley, 1855).

form of public assistance, and it was largely the prerogative of indigent men. (Relief in kind went to a great number of people, but it provided each with a very small amount that did not compare to full room and board in the almshouse.) Therefore, men were the chief recipients of the single, surviving, comprehensive form of public assistance—institutionalization.

Among men and women in the almshouse, there was one significant difference: men were most likely to fall into the older age groups—63 percent were thirty-one or older. Females were more evenly distributed across the age spectrum. Perhaps men, whose earning power was greater than women's, were simply able to manage on their own longer. During their younger years, men could earn enough to survive; it was only when older and facing competition from younger laborers that they had to seek asylum in the almshouse.

As for the racial makeup of the almshouse's population, between 1828–50, 13 percent of the inmates were black, although only between 6–9 percent of the residents of the city and districts were in these years non-white. Not surprisingly, blacks, who were generally relegated to the lowest wage jobs, often had to apply for welfare. They included men like forty-four-year-old Abraham Jackson, a laborer who became ill in 1830 and reentered the almshouse for the third time to seek medical aid; and Samuel Johnson, a thirty-nine-year-old laborer who, because of a sore leg, could not work to support himself, his wife, and child, so the whole family entered the almshouse in 1833 and stayed until Johnson had recovered.[66] Philadelphia's guardians of the poor routinely denied men like Jackson and Johnson outdoor relief, so black men had to enter the almshouse in order to obtain public aid.

There were also a large number of foreign-born in Philadelphia's poorhouses, and their proportion increased from 44 percent in 1829–35 to 57 percent in 1843–50. Other urban almshouses also admitted many immigrants. In 1830–31, 41 percent of Baltimore Almshouse inmates had been born abroad; in 1826, 40 percent and in 1837, 52 percent of New York paupers were foreign-born.[67] Most were Irish; of course, between 1829 and 1850, the rate of immigration from abroad, and particularly from Ireland, had also escalated. Nevertheless, in the old and new Philadelphia almshouses, the foreign-born occupied a disproportionately large share of beds. By 1850, less than 30 percent of the residents of the city and districts were immigrants, yet the foreign-born made up about one-half of the poorhouse population. Because of their limited economic prospects, immigrants, like blacks, were quite likely to require public assistance. Both groups certainly obtained an extremely large share of institutional aid, yet until 1835, immigrants actually received more public assistance, simply because they also secured a great deal of outdoor aid, while blacks obtained very little.

Regardless of racial or ethnic background, once most people entered one of Philadelphia's poorhouses, they remained for several months. Short stays of two weeks or less were slightly more common in the old almshouse than the new, perhaps because at Blockley, officials first began to make a conscious attempt to require inmates to work off the cost of their care before being discharged. Still, in both almshouses, the average length of stay was three months, and the largest proportion of inmates remained institutionalized for two months or more. The same pattern was characteristic in other almshouses. By 1814–15, most of Baltimore's poorhouse inmates stayed a few months, and by 1845 in Danvers, Massachusetts, three months was the average length of stay for paupers supported at state expense in the local almshouse.[68]

The age profile of paupers in nineteenth-century almshouses helps explain their typical length of stay: most inmates were neither very old nor very young. Had almshouses been filled largely with aged people and orphans, the average length of stay would have been much longer, perhaps even several years.[69]

Still, a three-month sojourn in an almshouse may seem like a fairly long time for a presumably able-bodied, thirty-year-old man or woman to remain institutionalized, but, in fact, most almshouse inmates were not able-bodied. Three-quarters of those who sought entrance to both Philadelphia almshouses from 1828 to 1850 were ill. Some were venereal patients, like Francis McNally, a twenty-three-year-old, unmarried Irish weaver who escaped in 1839 after a two-month stay in Blockley, and a few were obstetrical patients, like nineteen-year-old Elizabeth Chew, an unmarried black woman who stayed in the Bettering House about two months after having a baby. Guardians also admitted a few paupers whom they categorized as insane, like Margaret Carley, a thirty-six-year-old Irish widow with seven children who stayed at Blockley for about a month in 1840; and some who were injured or handicapped, such as Henry Reese, a forty-five year-old stonecutter who remained three and a half months at Blockley until his injured hand healed; and thirty-one-year-old Oliver Brown, a sailor who was lame and returned to the almshouse for the fifth time in 1829 to remain six months. In hospital wards, there were also a few alcoholics, like thirty-two-year-old Isabella Anderson, who entered the asylum for a second time in 1829 and lingered about a month. However, the vast majority of those admitted to Philadelphia's almshouses were, like Andrew Gillen, an Irish weaver who stayed at Blockley for three months and three days in 1838, simply labeled "sick."[70] It is likely that most ill, paupers suffered from chronic ailments from which recovery was slow. (The fact that most of the ill were assigned to medical rather than surgical wards supports this assumption.) Thus, the nature of many of the afflictions may also explain why such a large number of the inmates remained in the almshouse for so long.

Many probably remained in the almshouse, because they lacked jobs and comfortable homes to which to return. Among the men, the only inmates for whom occupational information was recorded, 45 percent were unskilled laborers, and another 13 percent held other very low-paying jobs. With poor financial prospects on the outside, inmates may have been reluctant to leave the asylum, and family ties probably did not draw them either. In all years from 1828 to 1850, about half of the new entrants were single, and another quarter were widowed.[71] As members of one charitable organization observed in 1851, young, single men who worked hard in shops or factories all day often returned at night to crowded boarding houses where they slept two in a bed. In such surroundings, disease could spread rapidly, and young men who became ill were often without family in the city to care for them. No wonder then that Allen Brown, a thirty-three-year-old, ailing laborer without wife or family, and Robert Reynolds, a thirty-eight-year-old, unmarried, Scots weaver with a sore leg, found it expedient to seek help in Philadelphia's almshouse.[72]

Between 1800 and 1828, managers who directed Philadelphia's public asylum for the indigent, the Bettering House on Spruce Street, demonstrated a good deal of humanitarian interest in the well-being of the needy in their charge. As in other facets of public poor relief administration during these years, a charitable outlook toward the poor was not atypical. Almshouse managers themselves regularly visited and assisted the poor in the asylum; provided particularly generous and individualized care for unmarried pregnant women and elderly married couples; encouraged a homelike atmosphere in the almshouse; saw to it that all inmates were given an adequate diet; passed out temporary leaves and permanent discharges willingly; and demonstrated no compunction about readmitting, should they request it, those least able to function independently outside of the public institution.

Later, almshouse managers found their humanitarian views challenged by a citizenry who objected even more loudly to pauperism during and after the Panic of 1819. With the whole welfare system under attack in the 1820s, almshouse officials found it expedient to deemphasize their former charitable approach to the poor. When the new Blockley Almshouse opened in 1835, welfare officials were inclined to treat the poor much less benevolently than before. Almshouse administrators visited Blockley infrequently; rarely concerned themselves with individual inmates; eliminated special wards for older married couples; insisted on a regimented atmosphere replete with uniforms and restrictions on movement inside the institution; rarely granted permission to leave the almshouse temporarily; and were reluctant to readmit inmates, no matter how worthy, who had previously been in the institution. Yet even though a charitable attitude toward the poor was less evident among Blockley's administrators than among managers of the Bettering House, humanitarian treatment did not vanish altogether. Some philanthropic interest in the poor is indicated by improvements made in the insane asylum and other divisions of the hospital, including establishing receiving wards; providing more privacy for patients; and employing a full-time resident medical officer to replace the former part-time, nonresident physicians and surgeons. These improvements possibly contributed to the lower death rate in the new almshouse in the 1840s.

While there is less evidence of a forebearing attitude toward almshouse inmates in Philadelphia after 1828, the desire to control the behavior of the institutionalized poor was always strong. Asylums have generally operated as instruments of social control, and the Philadelphia almshouses, 1800–54, were no exception. Indeed, the impulse to impose restraints on the poor grew more intense as the years went by. For example, although the Bettering House managers attempted to restrict inmate movement by fencing in the institution, they did not always keep the fence repaired. In contrast, Blockley administrators kept the stone wall around the new almshouse in good shape and ordered additional walls constructed within the institution itself to further restrict inmates' movements. Moreover, although at both institutions, sexual and racial segregation existed, there were many more rules that were consistently enforced at Blockley than at the old Bettering House. Measures to socially control inmates were adopted by both almshouses, but there were more measures instituted at Blockley; perhaps these added restrictions caused more inmates to escape.

Yet even as the desire to regulate inmate behavior intensified, officials found it next to impossible to realize their goal. Dependent as they were on inmates to keep both almshouses functioning properly, welfare officials could not afford to antagonize the poor unduly. Supervised only by a few employees, inmates probably enjoyed a great deal of freedom in both asylums. There was a considerable social group life in the wards and ready access to even the most forbidden articles, such as liquor. While social control was the chief objective of Philadelphia Almshouse adminstrators throughout the years between 1800 and 1854, they were never able to achieve this objective completely.

Even as social control grew more important to Philadelphia Almshouse officials between 1828 and 1854, so, too, did the need to economize. Of course, this need had never been altogether absent, but in the 1820s, welfare reformers put extra pressure on almshouse administrators not only to manage the institution more closely, but also to operate it more frugally. Nevertheless, both before and after the poor-law change in 1828, economical administration of Philadelphia's poorhouses was a goal only partially achieved.

Throughout the years between 1800 and 1854, Philadelphia Almshouse authorities enjoyed some success in promoting thrift by keeping medical expenditures low. Since both city poorhouses were principally hospitals, it was particularly important to manage hospital wards economically. Welfare officials achieved this goal by using inmates as nurses, medical student apprentices, and part-time, unpaid physicians and surgeons to minister to patients' needs. In 1845, officials abandoned part of this system when they hired a full-time, paid, resident physician to replace the physicians and surgeons who had previously donated their services free of charge in order to use the almshouse hospital as a clinic for their medical students. Employing a chief resident physician did not prove very costly, and retaining paupers as nurses and medical students to do most day-to-day medical work kept the almshouse medical programs fairly economical.

Some other economy measures were not quite so successful; the almshouse factory is a case in point. Ever since the eighteenth century, almshouse administrators had tried to defray part of the costs of running the poorhouse by selling items manufactured there by inmates. Nonetheless, only when city residents could not obtain higher quality textiles from abroad or from factories and workshops in Philadelphia at reasonable prices were they willing to purchase the cloth of low quality produced by inmates forced to labor in the almshouse, and such times were rare. As a consequence, by the 1820s, managers of the Bettering House never earned much from the sale of goods manufactured by inmates and usually used most of these goods within the asylum itself. When Blockley was built, welfare officials expressed renewed hope that with a new factory in a new institution, inmates might produce many goods that could be sold at a profit. Officials were disappointed and in 1845, shut down most of the factory and ordered the few items still manufactured in the almshouse to be consumed there. Even so, welfare officials at Blockley did manage to earn some money from inmate labor outside the factory. Paupers who worked on the farm harvested so many fruits and vegetables that they were able not only to provide fully the almshouse with these items, but also to market a lot of them to local residents. In this way, the Blockley farm, but not the factory, proved a financial success.

Yet when the factories in both almshouses failed to be money-making ventures, they were put to other uses. Beginning in 1823, welfare officials tried to make labor in the factories at the Bettering House and later, Blockley unattractive enough to dissuade people from seeking admission to either. Thus would a measure designed to promote social control— forced labor in the almshouse factory—promote economy as well. Eventually at Blockley, enforcing work requirements and other measures designed to limit inmates' freedom seemingly discouraged admission. Of those who did enter Blockley, most were men; few women, and even fewer children, entered the almshouse. This fact and other evidence of the declining commitment of Philadelphia's poor relief officials to caring for indigent children in an era of growing public concern for the needy young forms the subject of the next chapter.

(5)

Children and Welfare

Presumably, citizens respond more sympathetically to hollow-eyed children in dirty rags than to equally poverty stricken adults. The very helplessness of poor children and the fact that few of them are responsible for their indigence evidently stimulates public- and private-welfare authorities to extend the most generous and humane care to them.

These assumptions about children, poverty, and welfare, which are stated or implied in much of the literature on the subject, are proved false by the example of Philadelphia's public-welfare system, 1800–1854. Although before the War of 1812 ended, the Philadelphia guardians of the poor had demonstrated considerable charitable interest in needy youngsters and were their chief recourse in hard times, the demand for economy measures during the Panic of 1819 and the changing economic climate in the city in the 1830s and 1840s led guardians to reduce child-welfare programs in order to save money. Interestingly, many historians have argued that during these fourth and fifth decades of the century social concern for indigent children was on the upsurge, but in actuality, in Philadelphia, and to a certain extent in other cities as well, these were years when public officials reduced their commitment to aiding impoverished youth.[1] At this same time in Philadelphia, residents' concern about improvidence and laziness among the urban lower classes motivated welfare officials to expand programs for social control over young as well as old paupers. Thus, in child welfare as in all other public-welfare programs, the humanitarian spirit characteristic of the relatively prosperous years in the early nineteenth century gave way to a greater interest in social control and thrift during and after the depression following the War of 1812.

While public welfare for children was contracting, private welfare for the young was expanding. Beginning chiefly in the 1820s, in Philadelphia and other urban centers, sincere concern for impoverished youth prompted philanthropists to found a number of charities to serve the young. These agencies were also affected by the Panic of 1819, and they, too, emphasized social control over the youthful poor. As private child-care agencies grew in number, it might be assumed that they replaced public authorities in

118

assisting the needy young. However, in Philadelphia, and probably in other eastern cities prior to 1854, public officials abandoned the responsibility of child welfare much more quickly than private authorities assumed it. As a result, indigent children suffered.

In Philadelphia, as elsewhere in the United States before 1820, public welfare was almost the sole recourse of poor youngsters. There were then just three charities for children in New York City, three in Baltimore, and two in Boston.[2] In Philadelphia, there were two small private orphanages: one for Catholic and the other for Protestant youth. Catholic families organized an orphanage in 1797 to take in youngsters orphaned by yellow fever epidemics in the 1790s. By 1806, Catholics operated a small asylum called St. Joseph's, which came under the aegis of the Sisters of Charity in 1814. The Protestant orphanage was founded in 1815 by churchwomen partly in response to the War of 1812, which left many youngsters without one or both parents. The only other privately funded sources of assistance for poor children in the city at this time were three charities for women. They dispensed outdoor aid in the form of money, food, clothes, and medical supplies to indigent women, some of whom had children. These charities were, however, all small and did not supply substantial amounts of aid to youngsters. Neither did the two orphanages, which were also modest in size. By 1820, Philadelphia's private charities for children together cared for less than 18 percent of the children aided by the city's public-welfare system.[3]

Early in the nineteenth century, public authorities dispensed two types of aid to poor youngsters: outdoor relief, which was usually given in the form of public cash aid to mothers to enable them to support their children at home, and indoor relief, or institutionalization in the city's poorhouse. Because it permitted children to remain with their own family, outdoor relief was the most benevolent form of care, and by 1814, 70 percent of the youngsters on public-welfare rolls received outdoor rather than indoor aid (see table 2).

The census of outdoor-relief recipients made in Philadelphia in 1814–15 indicates that among the children then granted this form of public assistance, two-thirds were the legitimate sons and daughters of indigent widows On applying to welfare authorities, a needy widow like Eppy Bayment, who, when her husband died in 1814, found herself alone and unable properly to support her two young children, might obtain a weekly cash pension from the guardians. The amount of such a stipend depended on the number, health, and age of her children: for Bayment, it was 75¢ a week. Payments were greater for very young or ill children. Thus in 1814, Elizabeth Cummins accepted 75¢ a week for the care of her newborn infant and Elizabeth Hateruch, $1.25 a week for her lame youngster.[4] The re-

maining one-third of the youngsters on outdoor-relief rolls were foundlings or illegitimate children whose mothers applied for poor relief.
Philadelphia's public-welfare officials paid wet nurses to provide home care
for foundlings and sent unmarried pregnant women to the almshouse for
obstetrical care. After the birth of her child, such a mother could obtain a
weekly public cash stipend to enable her to care for the infant at home.
Even so, before she was entitled to such public assistance, the woman had
to go before a magistrate and swear to the identity of the father of her
unborn child. Pennsylvania law required that he pay for her lying-in
expenses and the support of their child for the first five to seven years of its
life. After that, the child could be indentured and begin to earn its own
keep. If the father could not be found or if he were too poor to contribute
anything to the maintenance of his child, only then did a public official
commence weekly relief payments to the dependents. The first recourse for
the needy was always assumed to be their immediate families; poor-tax
monies were only for those who had no relatives to care for them.[5]

Those children on Philadelphia's public-welfare rolls who were not
fortunate enough to obtain outdoor aid were sent to the almshouse. In
1807, almost one-half of these institutionalized youngsters resembled
three-year-old Alex Murphy, whose mother was in jail and whose father
had long since deserted the family: they were homeless. Such children
had no family to whom relief authorities could grant cash aid. One-quarter
of the institutionalized children consisted of the sons and daughters of
parents who had apparently left them temporarily in the institution, and
the other quarter consisted of children of almshouse inmates.

There is little evidence that Philadelphia Almshouse administrators
discriminated among children on the basis of race or ethnic background.
In 1807, almost one-third of the youngsters then in the almshouse were
black, although only 8–9 percent of the city's population was nonwhite. Of
course, free blacks in the city at this time faced considerable discrimination, and many lived in extreme poverty. Welfare officials responded to
need among black children and admitted them freely to the almshouse,
although fewer black adults were admitted to the asylum: only 8.5 percent
of pauper adults institutionalized in 1807 were nonwhite. Welfare officials
seemed to find it easier to sympathize with the young black poor.

The reaction to needy children from various ethnic backgrounds is
harder to determine. All of the children in almshouse nurseries in 1807 were
born in America, but what of their parents' birthplace, which was not
recorded? However, 68 percent of adult inmates in the almshouse in 1807
were foreign-born (more than two times the percentage of foreign-born in
the city at that time), and if officials did not discriminate against immigrant
adults, who, in this era, were often labeled lazy and blamed for their own
poverty, it is unlikely that authorities discriminated against children of the

Table 2
Number of Children Assisted by Public Welfare, Philadelphia, 1814–1850

Year	Almshouse[a]	Children's Asylum[b]	Total Institution-alized	Percentage of Institution-alized[c]	Bastards[d]	Outdoor Relief[e]	Total aided outside of institutions	Total
1814	417	—	417	17	46	1,079	1,125	1,542
1820	675	258	933	24	271	(532)	803	1,736
1826	751	192	953	23	249	414	663	1,606
1829	435	136	571	12	0	372	372	943
1835	293	—	293	12	0	0	0	293
1841	354	—	354	12	0	—	—	354
1847	260	—	260	6	0	—	—	260
1850	523	—	523	11	0	—	—	523

SOURCES: **Almshouse Admissions:** *Poulson's*, 19 October 1815, 22 May 1822; *Philadelphia Gazette*, 2 November 1827, 12 January 1831; *Pennsylvanian*, 7 December 1837, 27 January 1843; *Auditors Reports of the Accounts of Blockley Alms-House for the Years 1847 and 1850* (Philadelphia: Times and Keystone, 1848, Crissey and Markley, 1851); **Children's Asylum:** PCA, MGP, 20 November 1821, 28 May 1827; *Hazard's Register*, 5:345. **Bastards:** PCA, Guardians of the Poor, Register of Relief Recipients, 1814–15; *Poulson's*, 22 May 1822; *Philadelphia Gazette*, 2 November 1827. **Outdoor Relief:** For 1814, see PCA, Guardians of the Poor, Register of Relief Recipients, 1814–15; for 1826, see PCA, MGP, 30 August 1826 and for 1829, see *Hazard's Register* 6:267. For 1820, I estimated (in parenthesis) the number of children to be 40 percent of the total number of outdoor pensioners, which is about the proportion of children on relief rolls in 1826 and 1829. For the number of outdoor pensioners in 1820, see *Poulson's*, 22 May 1822.

[a] Includes new admissions of children only.

[b] The children's asylum opened in 1820 and became a part of the new almshouse at Blockley in 1835. Figures include new admissions only.

[c] Means the percentage of children (as opposed to the percentage of adult males and adult females) institutionalized by public authorities.

[d] Includes children with their mother and those with a nurse. Philadelphia's authorities stopped assisting bastards in 1829.

[e] Includes the number of young children living in the home of outdoor pensioners who received cash relief. The program ended in 1835, and although it was resumed in 1840, there is no evidence that any cash aid then went to children.

foreign-born, who were certainly not responsible for their indigence.[6]

In the almshouse early in the century, children of all racial and ethnic backgrounds were cared for similarly. Officials did not separate members of healthy, indigent families but assigned both mothers and children to beds in the same ward. In the long garret in 1807, Ann Gibbs kept her two children by her side; three other youngsters, the offspring of Rebecca Tiffin, Margaret McGill, and Eleanor Fairly, respectively, also slept beside their mother. Thus families were respected, and many children were spared separation from mothers and siblings. Even so, not all youngsters received humane care. The steward and matron placed sons and daughters of ill inmates, like five-year-old James Jones, whose mother was dead and whose father in 1807 was in a hospital ward, as well as youngsters without family in the institution, in special children's wards, called nurseries. Here, youngsters were apparently segregated by sex, but not by age or race. In 1807, there were more children in each of the two nurseries than adults in any but three of the other wards in the almshouse. Like almshouse nurseries elsewhere, the Philadelphia wards for children were overcrowded. In the Quaker City poorhouse and other similar institutions, these wards were staffed only by female paupers, some of whom were labeled feeble and aged or deranged. Only the boys received schooling, and in Philadelphia as elsewhere, they were taught by almshouse inmates, who were probably not the most skilled teachers. Almshouse managers themselves worried about "the adults whose habits and conversation form a vicious example which is too apt to leave a lasting impression on the susceptible mind of youth."[7]

Although between 1800 and 1820 some children remained in family groups within the Bettering House and probably had fairly decent care, a larger number received much less benevolent treatment in the overcrowded and inadequately staffed nurseries. Therefore, it is probably fortunate that only a minority of young public charges were then institutionalized; instead, most were beneficiaries of a much more helpful type of aid—relief in their own homes.

Later, after the War of 1812, the pattern of Philadelphia's child welfare changed dramatically: humane home-care programs, both public and private, were reduced and replaced by an expanded institutional-relief system for the young, which promoted regular habits in a controlled setting and preparation for self-sufficiency (which would save money by quickly readying needy children to earn their own keep). This change occurred after the Panic of 1819, when the number of poor in the Philadelphia area rose substantially and it became more and more troublesome for public-welfare authorities to collect poor taxes and private-charity, donations from an increasingly impoverished population. Charities for women, which had earlier supplied some outdoor aid to children, reduced their services. City officials also economized in the easiest way possible: between 1820 and 1826, they reduced by 25 percent outdoor cash pensions, which went almost entirely to women and children. Further reductions in outdoor aid to needy youngsters occurred in 1827 after a study revealed that Philadelphia's authorities aided many more mothers of bastard children than did officials in other eastern cities. Complaining that financial aid to bastard children "is an encouragement to vice, and offers a premium on prostitution," Philadelphia's officials eliminated welfare payments to illegitimate youngsters and paid their mothers or wet nurses only what money could be collected from the father for the children's support.[8] Finally, the new poor law passed in 1828 mandated the end of public cash aid to the poor as soon as a new almshouse was completed. When Blockley Almshouse opened in 1835, outdoor cash assistance to needy youngsters in their own homes ceased altogether.[9]

Thus, in the 1820s, in the face of much public criticism of high welfare costs, criticism that had not existed earlier in the century, some of Philadelphia's private-welfare officials curtailed outdoor aid to children, while public officials decided to sacrifice altogether home relief to women and children, who, since they were politically impotent, could not object. Still, poor children were not ignored altogether. When outdoor cash payments for them were contracted, the majority of young public charges were institutionalized (see table 2). In addition, private groups founded three asylums for indigent youth in Philadelphia in the 1820s. Welfare officials, public and private, came to prefer institutionalization because it gave them a greater measure of control over the lives of the needy young than did outdoor aid.

Although all three private children's institutions were begun by people with a genuine concern for needy youngsters, the purpose was to lock up children temporarily, educate them, and then indenture them, so that they could learn a trade. Thus, while humanitarian goals inspired the founders of Philadelphia's child-care asylums, once in operation, the institutions imposed social control as economically as possible.

The largest private asylum for children established in Philadelphia in the 1820s was the House of Refuge. Modeled after similar institutions in New York and Boston, it was founded by Quakers who were genuinely alarmed by the city's practice of incarcerating young vagrants with adult criminals in prison. After unsuccessfully trying to persuade the guardians of the poor to provide a separate facility for young vagrants, a private group of Friends was organized, solicited funds from state and county government, and opened the House of Refuge in 1828. It closely resembled a prison, where boys and girls, usually between ten and eighteen were incarcerated for about a year, given some schooling, and required to work eight hours a day under threat of punishment. Although labeled juvenile delinquents, most had committed only minor crimes. The purpose of the institution was to remove troublesome children from indigent families, discipline the children closely in a controlled setting—all as inexpensively as possible. Thus, the children remained in the House of Refuge only a year and then were indentured to local families to earn their own keep and presumably become self-supporting.[10]

The other two private children's asylums founded in Philadelphia in the 1820s were both smaller than the House of Refuge (which accommodated about 150 youngsters) and somewhat less restrictive. The Shelter for Colored Orphans, established in 1822 by female members of the Society of Friends, housed about a dozen children and was the first private children's charity in Philadelphia to admit blacks. The shelter was designed to provide more humane care for black children between eighteen months and eight years than they were likely to obtain in the public almshouse. In this goal, it probably succeeded, although the children were cared for in a disciplined, institutional setting, and after a short time, indentured in order to learn a trade—an economy measure. An even smaller children's charity was St. John's, the city's second Catholic orphanage. It was founded in 1829 to care for four Catholic children orphaned that year. By the very simple practice of accommodating few children, St. John's practiced thrift.[11]

As private charity officials relied more on institutionalizing of children in the 1820s, so, too, did public officials. Between 1820–35, needy youngsters in the city were admitted to one of two public institutions—the almshouse or the children's asylum. The former always accommodated more youngsters, most of whom entered with their parents. While in 1807, one-half of the youngsters in the almshouse were homeless and only one-quarter were admitted with their parents, the reverse was true by 1822. Then, most youngsters entered the institution as did four-year-old Manuel Embry—in the company of their mother.[12] This change probably occurred because of first the reduction, and later, the elimination of public home relief. Without an adequate outdoor pension to sustain them, many destitute parents found that they and their children could not survive unless the entire family accepted institutional care.

Throughout the last fifteen years that the old Bettering House existed, children were cared for there much as they had always been. Some slept beside their mother in general wards and others lived in overcrowded and understaffed nurseries. In 1819, private-charity officials criticized the inadequacy of almshouse nurseries and persuaded public officials to provide better care for very young white children. Hence, in 1820, guardians of the poor, acting out of concern for the city's needy young, established, some distance from the almshouse property, a separate children's asylum for healthy white children of all nationalities between eighteen months and seven years. (Black children were still willingly given aid but only in the less attractive almshouse.) The Philadelphia Children's Asylum was only the second public orphanage founded in the United States (the first was opened in Charleston in 1794), although following Philadelphia's example, New York established a similar separate institution for children in 1833.[13]

In all the years it was in operation as a separate institution, the children's asylum took a minority of its inmates from almshouse nurseries, but the majority came directly from their natural families to the new asylum. The parents of these children were probably slightly better off than indigent parents who, because of the reduction of cash pensions after 1820, had no alternative but to enter the almshouse with their children. Parents of children's asylum inmates probably discovered that with the cut in public outdoor aid, they could manage to get by outside of the almshouse but could not adequately provide for their children at home.[14]

The Philadelphia Children's Asylum was in many ways a much better home for the young than the city's almshouse. Established for benevolent reasons, as were private children's charities in this era, the new public institution also embodied certain features that reveal that a genuine desire to provide "a comfortable situation" for the city's indigent young remained important to public-welfare officials in the 1820s. For example, the new asylum was adequately staffed with a number of salaried employees, including a matron, a teacher, several nurses, domestics, and assistants; and children were attended by professionals, not by a few paupers working as nurses, as in the almshouse. Notwithstanding, there was one serious disadvantage to introducing a professional staff: its high turnover rate. In the first five years the institution was in operation, there were six different matrons and in the first decade, nine male teachers. Each new matron hired new nurses, domestics, and assistants. The guardians' desire to economize by paying low salaries to children's asylum employees probably contributed to this turnover rate. Many no doubt left asylum employment as soon as they could find better paying jobs. For the children, these constant changes in staff must have been confusing and upsetting.[15]

Guardians also economized on medical care for children. Although welfare officials admitted only those in good health to the children's asylum, many became ill after they arrived. Diseases common to most institutions, including measles and ophthalmia, flourished in Philadelphia's children's asylum. At first, the asylum's medical staff was organized much like the hospital staff at the almshouse: four physicians attended to ill youngsters on a rotating basis, and a live-in medical student carried out physicians' orders on a day-to-day basis. Then in 1827, amidst public furor over the high cost of poor relief, guardians discharged from the children's asylum all four attending physicians, who had been paid for their services since 1822, and replaced them with one full-time, salaried physician. The new doctor encouraged the children to brush their teeth, a practice that presumably reduced the incidence of "sore mouth" (probably cankers), a persistent medical problem at the children's asylum. Yet the cutback in medical staff to one doctor may not have been wholly beneficial, for accompanying it was a doubling of the death rate in the children's asylum from 5 percent in 1820–26 to 10 percent, 1828–33.[16] This growing mortality rate no doubt resulted from many factors, but one of them may well have been inadequate medical care.

Of considerable benefit to children in the asylum was the school program. Experienced teachers instead of pauper inmates instructed not just boys, as in the almshouse, but also girls, using special asylum classrooms. By 1825, all youngsters learned their lessons in a newly constructed school building on the grounds of the children's asylum. Publicly funded schools for poor children existed in Philadelphia in the 1820s, but neither public- nor private-welfare authorities patronized them. Poor relief officials preferred to educate their young wards outside of the city's common schools to avoid association "with those whose morals were not properly controled [sic] when out of school."[17]

This statement clearly reflects another purpose of the children's asylum between 1820 and 1835—to serve as an instrument of social control.

To function in this fashion, child-care agencies regulated their wards' companions, and not just in school. Parents and relatives were permitted to see children just once a week and then only in a special visiting room in most asylums. Children did not leave the asylum at all until they received official discharge. Both guardians of the poor and managers of the House of Refuge ordered the construction of fences around their buildings to enforce this regulation.[18]

In public and private institutions for children, discipline and order were enforced in other ways as well. Each day, officials woke youngsters at 6:00 A.M., then saw to it that they said their prayers, washed, and dressed. All children wore uniforms and customarily marched in single file about the institutions. In Philadelphia's orphanages, almshouse, and children's asylum, youngsters performed little more than maintenance chores, but in the House of Refuge, they worked all day at various manufacturing tasks. Philadelphia's officials expected children's asylum inmates to eat their three daily meals in silence, standing up. In both this institution and the House of Refuge, children consumed a little cold meat and a considerable amount of bread at breakfast and supper. They usually dined on bread or rice and molasses or soup; more rarely did they find meat and vegetables on their plates.

Once "children ... [had been] taken from the haunts of vice and wretchedness ... into habits of order and discipline" and "instructed in the rudiments of education," both public and private officials expected to indenture them or place them "in situations calculated to insure their future respectability and usefulness." Like private child-care agencies, Philadelphia's public children's asylum was never intended to be more than a temporary home for poor children. An institution for long-term care of the young would be costly, and by the 1820s, guardians of the poor were very concerned about economy.[19]

In the 1820s, when Philadelphia's welfare officials tried to impose social control and save money by indenturing youngsters from the children's asylum, they found, much to their dismay, that parents of young asylum inmates thwarted them. Before 1828, unlike the city's private institutions, the children's asylum did not become the legal guardian of youngsters it admitted. This meant that children could not be indentured out of the public institution without their parents' permission. As it turned out, few parents gave their consent, since most wanted the family to be reunited. Parents preferred to use the children's asylum as simply a temporary shelter where their children could obtain the food, clothing, medical help, and education that parents during the depression years of the 1820s were unable to provide. Public indenturing programs were disadvantageous to the poor, because such programs both broke up families and prevented parents from profiting from their youngsters' labor. Needy parents who avoided indenturing and reclaimed their children from the asylum could put them to work at home or hire them out for wages, which is exactly what these parents did. During the first six years that the institution was in operation, over half of the children were removed by their family and only 20 percent signed indenture contracts.[20]

This situation angered welfare officials, who did not want the children's asylum to be simply a "house of convenience" for poor parents, a mere source of free food and clothes. How could officials truly rescue needy children if most youngsters returned to their impoverished family after a short stay in the institution? To correct this problem, welfare officials wrote into the new 1828 poor law the requirement that parents pay their children's board before withdrawing them from the institution. If parents could not pay, their offspring could be indentured without prior parental consent.[21] This new legal contrivance served a dual purpose. It was economical, because if could provide a source of income for the asylum or that failing, at least remove children from the welfare rolls and place them in homes where they would learn to become self-sufficient. This law was also a method of social control, a way of permanently removing children from the home of their poverty-stricken parents to a better environment.

For the poor, the new restrictions promoted hardship. Many impoverished parents could not afford to pay for their youngsters' care in the children's asylum, yet they still wanted them home rather than indentured to strangers. Some emulated Catherine Howell, who "purloined or enticed" her grandson, Charles Finnemore, from the home of the shoemaker where he had been placed. Others went to the children's asylum to beg officials for their youngsters. Some parents became desperate. Mary Diviney actually hid in the asylum in the hope of contacting and rescuing her son. The matron and a guardian of the poor discovered her and turned her out into the street, where she threw stones and shouted abuse at the asylum. Eventually, welfare officials secured a warrant for Diviney's arrest and she was "committed."[22]

Diviney and others like her suffered when a firm commitment to social control and economy largely replaced charitable interest in the plight of poor children for Philadelphia's welfare officials. Between 1820 and 1835, the most benevolent welfare program for indigent youngsters, financial assistance to enable them to remain with their family, was, for the most part, replaced by institutional care in private orphanages, the House of Refuge, the public almshouse, or children's asylum. After 1835, to save even more money on welfare, public outdoor cash aid to children and their family was eliminated entirely; so, too, was Philadelphia's one unique public institution for the needy young—the children's asylum. Although this institution had been a means of control, it had also provided more benevolent and specialized care for youngsters than the public poorhouse. Nevertheless, when the new Blockley Almshouse opened, guardians of the poor closed both the old almshouse and the children's asylum and transferred all youngsters from the two institutions to the new poorhouse. Officials named one division of Blockley the children's asylum, but it was very unlike its namesake, for this new children's asylum was not physically or administratively separate but a part of the almshouse. By 1835, the dedication of Philadelphia's welfare officials to frugality had led them to abolish the two welfare programs most clearly designed to meet the special needs of the indigent young: cash relief to families of needy children and room and board for them in a unique, separate children's asylum.

Philadelphia was not the only city where officials, in the middle years of the nineteenth century, sought to economize on public child welfare. Elsewhere outdoor cash relief was not entirely abandoned, but special public asylums for youngsters were discontinued in New York as well as Philadelphia. New York supported a separate public institution for indigent children only between 1833 and 1848.[23] Apparently, detached children's asylums were expensive, and as public officials in the 1830s and 1840s grew more cost conscious, they decided to save money by caring for all the poor under one roof. While officials did attempt to keep children somewhat separated from adults in almshouses, as it turned out, such separation was incomplete. The antebellum reform impulse did not prevail for long in public welfare. Private charities that opened their doors before midcentury consistently segregated children in orphanages, but public attempts to do the same failed, apparently because they proved to be too great a tax burden.

In Philadelphia after 1835, while the care given children in the Blockley Almshouse was in many ways distinctly disadvantageous to them, it was not in all ways unsuitable. City-welfare authorities retained some understanding of, and solicitude for, needy children. Officials demonstrated their sympathy by respecting the family unit and keeping some mothers and children together in asylum wards. If a mother entered Blockley with a young child and they were in good health, as in the case of Jane McCommery who in 1840 brought her fourteen-month-old son with her to the almshouse, officials assigned them to adjacent beds in one of the nursery wards. Such family groups were able to remain together in the new almshouse just as they had in the old one. Still, this type of ward assignment affected only a few. While the majority of youngsters admitted to Blockley before 1854 came with a parent, on entering, most were separated from their parents and sent to different sections of the institution. Mothers in ill health, as well as those with more than one child, and all fathers were customarily denied access to their offspring inside the poorhouse. Youngsters under ten, like Mary and Bridget Ross, five and two, respectively, and James and William Lockery, eight and two, all of whom entered with their mother between 1839 and 1844, were sent to the Blockley children's asylum. Older children, like ten-year-old Catherine Smith, who was admitted to Blockley in 1844, entered regular asylum wards.[24]

As for racial or ethnic discrimination against children, there seems to have been as little at Blockley as there had been in the old almshouse. Between 1835 and 1850 one-quarter of the children in the institution were black, and 13 percent of adult paupers were nonwhite. In this era, there were a number of racial confrontations in the city, and the proportion of the city's population that was black shrank to 6 percent, but welfare officials still responded willingly to poverty among nonwhites and admitted a large number to the almshouse. As for foreign-born children, their number was small (about 9 percent), but many young inmates may have been the American-born children of immigrants. Since the ethnic background of parents was not usually recorded, we cannot determine the racial background of most children. Still, about half of the adults in the institution were foreign-born, yet less than a third of the city's total population had been born abroad. There was much nativism in the city in the 1840s, but that did not prevent Philadelphia's officials from admitting foreign-born adult poor to the almshouse, and there is no reason to suppose that officials were any less willing to admit immigrant children.[25]

While most children at Blockley benefited from the policy of admitting them with little regard for color or ethnic background and a few profited from the practice of keeping healthy mothers and children together, boys and girls assigned to the Blockley children's asylum enjoyed another advantage, the singular continuity of management in this division of the poorhouse. At the old children's asylum, personnel had changed yearly, but in the new children's wing at Blockley, only three matrons served during the first fifteen years of its existence. The one who remained the longest was Martha Dungan, whom visitors described as a firm person who used mild discipline and exhibited parental deportment. Apparently children were fond of her, and one girl, Margaret Murray, even voluntarily returned to Dungan's care after having been forcibly removed from the almshouse by her parents.[26]

Yet even though some policies at Blockley, for example, retaining an able children's asylum matron like Dungan, indicate interest in the young, other actions reflect more of a commitment to social control. Thus, guardians at Blockley continued as at the old children's asylum to maintain a strict daily regimen for boys and girls. Young inmates at Blockley still rose early, dressed in uniforms, and marched through the institution in military style. Occasionally, they attended civic gatherings, such as the fifth-birthday celebration of the Philadelphia-area Sunday Schools in Washington Square in 1842. At that time, an observer noted how "neat but sad" all the young inmates appeared and how much more "disciplined" they were than other, more fortunate youngsters.[27] In the 1830s and thereafter, just as in the 1820s, social control remained a key feature of public child-welfare programs.

Economy, too, lost none of its former appeal and, in fact, grew ever more important to Philadelphia poor relief officials as the years passed. When Blockley first opened in 1835, the willingness of welfare authorities to economize on the care of indigent children was evident in the refusal to employ special medical attendants other than paupers as nurses, who even guardians acknowledged were "ignorant and unprincipled," to minister to ill youngsters in the children's wing. Almshouse administrators found it cheaper to do without even the one doctor employed in the old children's asylum. Unfortunately, saving money on child care had disastrous results; within a month after the new Blockley children's asylum opened, twenty youngsters died. To their credit, public authorities in April 1835 replaced inmate nurses with professional ones and rehired long-time children's asylum physician, Dr. Matthew Anderson. In May, Officials also appointed a resident medical student to attend to ill youngsters. In essence, officials recreated in the new children's division in Blockley about the same medical program used at the old children's asylum. Despite these precautions, disease continued to claim the lives of many children. In 1838–39, there were severe outbreaks of ophthalmia and measles, which left thirteen children either totally or partially blind. Ten years later, within a two-month period, seventeen youngsters succumbed to ophthalmia, scarlet fever, and other old ailments. The death rate, which had been 10 percent in the old asylum, soared to 18 percent in 1848–49 in the new asylum. Institutional diseases existed in both asylums, and the means of coping with them were similar, too. The difference appears to be that since the older institution was separated from the almshouse, it avoided exposing youngsters to ill adults and also admitted primarily healthy children, most of whom proved strong enough to withstand the epidemics of juvenile diseases that periodically struck the asylum. In contrast, the new children's division of Blockley Almshouse occupied one wing of the hospital, and children were all too frequently in contact with ailing adults. Furthermore, since ill as well as healthy youngsters were admitted to Blockley children's asylum, disease spread rapidly there, and as guardians noted, those with the "miserable constitutions" common to the young who live in poverty, all too quickly perished from measles, scarlet fever, or ophthalmia.[28]

Just as welfare officials, in order to save money, ignored the physical well-being of young paupers by housing them all, regardless of health, in wards adjacent to those for ill adults, and for a time, denied children proper medical attendants, so, too, did officials sacrifice the youngsters' education in the interest of economy. Although there had always been a school in the old children's asylum and there was one established at Blockley when it opened in 1835, by 1844, when reformer Dorothea Dix visited the institution, she found children without a teacher. Instruction may have ceased when Matron Dungan left in 1843, since her daughter, who had been the schoolteacher, probably resigned then also. Of course, welfare officials could have replaced the teacher just as they did the matron, but they chose not to, apparently because they found the school unnecessarily costly. Eventually, authorities reopened the classroom in 1849, but for six years, children at Blockley received no formal education.[29]

While medical and educational programs for children at Blockley are two indications of the increasing interest of Philadelphia's welfare officials in thrift, the best evidence of a growing commitment to frugality in the decades before midcentury, is the policy of assisting a decreasing number of needy youngsters. Whereas over 1,700 children were on the welfare rolls in 1820, less than one-third of that number were receiving public aid in 1850.[30] (See table 2.) A portion of this decline is accounted for by the elimination of outdoor cash aid to children and their family, but much also resulted from officials' decision to admit a smaller percentage of children to public institutions. In 1820, 24 percent of the paupers in city asylums for the poor were children, but by 1829, it was 12 percent and by 1850, 11 percent (see table 2).

Because the number of youngsters in the almshouse and children's asylum first dropped sharply in 1829, perhaps the new poor law of 1828 was responsible. Since the law required parents to pay room and board for their children before being able to withdraw them from a public institution, many impoverished parents may have elected to endure extreme want rather than have their offspring enter a public asylum.[31] Thus, the decline in the number of poor youngsters institutionalized in Philadelphia's public asylums may be due in part to the conscious choice of indigent families, and if they made such a choice, it was because, at least from 1829 to 1839, public officials really enforced the law and separated members of impoverished families indefinitely.

Yet, although provisions of the 1828 poor law may in part explain the diminishing number of youngsters in Philadelphia's poorhouses between 1829 and 1854, the law alone cannot account for this remarkable decline. By 1841, welfare officials ceased requiring needy parents to pay room and board for their youngsters before withdrawing them from the Blockley children's asylum and actually began returning most children to their family; hence indigent parents no longer had quite so compelling a reason to refuse to let their children enter the public-welfare institution. Yet admissions of the young to the almshouse did not then increase substantially. Of course, poor parents may not have been fully aware of the change in institutional policy, or they may have distrusted it, and continued to keep their children out of the poorhouse.

On the other hand, while the declining number of children in Philadelphia's public asylums between 1829 and 1854 may, in part, be explained by poor parents keeping their youngsters at home, the drop in admissions was also the result of a conscious choice made by public authorities, for they decided to enroll fewer children in city asylums in order to save money. Such an economy measure was necessitated by the diminishing popularity of indenturing. When poor relief officials discovered that they could not easily place children from the almshouse and children's asylum in the home of responsible citizens to learn a trade, officials realized they would have to maintain youngsters in the institutions indefinitely at public expense. To avoid such a costly alternative, officials began to admit fewer children to public asylums and to return rapidly those few they did admit to the family.

Ironically, public-indenturing programs like the one in Philadelphia had originally been devised as an economy measure. From the seventeenth to the nineteenth centuries, public aid to children, either in their own home or in asylums, was always temporary; it lasted only until the child was old enough to work—sometime between the ages of six and ten. Then, either financial aid to the mother or accommodating the child in the almshouse ceased. If the natural parents could still not care for the child, welfare officials indentured the youngster to an adult in the community who promised to provide her or him with room, board, clothing, an elementary education, and a cash reward (called freedom dues) in return for labor until age eighteen, if a girl, or twenty-one, if a boy. Such a program was economical, because it limited the number of years a child had to be supported at public expense, and by preparing the child to be self-supporting, the program presumably precluded the possibility of her or him ever again requiring public aid.[32]

Although indenturing was supposed to be the ultimate solution to the problem of poverty among children, the system worked less and less well in Philadelphia as the century progressed. In 1805, of all the children welfare officials indentured, one-third remained with the masters to whom they were first assigned and returned to the almshouse to have their contracts officially terminated. These children obtained the education, skills, clothes, and money promised them; they included youngsters like Catherine Catharill, who at the age of nine in 1805, was indentured "to learn the art of housewifery" to a family in Philadelphia. She served the family for eight years, attended school every year, and when her indenture contract expired, she received two suits of clothes, one new, and $20.[33] Of course, children like Catharill might have occasionally been treated cruelly, but within the limits of public officials' expectations and knowledge, the indenturing system seemed to work, saving the public money and rescuing children from poverty. Nonetheless, over the years, fewer and fewer children successfully fulfilled their indenture contracts in this way. By 1820, just 16 percent and by 1850 only 8 percent of the youngsters indentured completed their terms of service.

Meanwhile, the number of children whom masters brought back to the almshouse after a few months or years of service grew. In 1805, 23 percent; in 1820, 28 percent; and by 1850, 33 percent of the children officially indentured reappeared at the institution. Many were reindentured, like six-year-old Elizabeth Dreeves, who after having been indentured in 1850 to a Philadelphia family to learn housewifery, was returned by that family within two months and promptly indentured again. With Dreeves and other children like her, the indenturing system did not work very well. Frequent returns to the almshouse were costly, and it is questionable how many useful skills children acquired as they moved from place to place.

In addition to those who either completed their first contracts or were reindentured, there were large numbers of boys and girls who simply left the almshouse with their master and were never heard from again. In 1805 and 1820, respectively, 35 percent so disappeared, and by 1850, the percentage had risen to 49. Such children included ten-year-old Peter Aldrey, who was indentured to a farmer in Montgomery County, and eleven-year-old Mary Kennedy, who was indentured as a house servant in Philadelphia. Both left the almshouse with their master and never returned to have their contract officially terminated.[34] It is possible that these children and others served out their term, obtained some education, learned some skills, and were granted their freedom dues. Conversely, many youngsters may have been treated unfairly, some may have died, others, absconded.

In all probability, the problems Philadelphia's public officials faced in indenturing indigent children in the first half of the nineteenth century were due to the decline in apprenticeships throughout the United States. By 1800, the paternalistic labor system was on the wane; commercialism had begun to undermine the relationship between master and apprentice. In the 1840s, "surplus labor and low wages" had the same effect. With so many cheap adult laborers available as the century progressed, many employers did not care to take on children, train them carefully, send them to school, and give them freedom dues. This may explain why fewer children were successfully indentured in nineteenth-century Philadelphia.[35] Of course, children could perform simple tasks adequately, and some masters took them on to do just that and then returned them to the almshouse before they completed their contracts. Thus, employers obtained free labor and spared themselves the expense of schooling and giving the children freedom dues. Masters could achieve the same results by simply dismissing children or paying them off and not bothering to bring them back to the almshouse at all. This may explain the large number of children who simply disappeared after their contracts were signed. In all likelihood, many never secured what was promised to them and instead were simply a source of cheap labor for their master for a few years.

Of course, the public-indenturing program was in trouble as early as 1820, but welfare officials did not react to its failure until economic considerations assumed an overwhelming importance after passage of the 1828 poor law. Philadelphia's officials then faced the prospect of maintaining a number of indigent children in the almshouse at public expense for indeterminate periods of time. To avoid such a costly alternative, the city's poor relief authorities took two actions. First, they reduced the number of youngsters admitted to the almshouse, and second, by 1841, they reversed their earlier policies and began to release the majority of indigent children into the custody of their family, whether or not the family had paid room and board.

An examination of youngsters who left the children's asylum and almshouse in the 1830s and 1840s shows the effect of this change. In the earlier decade, officials prevented most children from returning to their family by demanding strict enforcement of the 1828 poor law, which required indigent parents who wanted to regain custody of their children to first pay the youngsters' room and board in the public institutions. Parents who could not make these payments found their children indentured to more affluent families by authorities. In 1832–33 and 1838–39, over half the children who left the children's asylum or the almshouse entered into indenture contracts, while about one-quarter returned to parents or other relatives, and the rest died or escaped. However, by 1841, the situation had altered dramatically: only 40 percent of those discharged were indentured, while almost half returned to their family whether or not their room and board had been paid. By 1848, 51 percent of the youngsters who left the new Blockley Almshouse returned to their family, one-quarter were indentured, and the remainder died, escaped, or entered other institutions.[36]

Possibly, the reduction in the number of children aided by Philadelphia's welfare authorities after 1828 was simply part of a general reduction in the number of people entitled to public assistance. To a certain extent, this is true, for the actual number of people receiving substantial types of public aid, such as cash relief or institutionalization, did decline after passage of the 1828 poor law (see appendix 2 and chapter 2). Even so, aid to children was curtailed much more sharply than assistance to adult paupers. Besides needy youngsters, poor women were the greatest losers when welfare authorities cut outdoor cash aid. Yet after 1828, when institutional aid remained the most comprehensive form of public assistance dispensed in Philadelphia, men became its foremost beneficiaries, and institutional assistance to men expanded even as aid to children was being cut back. The dimensions of this change are illustrated in figure 3 in chapter 4. From 1800 through 1854, there were always more men than children in the almshouse, but beginning in 1830, the proportion of males in the asylum began to rise and the proportion of children to drop. After 1825, the percentage of youngsters in the almshouse never again approached 20 percent and was usually closer to 10 percent, while men generally made up over half of the poorhouse population.

Although figures for other cities are more difficult to obtain, it appears that roughly the same pattern prevailed in Boston and Baltimore as in Philadelphia. In Boston, by 1854, just 13 percent of all inmates admitted to the city's almshouse or House of Industry were children. In Baltimore in 1849, fewer than 200, or 10 percent, of those in the almshouse were 15 or younger. In New York, children comprised a larger proportion of the almshouse population than in any of the other cities, although the percentage of youngsters in public institutions did decline by the 1840s. Thus in 1826, there were about 600 children, comprising almost 30 percent of total inmates, in the New York Almshouse, but by 1843, while the number of children in this poorhouse had grown somewhat, their proportion of the entire inmate population had shrunk to 24 percent largely because of the rapid influx of male paupers.[37]

In Philadelphia after 1828, the greater willingness of welfare officials to aid adult, male paupers rather than indigent children may in part be explained by financial considerations. Institutionalization of a child, who in all probability could not by then easily be indentured, might last for years and be quite costly, while public aid to a man in the almshouse usually lasted for only about three months. Welfare officials may have also been more willing to aid needy men, because public welfare was virtually the sole recourse of adult males; there were almost no private charities in Philadelphia that would assist them. (More will be said about the discrimination practiced by private charities in chapter 6.) In contrast, a growing number of private agencies had begun to relieve indigence among children.

In Philadelphia in 1820, there were two private charities caring exclusively for children; in 1830, there were five; and by 1850, there were eight.[38] In addition, by midcentury, many of the city's private orphanages were quite large. St. John's and St. Joseph's had expanded in response to the migration of indigent Irish Catholics in the 1840s and in 1850 together accommodated 350 children. The House of Refuge contained the same number of juveniles after it added a division for black children in 1850. The Girard College, which began operating in 1848, thanks to a generous bequest from Philadelphia merchant Stephen Girard, enrolled 200–300 poor white orphaned boys between the ages of six and ten. For four to eight years, these boys lived in comfortable dormitories, were educated by a corps of teachers, and then released to relatives or indentured. Somewhat smaller was the Southern Home for Destitute Children, which opened in 1849 and accommodated a little less than a hundred needy boys and girls who were indentured in the country as soon as possible. Even older charities that had once been small expanded considerably by 1850: the Shelter for Colored Orphans housed sixty-seven, and the Orphan Asylum, eighty-four boys and girls. In fact, at midcentury, the only rather small charity for children in Philadelphia was the Foster Home Association, which opened in 1839 and assisted a couple dozen children on a temporary basis until their family could provide for them or until the youngsters could find jobs.[39]

Interestingly, none of these private charities seemed to have the problems with indenturing that troubled public authorities. The Catholic orphanages avoided such difficulties by entrusting their charges to the care of nuns until the boys and girls were old enough to find work on their own. Since most Catholic families in the city were not well off, it was difficult to find suitable placement for youngsters, so that they were rarely indentured. For other reasons, Girard College, too, did not rely much on indenturing. Because of ample funds at the disposal of the college's trustees, it was possible to retain children in the institution if satisfactory homes could not be found. Some children's asylums that did indenture, like the Orphan Asylum, placed so few children each year that it was probably easier for it to find homes for youngsters than for public authorities. On the other hand, the House of Refuge indentured about seventy children a year from 1840 to 1850. It may have been fairly successful in placing them, because the House of Refuge indentured principally large able-bodied boys to local farmers. In addition, many well-connected managers of this and other private children's charities may have been better able than public authorities to find families willing to take children, and such families may have also been more amenable to applying for child laborers from respectable private charities than the public almshouse.[40]

At the same time that charities for children in Philadelphia were growing in number, and many also in size, they were increasing in other cities too: by 1850, New York and Boston each had ten charities for children and Baltimore, nine.[41] At midcentury in all four cities, the position of public welfare, vis à vis private charities for children had been reversed, and private-charity officials, not public authorities, assisted the vast majority of indigent youth.

In Philadelphia, the only city for which complete figures are available, public authorities reduced aid to indigent children much faster than private groups expanded such assistance. This development can best be explained by reference to figure 4, which reveals how dramatically aid to indigent children in Philadelphia decreased from 1829 to 1850. Private charities cared for progressively more children, whereas public welfare cared for many fewer. After cutbacks in public child welfare initiated in 1829, it took twenty-one years for private charities to increase the number of youngsters they aided to the point where they and public authorities together once again served as many children as in 1820. Meanwhile, in these very same decades of the 1830s and 1840s, when public child-welfare programs contracted and private charities gradually expanded, by most accounts, the number of impoverished children in the city grew astronomically.

From 1800 to 1854, Philadelphia's public child-welfare program reflects the same values evident in other aspects of public poor relief: sympathy and concern for the poor, a desire to control and alter their life style, and a commitment to assisting the needy in an economical manner. As with outdoor and indoor relief, benevolent programs were gradually abandoned in favor of those that imposed social control and, most importantly, were inexpensive. Nonetheless, at no time was sympathy for young paupers entirely absent, nor for that matter were frugality and social-control aims peculiar to one decade or another. Rather, as the economic climate of the city altered for the worse, particularly in the 1820s, the desire to reform the youngest of the poor and save money on welfare programs designed for them took precedence over humanitarian concerns among public poor relief administrators.

Early in the century, at a time when private-charity aid to children was minimal, public authorities had been more willing to emphasize home-relief programs that were particularly beneficial for children. From 1800 to 1820, most young public charges remained in their own home with their mother, who received cash pensions for the youngsters' support. A mi-

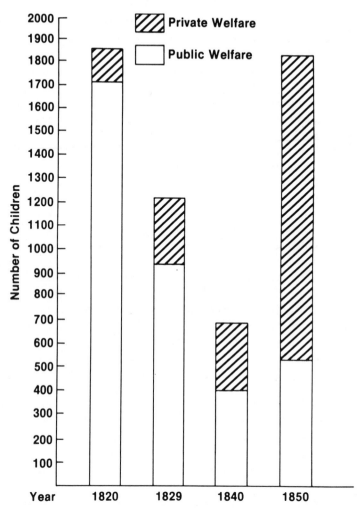

Figure 4
Number of Children Cared for by Public and Private Welfare,
Philadelphia, 1820 to 1850[a]

SOURCES: For public welfare, see *Poulson's*, 22 May 1822, *Philadelphia Gazette*, 12 January 1831; *Auditors' Reports of Blockley Alms-House, 1840, 1850*. For private charities in 1820, see *Philadelphia in 1824*, p. 65 (St. Joseph's Orphan Asylum) and *Poulson's* 12 January 1821 (Orphan Asylum). For private charities in 1829, see *Hazard's Register*, 5:197 (Orphan Asylum); *Poulson's*, 1 April 1830 (St. Joseph's Orphan Asylum); Scharf and Westcott, *History of Philadelphia*, 2:1483 (St. John's Orphan Asylum); Porter, *Picture of Philadelphia*, p. 44 (House of Refuge). Because the number in the Shelter for Colored Orphans in 1829 was unavailable, I used the number in the Shelter in 1824. See *Poulson's*, 3 November 1824. For private charities in 1840, see *Statistics of Philadelphia*, 1842, pp. 4, 6–7, 10–11 (Orphan Asylum, St. Joseph's, St. John's, Shelter for Colored Orphans); *Public Ledger*, 15 March 1842 (House of Refuge). For private charities in 1850, see Smith, *Philadelphia As It Is in 1852*, p. 275 (St. John's, Orphan Asylum, Shelter for Colored Orphans); House of Refuge, *Twenty-Second Annual Report, 1850*; St. Joseph's Orphan Asylum, *Report, 1850*; Girard College, *Fourth Annual Report, 1850*; Moyamensing Union School and Children's Home, *First and Second Annual Reports, 1850–51*; *Public Ledger*, 10 December 1850 (Foster Home Association).

[a]All numbers are aggregates and gleaned from annual reports. Admission lists for most private asylums are not available, so I could not check for overlap between them. However, since children usually did not move from one child-care agency to another but stayed within one, my use of aggregate admission figures should not inflate my totals too much.

nority of boys and girls were placed in a more regimented environment in the almshouse, where officials scrimped on their care by entrusting them to inmate nurses and teachers.

However, when the post-War-of-1812 depression led to extensive criticism of the city's poor relief system, public and private-welfare officials decided to place more emphasis on social control and thrift in administering child-welfare programs. Consequently, officials cut outdoor-relief payments and sought to enroll most young paupers in private orphanages, the House of Refuge, the almshouse or the new children's asylum, where behavior could be more closely monitored than in the family home. Although the disciplined routine of the children's asylum reflected the desire of the guardians of the poor to use the asylum for social control, the asylum's professional staff and its progressive educational program were also evidence of a philanthropic spirit that never altogether disappeared from public-welfare administration.

Nevertheless, in the 1820s and thereafter among public-welfare officials, sympathy for needy children gave way to an interest in how to provide for them as cheaply as possible. Therefore, to save money in 1835, officials eliminated all outdoor cash relief, closed the children's asylum, and sent all paupers, regardless of age, to the new Blockley Almshouse. Outdoor cash aid was costly and allowed mothers and children altogether too much independence, so it was abandoned. A separate institution for children alone was too costly to maintain, so it was closed.

After 1829, in order to save even more money, public officials began to admit fewer children to the one institution where they could receive public care—the almshouse. In this asylum, it had always been assumed that children were to be cared for temporarily until they could be indentured to an artisan to learn a trade. Institutional child-welfare programs were intended to be of short duration and thus inexpensive. Yet, as the public-indenturing program grew less popular, because artisans avoided taking children, whom they would have to train and educate, in favor of hiring an experienced adult willing to work for low wages, public officials faced the unpleasant prospect of having to spend large sums of money on extended institutional care for children who could neither be indentured nor released on their own. Accordingly, public officials began to admit fewer children to the almshouse and quickly returned to their family those few they did admit, a practice officials had once rejected, because it precluded reform. Clearly, when programs for social control, such as institutionalization and permanent separation of young paupers from their indigent family, became too costly, these programs were abandoned; the same was true of such humanitarian child-welfare programs as cash relief. By midcentury, thrift in public child-welfare administration was of preeminent importance.

Having cut back assistance to indigent children, it was comforting for public officials to assume that private-charity authorities would assume more responsibility for needy youngsters and largely replace public programs. Indeed, philanthropic aid to impoverished children was on the rise, but it took at least two decades for charities to assume completely the burden of child care so quickly abandoned by public authorities.

Although this chapter is essentially historical review and analysis of the first half of the nineteenth century, it has implications that are relevant today. For example, in the 1980s, the same pattern of events has been repeated with regard to child welfare. President Reagan has convinced Congress that the federal government must spend less and consequently reduce welfare programs, many of which, like AFDC, food stamps, and Medicaid, provide important benefits to children. Of course, neither in the 1830s and 1840s nor in the 1980s did a public official argue in favor of reducing welfare for needy, helpless children. Such an argument would be highly unpopular; nevertheless, to save money on welfare, it was necessary in both eras to reduce aid programs for children. Additionally, implicit in the actions of nineteenth-century officials, and explicit in the words of President Reagan, is the assumption that private-welfare agencies would take over where public ones had left off. Given the history of philanthropic concern among Americans, it is quite likely that charitable programs will grow in size and number. Yet, the experience of nineteenth-century Americans should demonstrate that it takes a while for private charities to expand and assume tasks formerly performed by public authorities. In the meantime, many indigent children are without help.

(6)

The Private-Welfare System

Just as private charities for needy children expanded in Philadelphia between 1800 and 1854, albeit slowly, so, too, did private-welfare agencies for
the older poor. This chapter deals with the agencies for the adult poor,
most of which were administered by small groups of concerned citizens
who visited the homes of the indigent and gave them money, food, or
clothing.

Alongside the public-welfare system in America, there has always been
another system of poor relief—the private-charity network. From 1800 to
1854 in Philadelphia, both public- and private-welfare officials dispensed
aid to the poor in their own home as well as in institutions, but public
officials always relied most heavily on indoor assistance and private
officials on outdoor aid. Those who administered the city's two welfare
systems also differed somewhat: managers of private charities generally
belonged to a higher social stratum than did public-welfare authorities. Yet
despite their differences, private- and public-welfare officials rarely competed and instead generally cooperated with one another. They also altered
some of their patterns of relief giving similarly in response to economic and
social changes in the city. The same three factors that affected the development of public welfare—humanitarian sympathy for the needy, the impulse to control the lifestyles of the poor, and the urge to economize on
poverty relief—determined the evolution of the city's private-welfare
system as well.

Yet the parallel between public and private welfare cannot be carried too
far. While the burgeoning growth of Philadelphia and public demand for
economy in poor relief required public authorities to relinquish their old
role as almsgivers, and as of 1829, become administrators instead, the same
development did not occur in private welfare. Philanthropic Philadelphians responded to the city's growth by simply creating many new private
charities, thus enlarging the network of citizens willing to attend to the
poor and enabling the private-charity sector to continue to serve the needy
on a personal basis from 1800 through 1854. Moreover, although the
demand for economy in welfare administration affected both public and

141

Soup House—Interior (*Courtesy of The Library Company of Philadelphia*). Poor applying for free food from one of nineteenth-century Philadelphia's many privately funded soup houses. They were open only in winter.

private agencies in Philadelphia, it had a greater impact on the public sector. Guardians of the poor worked to keep down welfare expenditures from 1820 on and so, too, did individual private charities. Yet, by the 1840s, the total number of private agencies in the city was so large that in the aggregate, private-charity officials spent considerably more than public authorities.

Before the War of 1812, Philadelphia possessed a network of private charities very similar to that in most towns and cities throughout both America and England. By this time, church-related charity was universal in both countries.[1] In Philadelphia, officials of many of the city's churches gave assistance to needy members of their congregations, and in the Quaker City, it is not surprising that the Society of Friends maintained one of the most elaborate welfare systems. Late in the seventeenth century, the Philadelphia Monthly Meeting began to appoint overseers of the poor to assist impoverished Friends. The overseers provided work, indentured children, distributed small amounts of money and gifts in kind, extended loans, and in 1713, erected an almshouse. This institution, which customarily housed poor, aged, and sometimes ill women, was always rather small, and by 1841, Quaker leaders ordered part of it torn down and replaced by office buildings. About four inmates occupied the smaller quarters.[2] Like the monthly meeting, Christ Church also supplied some outdoor assistance to poor communicants and in 1773, opened an almshouse called Christ Church Hospital. Between sixteen and forty Episcopal women, most of them widows of clergymen, annually received food, lodging, and medical care there.[3] The Friends' almshouse and Christ Church Hospital were, nonetheless, rather exceptional. Few Protestant churches relied on institutional relief; most furnished more informal assistance in the manner of the First Baptist Church, which paid doctors' fees and funeral expenses for some of its indigent members.[4]

Not only did churches commonly dispense relief in Philadelphia and elsewhere in America in the early nineteenth century, so, too, did ethnic societies. The Scots Charity Box was established in Boston as early as 1657, and in the next century, Scots' charitable societies appeared in New York, Alexandria, and Charleston as well as in Philadelphia. Germans, English, and Irish also formed emigrant-aid societies in many American cities by the end of the eighteenth century. These organizations functioned both as social clubs and relief-giving agencies. For example, the Philadelphia Hibernian Society sponsored annual dinners for its membership but also formed committees that met all ships coming from Ireland and granted assistance to impecunious passengers. The Welsh Society as well as the St. Andrews' and Scots Thistle Societies in Philadelphia were also organized for social and charitable purposes. Each provided relief to widows and children of its own members along with new Welsh or Scots immigrants. As for immigrants of other nationalities, in Philadelphia, needy Germans could appeal to the German Incorporated Society, French people to the French Society, and the English to the Society of the Sons of St. George.[5]

While various ethnic groups maintained their own charitable organizations in Philadelphia and elsewhere, so, too, did diverse occupational groups. Such groups organized mutual-benefit associations that occasionally dispensed poor relief in large eastern cities and also in smaller communities in rural areas. In Philadelphia by 1810, there were eleven organizations for skilled workmen, and by 1824, there were 150. Usually, their members paid an admission charge and monthly fees and in return acquired sickness benefits for themselves and their family. Such charity as these groups rendered was in the form of assistance to widows and children of former members. The Ship Masters' or Captains' Society kept a separate fund for this purpose and between 1806 and 1816 usually spent $1000–$2000 annually on charity to widows and children of ship masters. During the embargo, this society also gave extraordinary assistance to poor seamen through its Marine Benevolent Committee, which supplied 2,300

persons with cash, food, and wood. Still, the Captains' Society was unusual; occupational organizations in the city generally emphasized their
insurance, and not their charitable functions. Such societies assisted the
skilled worker, not the poor laborer.[6]

Before 1815, churches, ethnic societies, and occupational groups provided aid principally to their own members, but there were also philanthropic groups in Philadelphia and elsewhere in America that extended
aid not to others like themselves, but to certain types of people who were
frequently in need. Blacks, women, and the ill could all turn to special
charities created to serve their specific needs. Benevolent New Yorkers
established special schools and churches for free blacks, and in Philadelphia, impoverished blacks could indenture their children, find jobs for
themselves, or obtain temporary cash aid through a committee of the
Pennsylvania Abolition Society. However, this society grew less active
after 1806, and its members largely confined their activities to reading
lessons on morals in black churches.[7]

In contrast, needy women were able to appeal to a variety of charities
in Philadelphia as well as New York, Boston, and Baltimore. Following in
the tradition of evangelical English women, churchwomen in America
founded the first of these agencies.[8] In order to assist the many women
and children left impoverished by yellow fever epidemics in the 1790s,
Philadelphia's women Friends established the Female Society for Relief
and Employment of the Poor in 1793. A committee of its members visited
poor women weekly in their homes and brought them food and medicine.
Occasionally, members of the female society rented a house where they
attended to children while the mothers earned money spinning. From 1800
to 1818, this charity employed fifty to eighty women a year and allocated
outdoor assistance to another sixty-seven to one hundred families.[9]

By 1800, Protestant women in Philadelphia had launched the Female
Association for the Relief of Women and Children in Reduced Circumstances. Its managers visited and provided financial aid to the poor in the
form of monthly cash pensions. They also paid poor women for spinning in
their own homes until 1807, when the almshouse took over this work-relief
project. From 1802 to 1807, female association officials maintained a soup
house, which they later converted into an asylum for destitute widows and
children. It was not altogether successful and by 1815, had become a
private school for girls. Through its various programs, the female association aided between 500 and 600 women and children annually until the
1820s.[10]

Philadelphia's third church-related charity for women was the Female
Hospitable Society, founded in 1808 by wives of prominent ministers.
Concerned about the embargo, which left many fathers without jobs and
unable to support their families, members of the society granted assistance

to the wives and children of unemployed men and later to widows and orphans as well. Female managers of this charity visited poor families and if they were deemed worthy, issued orders that entitled the women to cash-relief, payment for home spinning, medical assistance from one of the doctors who donated his services to this charity, or relief in kind from the hospitable society's storeroom.[11]

Not only churchwomen, but churchmen as well established charities to assist women in the early nineteenth century. In both New York and Philadelphia, Friends and evangelical churchmen followed the example of philanthropists in London and Edinburgh and founded Magdalen societies to assist "those unhappy Females, who, in an unguarded hour, have been robbed of their innocence. . . ." In 1807, the managers of the Philadelphia society opened their first Magdalen asylum, to which they admitted between twenty-five and fifty women annually, and by 1847, they had moved to a second, larger building.[12]

Nineteenth-century Americans not only created more private charities for women, they established more agencies to succor the ill poor. Philanthropic Bostonians and New Yorkers as well as Philadelphians founded both hospitals and dispensaries to aid the ailing indigent. The oldest private medical facility in Philadelphia itself, patterned after comparable facilities in England, was the Pennsylvania Hospital. Founded in 1751, the Pennsylvania Hospital was originally designed to care primarily for the needy ill; nonetheless, by 1801, the hospital's financial situation made it necessary to admit about twice as many paying as needy patients. Not until the 1820s was the proportion of paying to indigent patients reversed; thereafter, the majority of patients in the hospital were needy people who could not afford proper medical care.

The Pennsylvania Hospital was organized much like the Philadelphia almshouse; managers appointed physicians and surgeons who used the hospitals as teaching facilities. Doctors at the private hospital attended to several hundred patients in the institution itself and over 1000 outpatients from 1800 to 1817 when the hospital's managers discontinued the outpatient department because the growth of the city's dispensaries had made it superfluous. There were also in the Pennsylvania Hospital, as in the city's almshouse, obstetrical, venereal, and insane wards. However, unlike public officials, managers of the private hospital admitted no one with infectious diseases nor any person who was chronically ill except lunatics.[13]

Another medical charity with counterparts in England, which, like the Pennsylvania Hospital, first opened its doors in the eighteenth century, was the Philadelphia Dispensary. Doctors donated their services to the dispensary in order to gain valuable clinical experience. In 1802, volunteer physicians visited 2,335 poor patients in their homes and by 1851, more than three times that number. The doctors treated "fractures, contusions, and lacerations," extracted teeth, and most importantly, prescribed medicines that were available to patients without charge at the dispensary office. Probably only those with minor ailments came to the Philadelphia Dispensary. Those with more serious diseases as well as indigent pregnant women entered the Pennsylvania Hospital or the almshouse. The dispensary also served a public-health function, inasmuch as its doctors vaccinated the indigent poor against smallpox.[14]

The third medical charity in Philadelphia was conceived in 1813 but did not officially open until 1817: it was the Friends Hospital for the Insane. In 1792, English Friends led by members of the Tuke Family started a rehabilitative institution for the insane at York, an asylum that was unique at the time in its emphasis on nonrestraint, understanding, and benevolent care. Philadelphia's Friends were impressed by the Tukes' example and founded their own Friends Asylum, which by 1821 housed about thirty patients and in 1837, sixty patients, some of whom were poor.[15]

From 1800 through the War of 1812, those who administered Philadelphia's various medical, religious, occupational, ethnic, and other charities were generally members of the city's established elite. For example, early in the century, Dr. Benjamin Rush, signer of the Declaration of Independence and one of the country's most distinguished physicians, served as president of the abolition society, and Stephen Girard, well-known Philadelphia merchant and benefactor, was a manager of the Captains' Society. The leaders of Philadelphia's private charities were much more likely to be upper-class professionals and merchants than were the city's public-welfare officials, who generally came from a step lower on the social scale: they tended to be businessmen and artisans.[16]

The difference in the social backgrounds of the city's public- and private-welfare officials may explain the conflict between guardians of the poor and managers of the Pennsylvania Hospital. In the late eighteenth and early nineteenth centuries, managers of the public almshouse frequently expressed resentment at the private hospital, founded by such a luminary as Benjamin Franklin and administered by some of the city's most distinguished citizens. Public officials grew particularly angry when the state legislature periodically voted to give funds to the Pennsylvania Hospital but granted no support to Philadelphia's larger public hospital. On one occasion, almshouse managers refused to hire any doctor who also served on the Pennsylvania Hospital staff. Not until 1815 did the two institutions agree to allow students who had paid fees at one hospital to attend lectures at the other without additional charge. Thereafter, enmity between the two hospitals diminished; they simply ignored one another.[17]

Still, this example of conflict between public- and private-welfare officials in Philadelphia is unique. In general, despite their different social backgrounds, officials from one system willingly cooperated with those from the other. Indeed, good relations between public- and private-welfare authorities was characteristic of most urban-welfare systems in nineteenth-century America. In many cities, including Philadelphia, private agencies commonly referred likely candidates for relief to public authorities, and the latter frequently extended financial and other types of assistance to urban charities. In 1807, the Philadelphia guardians of the poor agreed to take over a work-relief project, which involved employing poor women to do spinning in their own homes, from the Female Association for the Relief of Women and Children in Reduced Circumstances. Two years later, guardians enrolled and supported some young public charges in an orphanage for girls maintained by this same female association. The city's public-welfare administrators also permitted the female association and other private charities for women to purchase and distribute bread to the poor with the income from several small legacies left to public authorities. Managers of private charities sometimes assisted guardians of the poor. Between 1801 and 1810, managers of the Magdalen Society eased the burden on public authorities by removing a few women from the alms-house and accommodating them first in private homes and later in the Magdalen Asylum.[18]

Between 1800 and 1815 in Philadelphia, not only did public- and private-welfare officials generally cooperate with one another, they also both responded with humanitarian concern to the needs of the poor. The Christian doctrine of stewardship motivated public officials to meet and talk to the poor in their home, and the doctrine also prompted managers of the Pennsylvania Hospital to approve personally applications for admission. Female charity workers acted as God's almoners when they visited the indigent to determine the types of aid required. Both public and private welfare officials saw their role as assisting their needy brothers and sisters with whom they would stand before God on Judgment Day. Members of the Female Society for the Relief and Employment of the Poor stated that they were simply following Jesus' example by visiting the ill, clothing, and feeding the poor. And members of a Methodist-Episcopal Church group that called on and aided the poor in 1803 maintained that "he that giveth to the poor, lendeth to the Lord."[19]

When the city was relatively small and economic downturns were not so severe as they were in the 1760s or as they would be in the 1820s, when immigration and the ethnic conflict it sometimes engendered were reduced by war, and when there were few public expressions of distrust of the poor, private-charity officials, like public authorities, responded generously to medical and economic emergencies that affected the city's indigent. During the yellow fever epidemics at the turn of the century, guardians of the poor expanded their medical visitation program and the Female Society for the Relief and Employment of the Poor was launched to succor the widows and children of fever victims. During the embargo of 1807 to 1809, while public officials expanded employment opportunities in the almshouse, the Captains' Society extended special assistance to unemployed mariners and the Female Hospitable Society was organized to aid the wives and children of men without jobs. Both public- and private-welfare officials were also especially attuned to the needs of indigent women. Because employment opportunities for women were so limited and widowhood was for many equated with indigence, a large number of the poor were women. Accordingly, public officials dispensed outdoor aid almost entirely to females, and six of the city's private charities, the Friends' Almshouse, Christ Church Hospital, the three charities for women administered by women, and the Magdalen Society, all aided women exclusively. Even occupational groups like the Captains' Society extended a good deal of relief to women—specifically the widows of seamen.

The type of aid typically granted the poor by public- and private-welfare authorities from 1800 to 1815 also indicated sympathy toward the city's least fortunate. Private charities generally gave cash aid, which was particularly useful during depressions. Church leaders extended cash relief to their poorest communicants, members of ethnic societies waited on the wharves to dole out small amounts of money to impecunious arrivals from Europe; officials of the Captains' Society provided cash aid to widows and children of its members; and leaders of both the Female Association for the Relief of Women and Children in Reduced Circumstances and the Female Hospitable Society granted indigent women and their children cash pensions. Public authorities also gave a great deal of outdoor monetary aid during these years. Of course, public and private welfare officials also granted other types of assistance, including work and medical relief and some relief in kind in the form of free food, clothes, and fuel.[20] Nevertheless, in these years, cash aid was a viable, accepted mode of relief, and although it was granted with care, the fact that it was granted at all shows some faith in the poor's ability to manage money.

Although an understanding attitude toward the poor is more characteristic of private- as well as public-welfare authorities in Philadelphia before the end of the War of 1812, both groups of officials were also somewhat concerned about social control. Guardians of the poor exercised such control largely through the almshouse, but there were very few private institutions in Philadelphia at this time—only the Friends' Almshouse, Christ Church Hospital, the Magdalen Asylum, and the Pennsylvania Hospital, and all but the latter accommodated less than two dozen inmates apiece. It was not primarily through institutions that private charities exerted control over the poor but through rules and regulations they enforced and moral principles they attempted to inculcate in the needy.

The Female Hospitable Society, arguing that "immorality is too often the companion of poverty," refused to assist anyone the managers classified as immoral. Members of the Female Association for the Relief of Women and Children in Reduced Circumstances also preferred to aid women who were "honest and industrious, suffering under sickness and misfortune" and who were willing to send their children to school and indenture them to learn trades. Leaders of the Female Society for the Relief and Employment of the Poor insisted that those women to whom the society gave work be on the job by 9:00 A.M., "dress cleanly and decently and use no improper language, laugh, talk, sing, or smoke. They shall be satisfied with the work allotted them and the price paid them." Members of the Magdalen Society were also very specific about standards for the unwed mothers they assisted. The society planned "to inculcate the virtues of chastity, self-government, temperance, humility, and benevolence and to train to habits of useful industry." Young Magdalens would return to society "no longer disposed to injure and offend but to serve and oblige." [21]

By insisting that applicants be worthy, moral, hard working, obedient, agreeable to both themselves and their children, and learn habits of industry, private-charity officials established their own standards for the poor. Yet, early in the century, officials never carried their standards to extremes. The Female Association for the Relief of Women and Children in Reduced Circumstances promised to give soup to all poor "without discrimination," and members of the Female Society for the Relief and Employment of the Poor vowed to visit personally all needy, regardless of nationality or color, and assist everyone as best they could. In addition, managers of the Magdalen Society willingly released all women who demanded it, even if they were not, in the managers' view, "reformed." [22]

Nevertheless, private officials experienced financial constraints as they tried to be generous to the poor. Of necessity, economical administration of relief was a goal of Philadelphia's private-charity leaders from 1800 to 1815. Since all charities in the city were then relatively small with limited subscribers or financial supporters, the charities had to live within limited budgets. In fact, the median annual amount spent in 1810 by the nine private charities in Philadelphia for which records exist was just $1,296. All of the charities together spent $11,593, or approximately 13 percent of the outlay for public poor relief in 1810. It is unlikely that annual expenditures of the five other important charities in the city for which financial records are missing would substantially alter this picture. [23] In terms of dollars spent, public relief was the predominant form of welfare in Philadelphia before 1815. [24]

In the city, during the depression following the War of 1812 and the subsequent Panic of 1819, financial support for private charities, as well as public welfare, diminished. Not only did many citizens stop paying their poor tax, they also ceased voluntary contributions to charities. In addition, during these depression years, many blamed the poor for their own plight and attacked agencies, both public and private, that succored the needy. The war, the panic, economic constraints, and public criticism of poor relief, all substantially altered the pattern of private and public welfare in the 1820s.

From 1815 to 1830, approximately eleven new charities for adults and five for children were founded in Philadelphia. Significantly, all but two (the House of Refuge and St. John's Orphan Asylum, which opened in 1828 and 1829, respectively) were established before 1824, and most appeared in the years immediately following the War of 1812. By 1825, the city's private charities were so hard pressed for funds and the public clamor against welfare so great that almost no new charities were launched for several years.

The eight private-welfare agencies for the adult poor begun between 1815 and 1820 were all, in one way or another, responses to the war or the depression that followed. One such charity was founded by churchwomen, many of whom were Friends. It was the Indigent Widows' and Single Women's Asylum, opened in 1817 to accommodate older women, who had a difficult time surviving on their own in the postwar depression, or as managers of the asylum said, "During a season of almost unexampled pecuniary distress, when the pressure of the times has been universally felt." (A few of the new inmates may also have been widowed by the war or lost family in it who might have supported them.) Applicants gained admittance if they could pay an entrance fee that varied between $30 and $150, supply their own clothes, and furnish their own rooms. The asylum accommodated about fifty women, who sewed, knitted, and quilted to help defray the cost of their keep.[25]

Philadelphia philanthropists also responded to the war and Panic of 1819 by creating five soup societies, aimed at providing food for the poor during the winter months when jobs were scarcest and those who had been unemployed for a good portion of the year found their meager savings fast disappearing. These societies operated in various neighborhoods in the city and districts from January to March. Generally, their members served free soup and bread to the hungry once a day.[26]

After the War of 1812, two new medical charities, the Northern and Southern Dispensaries, were also formed in Philadelphia. In this economically depressed era, illness became an acute problem for the many who were without work and consequently without adequate housing or food. Philanthropists responded by founding dispensaries in the northern and southern districts in 1816. They, like the Philadelphia Dispensary, which continued to serve residents of the city proper, provided free medical care and medicine to the poor.[27]

Soup House—Exterior (*Courtesy of The Library Company of Philadelphia*). Note the diversity among the poor who applied for this form of charity.

The appearance of soup societies and dispensaries between 1815 and 1820 indicates the growing tendency of private-welfare officials to provide the poor with a necessary commodity—food, medicine, or a useful service, such as medical aid—rather than cash assistance. This pattern continued into the 1820s, when groups of churchwomen founded various Dorcas Societies to distribute free clothes to the poor. Work relief also became more popular with the formation of the Provident Society in 1823. Its male members visited poor women throughout the city and employed the most needy and worthy to sew in their own home or at the society's house of industry on Market Street. The women were paid small sums for making clothes that were subsequently sold by the society[28]

Still, private charities did not cease altogether giving cash aid in the 1820s. Churches and ethnic and occupational groups continued to give some money to the poor. Nevertheless, at this time, charities for women, which had previously granted many cash pensions, lost members to newer causes and substantially curtailed the number they had aided. The Female Association for the Relief of Women and Children in Reduced Circumstances rarely met in the 1820s, and members of the Female Hospitable Society complained that their declining membership rolls required them to limit the number of poor women they "relieved." [29]

Of course, this deemphasis on cash relief and growing reliance on relief in kind, and medical and work relief characterized not only private but also public welfare. Relief in the form of food, clothes, or medical supplies was less costly than cash relief, and during and after the Panic of 1819, both public and private charities were forced to economize. The general economic situation at this time not only led some Philadelphia residents to refuse to pay their poor taxes but also required others to limit their donations to private charities. Leaders of almost every charity in the city complained about lack of financial support in the 1820s. The Indigent Widows' and Single Women's Asylum limited admissions because of lack of funds, as did the Magdalen Asylum. The Female Hospitable Society discontinued work relief in 1829 due to lack of money; the Orphan Society had only $4.00 in its treasury in September 1820; and the Provident Society justified the low wages it paid indigent seamstresses by noting the limited funds at its disposal.

Before the War of 1812, most charities survived by investing legacies they occasionally received and then using the interest to defray part of their annual expenses. To finance the remainder of their costs, charities counted on $1–$2 annual donations from each of their subscribers. In the 1820s, the number of subscribers to almost every one of Philadelphia's private charities diminished and so, too, did their income. If even private charities of long standing in the city were in economic trouble by 1825, it is not surprising that, for the rest of the decade, few Philadelphians had the temerity to launch new philanthropic ventures. [30]

The economic constraints under which private charities operated can best be understood by looking at their expenditures. From 1810 to 1825, the median annual amount spent by the nineteen Philadelphia charities for which financial records are extant decreased 13 percent to $1,112. The total spent by all the private agencies did increase to $38,415, but that was because of the appearance, immediately after the War of 1812, of a cluster of new charities. Even if it were possible to include outlays from the four other charities for which financial records are missing, in all probability, expenditures for public welfare would still far outdistance those for private charity. As of 1825, guardians of the poor spent approximately two and a half times as much as their private-charity counterparts. [31]

In the 1820s, many Philadelphians justified their unwillingness to support financially private charities by using the same argument that had been directed against public relief: welfare agencies foster poverty by supporting the poor in their idleness. Many private-charity officials combated this argument, as did public officials of the era, by emphasizing the advantages of relief in kind and medical and work relief. Soup-society officials argued that giving a pauper an occasional meal was unlikely to foster permanent idleness, and dispensary managers made the same claim about a free occasional visit from a doctor. In addition, Provident Society leaders insisted that putting people to work actually prevented dependency.[32] Thus, the growing commitment of private-welfare officials to food, medical, and work relief not only indicated a ·desire to economize during difficult times, but also a willingness to control the poor by restricting the types of aid they received.

Economy and social control became more important to Philadelphia's private- and public-welfare officials in the 1820s, yet the humanitarian impulse did not vanish entirely. Charity officials frequently expressed sympathy for the poor in this economically troubled decade. In 1821, the Female Hospitable Society insisted that poverty was due largely to lack of work and not to intemperance, which was, in fact, the effect and not the cause of most indigence. Members of the Provident Society asserted in 1824 that "it is unworthy of us, as men and Christians, to sit still and condemn the poor.... They are not all confirmed in intemperance and indolence." And Carey argued that if the well-to-do would just accompany private-charity workers on visits to the poor, they would see places where,

> Every room contains a family, in many cases widows who have been reared with tenderness, and lived in affluence, but now have to earn a support for themselves and children by their needle, at the maximum of twenty-five cents per day. Could they behold their sorry fare, and the scantiness of the supply of even that fare—they would for ever cease to complain of the oppressive nature of the contributions to these societies—they would never join in the unfounded clamour against them, grounded on the absurd idea, that by their charities, they encourage idleness, and produce pauperism.... They often, by timely interference, prevent it.[33]

Nonetheless, private-welfare officials were on the defensive in the 1820s, and public pressure to economize and regulate the "improvidence" of the poor was so great that for these officials, such goals took precedence. The public distrust that produced such monetary constraint on private welfare is well demonstrated by the results of a fund-raising campaign launched in 1829. Spearheaded by the indefatigable publisher Carey, ninety-three leading Philadelphians, including most of the city's ministers, many of the guardians of the poor, and even William M. Meredith, erstwhile legislative critic of both public and private welfare, supported the drive. They employed a collector to solicit contributions door-to-door for the charity of the donor's choice. After three weeks, when the collector had amassed only $276.50, sponsors declared the campaign a failure. Just 137 persons donated money, and many of them were old subscribers to private charities. Carey refused to quit and continued to publish pamphlet after pamphlet describing the plight of the poor and urging people to subscribe to private charities. Even though he circulated his appeals in several cities, in four years, he raised only $92. Complaining that he was seventy-four years old and preferred to read rather than write, Carey despaired that "men with $20 for my one" would not respond to his pleas.[34]

In Philadelphia, public reluctance to support private charity persisted somewhat into the 1830s, when only eight new charities for adults and two for children were founded. The pressure to economize remained strong, and all the new charities were small, low-budget operations.

Three were medical charities. The Wills Hospital, opened in 1834 with a bequest from James Wills, treated poor patients with eye diseases. It could accommodate just forty-five patients, only a fraction of whom were indigent, since the hospital also accepted paying patients.[35] The other two medical philanthropies each provided attendants to needy pregnant women in their own home. Leaders of the Lying-In Charity, founded in 1831, and of the Nurse Charity, begun in 1839, sent doctors, midwives, and nurses to the home of indigent women to help deliver their babies. Thus, the women were spared entering either the Pennsylvania Hospital, where they would have been separated from their husband and children, or the almshouse, where they would have been branded paupers. In 1851, the two charities aided several hundred women and together spent less than $1,500.[36]

A fourth charity even more devoted to thrift was the Friends' Charity Fuel Association, founded in 1835. Its Quaker leaders intended to provide fuel for the poor in winter, but rather than give away coal and wood, they generally sold them at reduced prices. Thus, the poor would be able not only to warm their home but also to maintain their self-respect by avoiding dependence on free handouts.[37]

Equally economical in spirit were the four other charities established in Philadelphia in the 1830s. All emphasized moral advice rather than financial assistance to the poor. They were products of the evangelical religious revival movement that swept America in the 1820s, 1830s, and 1840s. Cities like Philadelphia were special targets for religious reformers, for rapid urban growth posed a challenge to the old moral order of the town:

> Would the web of community restraint be utterly swept aside, turning the emerging cities into seething cauldrons of licentious, brutalized creatures contemptuous of morality, responsible to no one, owning no master but the lustful dictates of their own wicked flesh?

Philadelphia reformers and others who were committed to the idea that every true Christian believer had an obligation to improve this world to make it more Godlike founded Bible and Tract Societies and Sunday schools in the 1820s. These organizations were intended to spread the good word to non believers from all walks of life. By the 1830s and 1840s, many reformers preferred programs aimed more directly at the urban poor, who were deemed especially in need of religious awakening, since so many lived in slums, where "riots, gang wars, and turbulent street brawls" were common and where "a debased urban lower class [was] not only surviving but flourishing as an encysted lump in the heart of the city, forever mocking its moral pretensions." [38]

In Philadelphia, the largest of these new agencies was the Union Benevolent Association, founded in 1831 and modeled after Thomas Chalmers' efforts to visit, advise, and aid the poor in Glasgow. Much like the Association for Improving the Condition of the Poor founded in New York City twelve years later, Philadelphia's Union Benevolent Association divided the city into districts, where in each, a corps of male and female visitors advised indigent men to be thrifty and avoid liquor and told needy women how to obtain needlework jobs and provide good, cheap food and clothing for their family. Occasionally the agency gave financial aid, but it preferred to lend money to the poor, hand out free fuel in winter, and help the unemployed find jobs for themselves and their children. [39]

A second smaller charity was formed in 1832 to bring religion and temperance to seamen who disembarked in Philadelphia. The Female Seamen's Friend Society, which had counterparts in other port cities, provided ill, poor, and disabled mariners with Bibles and temperance tracts as well as with food, fuel, and clothing. [40]

The other two religiously oriented charities founded in Philadelphia in the 1830s were both city missions. In 1830, the Philadelphia Society for Bettering the Condition of the Poor and in 1835, the Home Missionary Society began to send representatives into the streets of Philadelphia to extend moral advice to the unchurched poor. Both charities were patterned after clergyman Joseph Tuckerman's mission to the needy in Boston and closely resembled comparable missions in New York. Philadelphia's missionaries advised the poor on how to be clean and industrious and urged them to send their children to school. Missionaries also solicited alms and distributed them to the needy, usually in the form of food, fuel, or clothing and more rarely, cash. [41]

While a sympathetic concern for the poor and a Christian commitment to serving their needs certainly motivated founders of religious charities in Philadelphia in the 1830s, of equal or even greater significance was the charities' desire to oversee personally the activities of the impoverished. As leaders of the Union Benevolent Association stated, "Vicinity is of course important for the purpose of direct supervision of this class of people." [42] Visitors for this agency and city missionaries called on the poor, not primarily in the role of stewards of God's wealth who would distribute it in a benevolent fashion "even unto the least of these," but as moral advisers who could teach the indigent how to lead more upright and productive lives. Giving alms in any form was secondary to imparting religious counsel. If relief were granted, it was usually in the form least likely to be abused—relief in kind or medical or work relief.

Thus, in Philadelphia through the 1830s, social control remained the cardinal goal of private-welfare officials. At this time, the same goal motivated public-welfare authorities to replace cash relief with relief in kind and require all truly needy welfare applicants to enter the new, more tightly regulated almshouse at Blockley. Even so, the difference between social control in public and private welfare remained as it always had: public officials exercised control largely through an institution, the almshouse, and private officials, through personal moral supervision of the needy.

From 1840 to 1854, Philadelphia's private charities of long standing survived and prospered and were joined by fifteen new charities for adults and four for children. Among these new charities were several with a religious-reform bent, including two houses of industry, established by evangelical Protestants anxious to expand their proselytizing among the poor in sections of the city where many indigent lived. Tensions between American Protestants and immigrant Irish Catholics, which culminated in riots in 1844, called attention to intemperance, impiety, and poverty in immigrant neighborhoods. To deal with such problems in Moyamensing, evangelical Protestants and some Quakers formed the Christian Home Missionary Society in 1846, which promptly opened the city's first house of industry. Its chief object was to preach temperance and religious conversion, but it also provided practical assistance to the poor. In the house of industry, needy women and men labored to "cut and sew carpet rags" and weave them into rugs and mats, which the leaders of the Christian Home Missionary Society sold. They used the profits to pay the workers' wages. Later, this missionary society became the Philadelphia Society for the Employment and Instruction of the Poor, and by 1850, their Moyamensing House of Industry contained a soup house, dispensary, grocery store, and school as well as bathing facilities, lodging rooms, and workshops where forty to fifty people toiled daily. This first house of industry was so successful that Protestant philanthropists opened a second one in Northern Liberties in 1847. [43]

Another Protestant charity that pressed for moral reform among the poor in Philadelphia was the Pennsylvania Seaman's Friend Society formed in 1845. This was the male counterpart of the Female Seaman's Friend Society begun in 1832. While the latter charity employed the widows of seamen as seamstresses and used profits from the sale of clothing they made to aid impoverished mariners, the male contingent of the society, in cooperation with the female branch, built a boarding house for sailors on Lombard Street. Mariners paid a minimal fee to stay in the house, where they were plied with tracts and Bibles and urged to sign the temperance pledge.[44]

Somewhat less evangelical in spirit, but no less cautious about indiscriminate relief giving was the Grandom Institution, created by a bequest in 1841 and administered by the Society of Friends. Managers of this agency lent money to young, necessitous men hopeful of starting their own business and gave some free fuel in the winter to the "deserving" but not the "intemperate" poor.[45]

The numerous Protestant charities in Philadelphia and their attempts to proselytize among the poor, many of whom were Catholic, upset leaders of the Church of Rome in Philadelphia and stimulated them to form several charities of their own. Ever since 1806, Catholics had maintained one orphanage in Philadelphia, and they founded a second in 1829, but they broadened their charitable activity to assist many different types of poor only after the great influx of Irish immigrants and the riots in 1844. In 1848, Catholics opened St. Anne's Asylum to accommodate indigent widows and St. Joseph's Hospital for the ill poor and in 1851, two other agencies— the House of the Good Shepherd for unwed mothers and the Society of St. Vincent de Paul, which extended relief in kind to the poor in various parishes in the city.[46]

Just as religiously oriented charities increased in number in Philadelphia from 1840 to 1854, so, too, did medical relief programs. In 1841, the Pennsylvania Hospital moved and expanded its division for the insane. In the next eleven years, the new Pennsylvania Asylum for the Insane, located, as was the almshouse, outside the city in Blockley Township, admitted over 13,000 patients, roughly 71 percent of whom were indigent; the rest were paying patients. Somewhat later, in 1848, the Moyamensing Dispensary opened in the Moyamensing House of Industry and joined the Philadelphia, Northern, and Southern Dispensaries in providing medicine and medical diagnoses without charge to the city's poor.[47]

The ailing indigent were always objects of special concern to Philadelphia's philanthropists, as were needy women. All the old charities devoted to women's needs were still functioning by 1854, and six new ones had appeared in the previous eight years. Two of the new agencies were founded by Catholics, St. Anne's Widows' Asylum and the House of the Good Shepherd, and the others by Protestant women. Charities run by and for females had long been in existence in both America and England; they simply grew more numerous by the middle of the nineteenth century. With the growth of cities like Philadelphia, there were more and more affluent urban women, free from farm drudgery, who were encouraged, especially by male religious leaders, to devote their energies to charitable work.

The doctrine of women's separate sphere, popular during the nineteenth century, maintained that women had a special expertise in moral and religious matters and in managing households and children. Philadelphia's churchwomen who founded charities from 1800 to 1815 demonstrated this expertise by both preaching moral principles to the needy women they visited and teaching these women household skills, as did their successors who launched charities in the 1840s. For example, in 1847, philanthropic women established the Rosine Association to use moral suasion to reclaim prostitutes. Members of the association visited brothels and tried to persuade women to leave to enter the Rosine Asylum, where they would be taught to sew and directed into reputable jobs. The new institution was simply a household where former prostitutes learned many of the skills women were supposed to acquire at home.[48] Other female charities also emphasized labor traditional to women. In 1846, members of the Northern Association for the Relief and Employment of Poor Women and in 1847 the Western House of Employment opened workrooms where needy women were taught to sew and paid for their labor. In addition, female managers of the Temporary Home Association maintained a large house to accommodate unemployed mothers and their children. The association charged no rent while the women were out of work and helped find jobs for them and their children.[49]

While by midcentury, impoverished women in Philadelphia could seek aid from numerous charities devoted to their needs, indigent men were not so fortunate. Only the Seaman's Friend Society, which was not a very large or generous charity, and the Naval Asylum were specifically intended to assist only men. The latter institution served as a home for over a hundred aged, U.S. naval veterans, each of whom received clothing, tobacco, and a monthly pension from the federal government.[50]

Of course, both needy men and women in Philadelphia were assisted by many charities, churches, medical dispensaries and hospitals, soup societies, fuel associations, and ethnic societies. In the 1840s, the latter groups, most of which had been founded at least a half century earlier, became substantially more active. Before the War of 1812 stopped immigration for some years, Philadelphia's ethnic societies regularly sent committees to meet ships arriving from Europe and aid passengers in need. Although migration to America from abroad increased after the war, it accelerated most rapidly in the 1840s, when Germans and Irishmen, many of them quite poor, fled political and economic upheavals in their respective homelands for America. This vast increase in new arrivals provoked members of various long-dormant ethnic societies to expand their relief-giving function. In 1847 alone, such societies spent $20,000 to assist aliens. In 1848, as passengers landed at the wharves in ever-growing numbers, concerned citizens also formed a new, general Emigrant Aid Society to protect foreigners of all nationalities from fraud, provide them with temporary housing, and help them find employment.[51]

The formation of so many new private charities in Philadelphia around midcentury indicates a significant difference in the way that public and private welfare responded to the city's growth. The rapid increase in Philadelphia's population and its geographical dispersal challenged the monolithic public-welfare system. Instead of simply expanding the number of public officials as the city grew, and thereby complicating administrative procedures, public authorities created a welfare bureaucracy. In doing so, they inevitably separated themselves from the needy and concentrated more on management than interaction with the poor. In contrast, private charities reacted to the city's growth not by contracting and stressing efficiency, but by proliferating. Groups of citizens who became alarmed about poverty for whatever reason, created new charities, often much like those already in existence. Because the number of people engaged in private charitable work multiplied and because most charities assisted a relatively small group of people, personal almsgiving remained viable in private charities from 1800 through 1854, not only in Philadelphia, but in most other American cities as well.[52]

In the 1840s in Philadelphia, despite the depression with which the decade began, private agencies rapidly grew in number. During the general business depression from 1837 to 1843, some older city charities lost money when income from their investments decreased. The orphan asylum, the Northern Dispensary, and the Female Association for the Relief of Women and Children in Reduced Circumstances all complained of this problem. In addition, charities that provided work relief, like the Provident and Union Benevolent Associations lamented that during this business slump, they could not sell clothing made by the needy women they employed.[53]

Nevertheless, during the Panic of 1837, citizens' contributions to Philadelphia's charities, both old and new, remained fairly constant. The pattern of events that succeeded the Panic of 1819, when donations to charities declined and few new charities were formed, was not repeated for a variety of reasons. For one, in the 1840s, unlike the 1820s, Philadelphians were not overly burdened by public poor taxes. Ever since the 1828 poor-law reform, guardians of the poor had curtailed expenditures, and thanks to the rapid growth of the city, the poor-tax burden was spread over a large population and did not fall too heavily on most citizens. In addition, from 1829 to 1854, public welfare became increasingly the province of small-time politicians, who earned the distrust of Philadelphia's middle and upper classes, still the mainstay of private charity. Once the board of guardians became known as the board of buzzards, a group that cared more for themselves than the poor, the stage was set for "locally prominent bankers, merchants, editors and professional men" who were "evangelical in religion and conservative in politics" to expand private welfare and make it the chief dispenser of relief in the city.[54] These leaders may have also felt such an expansion necessary because of the very inaction of public-welfare officials who, to save money, did not expand aid to the unemployed nor to the flood of new immigrants who entered the city in the 1840s. The arrival of these immigrants engendered ethnic and religious conflicts in the form of several riots in 1844, which troubled Philadelphia's elite. Hence, city philanthropists, unencumbered by high tax bills, distrustful of public-welfare officials, yet concerned about the problems they ignored and motivated by a desire for religious reform that had abated little since the 1830s, set out to create a variety of new charities for the poor.

The founding of so many new agencies in such a short time reflects the genuine concern felt by many Philadelphians for the problems of the poor. The economic distress engendered by the Panic of 1837 prompted sympathetic citizens to establish numerous work programs in houses of industry and charities for women. In addition, the rapid inflow of indigent immigrants to the city stimulated some Philadelphians both to revive old and open new immigrant-aid societies. The readiness with which citizens expanded private poor relief programs in the 1840s is certainly a sign of their compassion for Philadelphia's needy. Especially when the private-charity response is contrasted to public welfare's which was negligible, the humanity of many managers of Philadelphia's charities stands out in bold relief.

Nonetheless, even though between 1840 and 1854, Philadelphia's charity leaders acted more willingly and quickly than public officials to aid recent immigrants as well as the victims of economic depression, the manner in which private authorities dispensed aid to the poor was the same as it had been since the 1820s and 1830s. Relief in kind and medical and work relief—forms of aid that officials believed could be used only to alleviate want—remained most popular. None of the new charities founded in Philadelphia between 1840 and 1854 dispensed cash aid. Moreover, not only through the forms of relief granted, but also through specific requirements made of recipients, private-welfare authorities continued their efforts to control the lives of the poor. Those who applied for charity had to be receptive to moral reform. Needy men and women were required to attend temperance meetings and send their children to Sunday schools if they wanted aid from a house of industry. Mariners who lodged at the boarding house run by the Pennsylvania Seaman's Friend Society were constrained to sign temperance pledges. Unwed mothers who enrolled in the new Magdalen Asylum were compelled to accept virtual imprisonment away from the temptations of the world for the term of their pregnancy. Those poor who sought fuel from the Union Benevolent Association were obliged to pay half price in order to build self-reliance. Women seeking jobs, who boarded free of charge at the Temporary Home Association, were expected to pay back their room and board fees once they found employment, so they could learn self-sufficiency.[55]

By midcentury in Philadelphia, private-welfare officials were sympathetic to the poor, but they were also determined to make the needy behave in a moral, upright manner. Social control was a firm objective of both private- and public-welfare officials, although the former still imposed control largely through rules and regulations and the latter through institutionalization.

Economy, too, remained important to private- and public-welfare officials in Philadelphia from 1840 to 1854. Almost all new agencies formed at the time were, like their predecessors, relatively small and practiced thrift out of necessity. By 1850, median annual expenditures of the thirty-seven charities in Philadelphia for which there are financial statements was $2,000, higher than the median amount spent by city charities in either 1810 or 1825, yet still not an extraordinarily large amount of money. When the sums spent by all thirty-seven agencies in 1850 are totaled, their expenditures equal $202,336, or 22 percent more than the amount spent by public welfare during the same year. Of course, if we had the financial records of the ten other important charities in the city in 1850, the disparity between private- and public-welfare expenditures would be even greater.[56] By midcentury in Philadelphia, the typical charity was still quite small, but because there were now so many of them and the guardians of the poor had worked to reduce public-welfare expenditures, private charity had become the dominant mode of relief.

By the time the private-welfare system had become paramount in Philadelphia, its interests and those of the public-welfare system had diverged somewhat. For example, as public officials economized, they reduced aid to women and children by giving them little cash aid and by admitting fewer of them to the almshouse. In turn, private officials took up where the public left off and began to expand aid programs to needy women and children. Yet private agencies generally refused assistance to indigent men, and as they became more numerous in the city due to industrial change and economic depression, public officials admitted more unemployed and often ailing men to the almshouse. Thus by 1854 in Philadelphia, impoverished men were most likely to obtain substantial forms of assistance, such as full room and board and medical care, from guardians of the poor, whereas needy women and children generally secured such aid from private groups.

Another sign of the growing divergence of public and private welfare in Philadelphia was the withdrawal of public support from some private programs. In the early 1820s, when the almshouse was frequently over-crowded, guardians of the poor had paid the board of some youngsters in the Shelter for Colored Orphans and some older women in the Indigent Widows' and Single Women's Asylum. Officials had also donated funds to the Provident Society on the condition that it employ a number of public outdoor pensioners. Later, when the new almshouse at Blockley, autho-rized by 1828 legislation, opened, welfare officials had plenty of space to accommodate both black and white children as well as old women. There-fore, guardians ceased paying the board of destitute old or young people in private institutions. In addition, with the termination of outdoor cash relief in 1835, there were no more pensioners for whom work had to be supplied by the Provident Society, and so the flow of tax dollars to this agency also ended.[57]

Yet even though public officials reduced aid to some charities in the 1840s, they expanded assistance to others. Thus, officials donated medicine to the Moyamensing Dispensary and money to several soup societies in return for medical and food relief for public-welfare recipients. On occa-sion, private agencies also helped public officials: when Girard College for orphans opened in 1848, its managers accepted a number of orphaned boys from the public almshouse.[58] Thus, between 1800 and 1854, although the city's two welfare systems did grow apart somewhat, they did not alto-gether cease to cooperate with and assist one other.

Throughout the years from 1800 to 1854, Philadelphia's network of private charities dispensed an increasing amount of outdoor aid to the city's poor. Although some private-charity institutions were formed in the city, they were never so important to the private-welfare system as the almshouse was to the public. At all times, those who applied to managers of private charities were most likely to receive a small cash handout, clothing, a load of wood, a bowl of soup, medicine, a visit from a physician, or a temporary job. In contrast, public paupers were customarily admitted to the almshouse.

While representatives of the city's two welfare systems generally granted diverse forms of aid to the poor, and even began to specialize in aiding various types of needy people, officials usually got on well together. Disputes between administrators of the two welfare systems were in-frequent. Even though private-charity officials were more likely to be members of the city's elite than public-welfare leaders, both groups often collaborated and supported each other's programs.

Furthermore, leaders of private- and public-welfare systems sympa-thized with the poor, yet still sought to administer relief programs that would be both economical and unlikely to encourage dependence on charity. Empathy, thrift, and social control were always concerns of welfare officials, but one or the other became more significant depending on social and economic conditions.

Hence, from 1800 to 1815, when Philadelphia was still relatively small and economic crises were not overly severe and the prevailing religious philosophy emphasized stewardship of the poor, the city's welfare authorities, public and private, dealt with the needy in a benevolent fashion. Private-charity leaders expanded relief programs during the embargo and dispensed a good bit of cash aid. They also responded promptly to the War of 1812 by founding a variety of new charities for the widowed, ill, and hungry.

However, the Panic of 1819 affected private and public welfare adversely. As the money supply decreased, many Philadelphians ceased paying their poor tax and stopped contributing to private charities. The city's two welfare systems not only lost financial support, but they were also criticized for encouraging dependence on charity. If unemployment were the result of the moral turpitude of the poor, as many believed, then those who aided the indigent were suspect. As a consequence of this criticism, both private- and public-welfare authorities in Philadelphia reduced expenditures and emphasized such forms of aid as medical and work relief and relief in kind that were both inexpensive and unlikely to encourage dependence. Such types of aid also gave donors a large degree of control over recipients. In addition, from the 1820–54, the growth of evangelical Protestantism, whose adherents established a number of charities in Philadelphia, furthered the trend toward close moral surveillance of the poor.

Yet, despite significant similarities, the history of private and public welfare in Philadelphia between 1800 and 1854 diverged somewhat. For example, public pressure to economize on poor relief, which began in the 1820s, thereafter continued to influence public welfare to a much greater degree than private charity. Furthermore, the growth of Philadelphia's population and the physical diffusion of its residents led guardians of the poor to become managers and hire employees to visit the poor directly. In contrast, private charity eschewed bureaucracy and attracted more volunteers, who continued to serve the poor as personal almsgivers long after public officials had relinquished this role.

The divergent ways in which public and private welfare responded to economic and population pressures can, to a large extent, be explained by structural differences. Since the public-welfare system was monolithic, as the city grew, so, too, did the system. Such growth produced an unwieldy welfare program that eventually, of necessity, had to be streamlined. Guardians of the poor gave up personal contact with the poor for pragmatic reasons. Further, simply because there was only one public-welfare system supported by one special tax, this welfare system was quite visible. Residents could and did demand and enforce economy on public relief with relative ease.

On the other hand, private charities were many and varied. As the city grew, more private agencies appeared, each one specializing in care for a particular group of poor, often in a limited section of the city. Because each charity remained small and distinct and attracted a dedicated corps of volunteers, personal almsgiving continued to be characteristic of private charities long after it had become historical artifact for public welfare. In addition, because there were so many charities, it was virtually impossible to keep abreast of total expenditures. Each charity published its own financial statement at different times in the year, and there was no general review of all these statements. Thus, private-charity officials did not feel public pressure comparable to that exerted on the guardians of the poor to economize. Of course, each private agency practiced thrift out of necessity, since each had limited resources, but all together, by 1850, they were spending a considerable sum of money.

Eventually, private charities were called to public account for their expenditures and the duplication of effort among them. In the 1870s, after another serious depression, loud objections to the extravagance of private charities were voiced and action was finally taken to enhance their efficiency by Charity Organization Societies. At about the same time, paid social workers began to replace volunteers who had previously staffed private charities.[59] Thus, public pressure for economy, efficiency, and bureaucracy in administering relief to the poor was felt first by public welfare in the 1820s and by private welfare in the postbellum years.

(7)
Nineteenth-Century Welfare: The Broader Perspective

Data for Philadelphia and corrobative evidence from other cities confirm that actions taken by welfare officials reflect a mixture of three motivations: a commitment to caring for the needy in a humane and understanding fashion, a desire to control and reform them, and dispense welfare as economically as possible. At any given time, the relative importance of a particular impetus was related less to the personal whims of welfare authorities than to factors in the larger society that inevitably influenced poor relief administrators.

Economic upheavals are decisive in promoting welfare change; the direction that change takes, however, depends on social and political factors. In the depressions that followed the Seven Years' War and the War of 1812, the number of poor in Philadelphia rose dramatically and so, too, did the cost of poverty relief. Consequently, officials in both eras instituted repressive welfare measures with a view toward saving money by reducing the number of poor receiving assistance. Nonetheless, in the earlier era, the city had not grown large enough to require bureaucratization of the welfare system; by the 1820s, it had. In addition, in the 1760s, Quaker leaders had the political clout to reform Philadelphia's welfare system by placing a segment of it, the almshouse, under their own private control. By the 1820s, political factors led not to the creation of a part private-, part public-welfare system, but to a smaller, more efficient public program.

Large-scale expansion of public relief to the poor and massive changes in welfare legislation are rare in American history. Economic dislocations in the eighteenth and nineteenth centuries usually produced either slight changes in relief giving or significant cutbacks in aid. In Philadelphia, the Embargo of 1807 and the Panic of 1837 were examples of the former. During the embargo, welfare officials expanded almshouse manufacturing somewhat, and during the panic, they gave small amounts of fuel to thousands of needy citizens. Yet, in neither case was the increase in public relief very great. In contrast, the depression following the Seven Years'

165

War and the Panic of 1819 were times when public welfare, particularly outdoor relief, was markedly curtailed. Depressions later in the century, in 1873–78, 1882–86, and 1893–97, confirm this pattern, for they, too, occasioned contractions of public outdoor relief in several U.S. cities, including Philadelphia.[1]

Not until the twentieth century in the United States were there two major exceptions to the dictum that equates economic upheavals with reductions in welfare. The first was the Great Depression of the 1930s. Then, through work-relief programs, unemployment and old age compensation, and aid to families with dependent children, public-welfare programs multiplied. Frances Fox Piven, a political scientist, and Richard Cloward, a sociologist, suggest in their book *Regulating the Poor* that social protests by the indigent, who marched on local welfare offices and demanded aid, combined with the willingness of Democrats to help the unemployed, whose votes Democratic politicians coveted, produced the first massive increment in federal aid programs to the poor. The new measures were not wholly successful and did not eliminate all poverty, but they did involve expansion rather than contraction of welfare. Piven and Cloward believe that the depression in the 1930s was unusual in U.S. history because of the way protests by the poor interacted with politics to produce a welfare explosion. The authors argue that even though depressions in the 1870s, 1880s, and 1890s were also accompanied by rioting by the poor, politicians were unwilling in those years to respond to protest.[2] The important point to note here is that there is a political component in every change in welfare policy. Politicians may find it expedient to respond to the poor at some times, but not at others.

There are other explanations for the welfare explosion that accompanied the depression in the 1930s as well. Historian James Patterson rejects the Piven and Cloward emphasis on protest and politics. Although Patterson agrees that the consciousness of national politicians was raised, it was not by protests, for the poor during the depression were remarkably quiescent. Ultimately, Patterson emphasizes dislocation in the economy in the years from 1929 to 1933, when the number of unemployed rose to 25 percent of the labor force. Local relief arrangements simply could not suffice to handle both the newly unemployed and all the "old poor," including blacks, the aged, small farmers, and the disabled. Patterson believes that structural problems exacerbated by economic and social changes best account for the outpouring of federal government aid after 1933.[3]

The explanations of Piven and Cloward and of Patterson for the growth of welfare during the depression of the 1930s are irreconcilable. Although all of the authors agree that the economy, politics, and social protests or social changes played a part in this welfare explosion, they disagree on the relative importance of each component. Yet, however the expansion of relief giving in the 1930s is explained, it was an era when welfare officials took a more charitable approach to the poor than they had previously. By February 1934, federal relief programs "reached nearly 8 million households, or 28 million people. This was 22.2 percent of the population—a high in public welfare for any time in American history." [4] Nonetheless, the need to control the poor and economize on assistance to them remained viable issues for public officials. Work-relief programs like the Works Progress Administration served not only "to alleviate distress," but also to "enmesh ... people in the work role, the cornerstone of social control in any society...." [5] And as for saving money, by 1935, President Roosevelt had persuaded Congress to reduce direct relief for "so-called unemployables" and leave such programs to the states. In turn, "the states and localities did not provide enough money."

> Many communities stopped providing any allowance for clothing, rent, or medical assistance; others tried to make unemployables work for their check. Some reverted to paying people in goods rather than cash. Many tightened residency requirements or enforced statutes that had been on the books since the seventeenth century. There were great variations in payments for general assistance. In April 1939 the average was $23.86 per month for 4 million families, as opposed to $28.96 four years earlier under FERA. [6]

The second time in this century when welfare programs were enormously augmented was in the 1960s. At first glance, the expansion of welfare in this decade seems to disprove the thesis that sizable welfare changes occur only during periods of economic upheaval: the 1960s was a prosperous decade in America. Yet Piven and Cloward argued that agricultural modernization in the South in the 1940s, forced blacks to migrate to cities in the North, where they faced severe social and economic deprivation. By the 1960s, many of these blacks had participated in riots in U.S. cities to protest their lot. Again, there was a political response. Democrats at the national level found it politically expedient to appease northern urban black voters, on whom the party's continued success at the polls depended to a large degree, by augmenting relief through the War on Poverty. [7]

Again, Patterson disagrees with Piven and Cloward and instead maintains that the most important economic factor was the very prosperity of the 1960s, which made it more feasible for concerned liberals like John Kennedy and Lyndon Johnson to spend more on welfare—and so perhaps enhance their national political appeal. In addition, "an increase in the percentage of the poor who were aged, members of female-headed families, or minorities," as well as bureaucratic pressure from members of the government's welfare establishment and the desire of local officials to have Washington shoulder more of the welfare burden, also contributed to the welfare explosion in the late 1960s and early 1970s.[8]

As in the growth of poverty-relief programs in the 1930s, interpreters of the era agree that politics played a part in the 1960s, but was it in the form of Democrats courting black voters or concerned liberals appealing to a national electorate? And what of the economy? Was it agricultural modernization in the South in the 1940s or prosperity everywhere in the 1960s that precipitated the War on Poverty? Concerning social forces, was it rioting in northern cities or the growth of the number of poor that conditioned responses to poverty in the 1960s?

Once again, even though reasons for a welfare expansion may be in dispute, the tripartite mixture of concerns that motivated the actions of welfare officials is not. By the 1960s, humanitarianism was again at center stage. Relief expenditures soared from 7.7 percent of the gross national product in 1960 to 16 percent in 1974. "Public assistance payments per recipient increased both in constant dollars and in comparison to average wage rates." Yet some concern about social control and frugality were still evident—thus the emphasis in the War-on-Poverty programs on "doors," or relief programs to open job opportunities to the poor. Such relief measures as those embodied in the Job Corps and in later Office of Economic Opportunity (OEO) measures were designed to reform the poor, convince them to accept the work ethic. Rehabilitation programs were also expected to save the taxpayers' money by permanently relieving poverty. Economy was also evident in other aspects of welfare in the 1960s. The OEO, a key agency in the War on Poverty, "never got much money to do what it proposed to do. Funding was low from the start . . . and after 1965 money became even harder to get."[9]

The history of welfare in the twentieth century demonstrates the persistence of the three basic concerns of welfare administrators since the eighteenth century—charity, social control, and frugality. In addition, while economic, political, and social factors all affected changes in welfare policy in this century, defining the nature of each factor and what part each played in determining the course of reform is difficult. In the nineteenth century, substantial changes in welfare practice occurred only in response to economic distress, with social and political forces serving simply to influence the form changes took. In addition, huge increases in welfare programs in the 1930s seemingly prove that the old connection between a depressed economy and welfare reduction has been broken forever. Here, events in the early 1980s should give us pause. When inflation and recession disrupted the American economic system, the federal government, which, as of 1980 was controlled by an economy-minded Republican administration headed by President Reagan, cut a number of poverty-relief programs, including food stamps, AFDC, and Medicaid. Once again, as in earlier centuries, those beset by economic woes accepted reduction of costly welfare programs, and the poor themselves did not immediately organize to protest the changes.[10] Unquestionably, the level of relief giving is higher now than in the past, yet decreases in welfare programs can still be made, and they may well occur in response to predictable phenomena. At the same time, not even when welfare is most reduced, are humanitarian programs likely to disappear entirely (although the Reagan Congress has cut programs, it did not eliminate them entirely); nor when relief measures are increased, are social control and thrift likely to be completely ignored.

Just as there are similarities between periods of reduction in relief in the nineteenth and twentieth centuries, so, too, are there parallels betwen recipients of welfare, public and private. For the sake of convenience in the discussion that follows, I treat various categories of the poor as distinct, although in reality they were not. At one and the same time, an indigent person could be aged, ill, and female, but I deal with these groups separately in order to clarify the specific forms of welfare granted to each.

In the last century, impoverished, unskilled male laborers sometimes accepted a bag of groceries or a load of wood from private- or public-welfare officials or a visit from a dispensary or publicly employed physician, but the most conspicuous type of relief available was institutionalization in the almshouse. This most unattractive form of public relief was intended to encourage indigent men to work rather than rely on welfare. Interestingly enough, in view of the strong prejudices of nineteenth-century Americans against granting poor relief to men, the virtual elimination of outdoor cash aid in Philadelphia in the 1830s and 1840s made them the major recipients of the most comprehensive and useful form of public welfare left: institutionalization in the almshouse. Because needy women had always received most outdoor cash aid and poor men most indoor relief, when the Philadelphia guardians curtailed pensions, impoverished men in the almshouse remained the major beneficiaries of the largest public-welfare program.

Even today, there remains some prejudice against granting public cash assistance to men. Families headed by men constitute only a small percentage of those receiving the most conspicuous form of public cash-transfer payments today, AFDC. Medical relief through Medicaid also goes largely to women; in 1981, only 27 percent of the beneficiaries of Medicaid were men. In 1981 male-headed families also made up just 27 percent of the households participating in the federal Food Stamp Program. Nevertheless, although public assistance is still not so freely extended to men as to women, men do benefit considerably from various forms of social insurance, which are, however, not intended strictly for the poor. Over half of the recipients of old age insurance, unemployment insurance, and worker's compensation in 1977 were men.[11]

While in Philadelphia in the last century, destitute men gradually secured a larger proportion of the major forms of public welfare than needy women, women always constituted the bulk of public-relief recipients. From 1800 to 1828, impoverished females collected almost all of the cash aid granted by guardians of the poor; women were the exclusive beneficiaries of the guardians' outdoor spinning project; and women were also entitled to fuel and food relief as well as admission to the almshouse. By 1835, when work and cash aid were suspended, women were eligible for only indoor relief in the almshouse and fuel aid. Not many claimed indoor assistance, but thousands obtained free wood and coal, and since relief in kind had become the most popular form of public welfare, women continued to compose the majority of public-relief recipients. At the same time, they received an extraordinary amount of aid from private welfare as charities for women proliferated in Philadelphia from 1800 to 1854.

Subsequently, in the late nineteenth century, other cities followed Philadelphia's example and reduced outdoor cash aid on which so many indigent women counted. Private charities furnished the only noninstitutional form of welfare for women until the early twentieth century, when many states devised mothers' pension plans, which, while not altogether generous, did allow some women outdoor aid once again. Finally, in the 1930s, mothers' pensions were federalized with AFDC, which is the major welfare program today.[12] This aid goes almost entirely to women and their children. Indigent women constitute the majority of public-relief recipients today just as they did in early nineteenth-century Philadelphia. In the last century and a half, we have not been able to solve the problem of poverty among women, and we have not even formulated very many creative welfare programs to deal with it. In form if not in amount, AFDC payments differ very little from nineteenth-century outdoor cash pensions.

In the past, cash pensions went not only to women but also to children. Actually, in nineteenth-century Philadelphia, there were three types of welfare available to indigent boys and girls—home care, institutionalization, and indenturing. Until the 1820s, guardians of the poor used all three: they assisted most needy children in their own home by making cash payments to their mother or wet nurse; officials accommodated a few homeless youngsters in the almshouse; and they indentured all young public charges when they reached working age.

As a part of their economy drive in the 1830s, Philadelphia's welfare officers eliminated publicly funded home care for the young. Instead, they emphasized programs that permitted maximum social control over poor children—institutionalization and indenturing. By the 1840s, the declining practice of indenturing required guardians to choose betwen incarcerating youngsters for long periods until tradesmen finally applied for their services or returning them after a brief stay in the children's asylum to their family. Welfare officials chose the latter and cheaper of the two alternatives. In the meantime, private charities for children in Philadelphia grew in number, but they were not immediately able to take over the care of all the indigent young dropped from public-relief rolls. The Philadelphia experience should teach us that a decline in public aid, even to a group as deserving as children, is not likely to be offset immediately by an increase in private philanthropy.

By the late nineteenth century in the United States, public welfare to children was minimal; private charities had literally assumed charge of most youngsters in need. Private agencies secured passage of legislation to remove children from almshouses; they built their own orphanages and reform schools; and they devised foster-care programs. Not until the twentieth century and the appearance first of mothers' pensions and later of AFDC did public welfare for the young once again regain the status and significance it had had in the antebellum era. In 1977, of every 1,000 children in the United States under the age of eighteen, 118 lived in families that benefited from AFDC.[13] Today, as in the earliest years of the nineteenth century in Philadelphia, public welfare is the mainstay of needy children and their mother.

In nineteenth-century Philadelphia, poor blacks obtained assistance largely from public-welfare authorities. There were a few private charities for nonwhites in the city, but they aided a small number. Actually, public poor relief officials granted few outdoor pensions to blacks, but they more willingly admitted them to the almshouse, where between 1828 and 1850 the percentage of black inmates was almost twice as great as the proportion of blacks then living in the city and districts.

Today, blacks receive an even larger share of public welfare than they did in the last century. Although blacks do not now constitute the majority of AFDC recipients, the proportion of blacks on the AFDC rolls is four times the percentage of nonwhites in the total population. Beginning in the 1940s, many blacks, displaced by the mechanization of cotton farming in the South, moved North. There, unequipped for industrial labor, blacks often sought work in vain, and by the 1960s, thousands of them had applied for and obtained public relief. Although the economic position of blacks has improved somewhat and the proportion of blacks on AFDC has declined, nonwhites in the 1980s, as in the last century, depend significantly on public welfare.[14] Quite obviously, the question of how to alleviate poverty among them remains unsolved.

Immigrants formed a consistently large portion of public-relief recipients in Philadelphia between 1800 and 1854—about one-half of the almshouse inmates and one-third of the outdoor-relief recipients were foreign-born. Charities like the immigrant-aid societies also assisted many foreign-born; so, too, did other private organizations, including the Pennsylvania Hospital: at midcentury, a majority of its patients were foreign-born. All these facts simply confirm the truth of the often-made observation that immigrants arrived poor and frequently ill, earned little in the low-wage jobs to which they were relegated, and when they lost these jobs because of a depression, illness, or old age, they required public or private relief.

Among those poor completely dependent on welfare, the incurably ill and those with chronic ailments sought help from public officials, because private charities consciously excluded them. There were always special wards for incurables in the Philadelphia almshouse between 1800 and 1854, and probably the majority of the patients in its hospital wards suffered from chronic ailments.

The aged poor also relied heavily on public welfare, since there were only a few small private charities available to them in the city before 1854. Usually, 18 percent of those who entered the almshouse were aged, and an even larger portion of those receiving outdoor pensions were over fifty.

Today, the foreign-born make up only about 6 percent of our population, and poverty among them is no longer so serious as it was in the last century. In addition, while medical advances have reduced the number of incurably ill, those who are hopelessly ill today may qualify for aid under the disability insurance provisions of social security. Some may also be eligible for federal categorical assistance. The aged poor today have access to more public-welfare programs than in the nineteenth century. Now the elderly needy may be entitled to old age insurance under social security, and if this proves insufficient, they can apply for supplemental public assistance. Medicare, Medicaid, and food stamps are also available to indigent aged Americans.

Clearly, there are differences in the composition of public-welfare rolls today and in the last century, although there are depressing similarities as well. Moreover, while there are considerably more public-welfare programs in existence now than in the past, many of the relief-giving methods that we presently employ are much like those of the nineteenth century. Although we no longer call them indoor and outdoor relief, both of these forms of public-welfare persist. The old undifferentiated almshouse is indeed an artifact of the past, but some groups of poor, such as the mentally ill and the handicapped, are still placed in asylums, although there has been a strong movement in many states toward deinstitutionalization. The medical function of early almshouses has become so important that many evolved into public hospitals. The Philadelphia Almshouse became Philadelphia General Hospital, which served the ailing indigent until city officials decided to close it in 1976, ironically for reasons of economy.

Outdoor relief in the form of cash payments is still made, largely by the federal government through AFDC. These welfare payments are often the object of criticism today, as in the past, while outdoor relief in kind, which endures in the form of food stamps, was until the early 1980s, praised as much as fuel aid had been in nineteenth-century Philadelphia.[15] Apparently, many Americans still make the same moral judgments about the poor as their nineteenth-century ancestors and find it more acceptable to give the indigent some obvious necessity that cannot be misused, such as food or fuel, rather than money, which presumably the poor may spend on liquor, tobacco, or drugs. Finally, special indoor or outdoor relief in natural disasters remains as popular today as it was in the past. The Philadelphia guardians of the poor always responded energetically to poverty caused by disease and freezing winters. Today, as in the past, epidemics, fires, and floods all elicit immediate responses from governments: emergency evacuation centers are established, and money is lent to victims. Perhaps we act rapidly to relieve this kind of poverty, because we know that individuals are not responsible for destitution caused by acts of God and we can easily see ourselves as victims of some natural disaster.

It is also interesting that the trend toward bureaucracy in public welfare, which began in Philadelphia in the early nineteenth century, has never been reversed. As state and federal governments have assumed more responsibility for relief giving, they, too, have adopted bureaucratic administrative systems. The size of first city and later, state and national governments and their poor constituencies made bureaucratic arrangements appear the most logical.

Ultimately, the history of public welfare in the nineteenth century should make us aware of striking resemblances between public-relief recipients, the forms of aid they received, and the pattern of welfare administration in the past and present. And this history should also alert us especially to economic as well as political and social factors that are likely to alter substantially relief practices in the future as they did in the past.

Appendix 1

Tax Assessments and Expenditures for the Poor, Philadelphia, 1800–1854

Year	Poor-Tax Assessment[a] ($)	Almshouse Expenditures[b] ($)	Percentage of Total (%)	Outdoor Expenditures[c] ($)	Percentage of Total (%)	Total Expenditures ($)
1800–01[d]	50,000	25,329.92[f]	54	21,882.38	46	47,212.30
1801–02	75,000	37,568.07	63	22,261.74	37	59,829.81
1802–03	60,000	38,004.41	52	35,503.07	48	73,507.48
1803–04[e]	75,000	50,191.62	63	29,492.26	37	79,683.88
1804–05	70,000	55,202.38	60	36,499.86	40	91,702.24
1805–06	90,000	62,308.78	65	33,715.76	35	96,024.54
1806–07	90,000	57,941.59	65	31,853.85	35	89,795.44
1807–08	91,160	67,537.48	65	36,318.24	35	103,855.72
1808–09	90,000	79,414.08	70	34,537.48	30	113,951.56
1809–10	83,000	76,704.25	68	36,344.52	32	113,048.77
1810–11	88,000	58,153.95	63	34,048.69	37	92,202.64
1811–12	102,954	49,022.93	56	39,066.81	44	88,039.74
1812–13	102,595	—		—		—
1813–14	90,000	45,408.90	44	58,571.76	56	103,980.66
1814–15	100,000	64,423.90	53	56,063.77	47	120,487.67
1815–16	110,000	70,787.58	57	53,872.23	43	124,659.81
1816–17	110,000	63,222.42	54	54,670.03	46	117,892.45
1817–18	150,000	52,031.16	48	55,566.51	52	107,597.67

Year						
1818–19	135,000	42	48,811.35	67,596.36	58	116,407.71
1819–20	135,000	52	51,392.90	46,620.87	48	98,013.77
1820–21	140,000	54	51,501.08[g]	43,509.00	46	95,010.08
1821–22	130,000	52	50,510.76	47,336.66	48	97,847.42
1822–23	105,940	54	59,505.83	51,529.57	46	111,120.14
1823–24	114,468	44	57,226.76	71,898.16	56	129,124.92
1824–25	132,317	49	52,422.87	55,597.02	51	110,019.89
1825–26	129,383	52	52,841.61	47,328.79	48	100,170.40
1826–27	89,961	59	70,789.09	49,008.94	41	119,798.03
1827–28	80,000	63	52,419.29	30,668.77	37	83,088.06
1828–29	90,000	67	55,189.70	26,964.05	33	82,153.75
1829–30	90,000	65	53,877.07	29,631.13	35	83,508.20
1830–31	80,564	63	54,494.05	32,119.73	37	86,613.78
1831–32	91,828	66	69,513.21	36,626.20	34	106,139.41
1832–33	139,871	61	64,814.09	41,437.72	39	106,251.81
1833–34		67	68,308.10	33,289.08	33	101,597.18
1834–35	—	—	—	—	—	—
1835–36	168,942	86	97,720.04	16,371.63	14	114,091.67
1836–37	—	89	100,296.87	11,809.69	11	112,106.56
1837–38	—	88	114,932.95	15,426.99	12	130,359.94
1838–39	169,043	86	105,920.63	16,691.11	14	122,611.74
1839–40	—	76	84,902.07	26,389.74	24	111,291.81
1840–41	—	72	70,620.65	28,142.27	28	98,762.92
1841–42	181,094.16	74	88,910.37	31,125.04	26	120,035.41
1842–43	178,003.25	70	80,755.41	34,755.55	30	115,510.96
1843–44	194,824.58	70	79,488.56	33,545.70	30	113,034.26
1844–45		—	—	—	—	—
1845–46	161,025	73	105,245.10	38,828.90	27	144,074.00
1846–47	197,265.31	71	91,463.26	37,881.85	29	129,345.11
1847–48	191,012.66	73	106,206.62	38,391.20	27	144,597.82
1848–49	189,425.41	68	100,683.04	47,613.48	32	148,296.52
1849–50	191,036.96	70	117,758.52	48,587.40	30	166,345.92

Year	Poor-Tax Assessment[a] ($)	Almshouse Expenditures[b] ($)	Percentage of Total (%)	Outdoor Expenditures[c] ($)	Percentage of Total (%)	Total Expenditures ($)
1850–51	208,018.00	121,485.31	73	45,719.27	27	167,204.48
1852–53	259,583.04	120,877.50	69	55,557.01	31	176,434.51
1853–54	—	127,558.33	66	65,718.71	34	193,277.04
1854 (May to Dec.)	—	115,664.74	80	28,107.03	20	143,771.77

SOURCES: **Poor Tax Assessments:** 1800–01—PCA, MAHM, 7 May 1800; 1801–02—PCA, MAHM, 22 March 1801; 1802–03—PCA, MAHM, 22 March 1801; 1802—03—PCA, MAHM, 12 April 1802; 1803–04—PCA, MAHM, 25 April 1803; 1804–05—PCA, MAHM, 23 March 1804; 1805–06—PCA, MAHM, 15 January 1805; 1806–07—PCA, MAHM, 7 February 1806; 1807–08—PCA, MAHM, 1807–12 vol., pp. 222–34; 1808–09—PCA, MAHM, 18 February 1808; 1809–10—PCA, MAHM, 16 February 1809; 1810–11—PCA, MAHM, 26 February 1810; 1811–12—*Poulson's,* 19 February 1812; 1812–13—*Poulson's* 19 November 1812; 1813–14—PCA, MAHM, 23 February 1813; 1814–15—PCA, MAHM, 10 March 1814; 1815–16—PCA, MAHM, 4 March 1815; 1816–17—PCA, MAHM, 12 February 1816; 1817–18—PCA, MAHM, 23 January 1817; 1818–19—PCA, MAHM, 2 April 1818; 1819–20—PCA, MAHM, 11 February 1819; 1820–21—PCA, MAHM, 9 March 1820; 1821–22—PCA, MAHM, 12 February, 1821; 1822–23—*Accounts of the Guardians of the Poor . . . 28 May 1822 [to] 27 May 1823* (Philadelphia, 1823); 1823–24—*Philadelphia Gazette,* 6 November 1824; 1824–25—*Philadelphia Gazette,* 20 December 1825; 1825–26—*Philadelphia Gazette,* 7 November 1826; 1826–27—*Philadelphia Gazette,* 2 November 1827; 1827–28—PCA, MAHM, 1 January 1827; 1828–29—PCA, MAHM, 11 January 1828; 1829–30—PCA, MGP, 5 January 1829; 1830–31—*Hazard's Register* 6:124; 1831–32—*Hazard's Register* 8:88; 1832–33—*Hazard's Register* 10:10; 1835–36—PCA, MGP, 12 January 1835; 1839–40—PCA, MGP, 11 February 1839; 1842–43—*Pennsylvanian,* 27 January 1843; 1843–44—*Auditors' Report of the Accounts of the Guardians . . . for the Fiscal Year Ending May 15, 1843* (Philadelphia: Office of the American Sentinel, 1843); 1844–45—*Auditors' Report of the Accounts of the Blockley Alms-House for the Fiscal Year Ending May 20, 1844* (Philadelphia: Mifflin and Parry, 1844); 1845–46—PCA, MGP, 2 June 1845; 1846–47—*Auditors' Report of the Accounts of the Blockley Alms-House, for the Fiscal Year Ending May 18, 1846* (Philadelphia: Daily Sun, 1846); 1847–48—*Auditors' Report of the Accounts of the Blockley Alms-House for the Fiscal Year Ending May 18, 1847* (Philadelphia: Times and Keystone, 1847); 1848–49—*Auditors' Report of the Accounts of the Blockley Alms-House for the Year, 1848* (Philadelphia, 1849); 1849–50—*Auditors' Report of the Accounts of the Blockley Alms-House for the Fiscal Year Ending May 12, 1849* (Philadelphia, 1849); 1850–51—*Auditors' Report of the Accounts of the Blockley Alms-House for the Fiscal Year Ending May 21, 1850* (Philadelphia: Crissy and Markley, 1851); *Auditors' Report of the Accounts of the Blockley Alms-House for the Fiscal Year Ending May 21, 1851* (Philadelphia: O. I. Search, 1852).

Almshouse, Outdoor Relief and Total Expenditures: In the annual statements of the Guardians of the Poor. For 1800–01—PCA, MAHM, 22 March 1801; 1801–02—PCA, MAHM, 12 April 1802; 1802–03—PCA, MAHM, 25 April 1803; 1803–04—PCA, MAHM, 23 May 1804; 1804–05—Supplement to the *Aurora*, 30 August 1805; 1805–06—*Aurora*, 1 August 1806; 1806–07—PCA, MGP, 25 May 1807; 1807–08—PCA, MAHM, 1807–12 vol.: 222–34; 1808–09—*Aurora*, 8 November 1809; 1809–10—*Aurora*, 31 October 1810; 1810–11—*Poulson's*, 19 February 1812; 1811–12—*Poulson's*, 19 November 1812; 1813–14—*Poulson's*, 3 November 1814; 1814–15—*Poulson's*, 19 October 1815; 1815–16—*Poulson's*, 19 November 1816; 1816–17—*Aurora*, 29 November 1817; 1817–18—*Aurora*, 24 September 1818; 1818–19—*Aurora*, 25 October 1819; 1819–20—*Poulson's*, 17 October 1820; 1820–21—*Poulson's*, 22 May 1822; 1821–22—*Poulson's*, 16 May 1823; 1822–23—*Accounts of the Guardians of the Poor …28 May 1822 to 27 May 1823* (Philadelphia, 1823); 1823–24—*Philadelphia Gazette*, 6 November 1824; 1824–25—*Philadelphia Gazette*, 20 December 1825; 1825–26—*Philadelphia Gazette*, 7 November 1826; 1826–27—*Philadelphia Gazette*, 2 November 1827; 1827–28—PCA, MGP, 26 May 1828; 1828–29—*Philadelphia Gazette*, 19 January 1830; 1829–30—*Philadelphia Gazette*, 12 January 1831; 1830–31—*Philadelphia Gazette*, 13 January 1832; 1831–32—*Philadelphia Gazette*, 1 January 1833; 1832–33—PCA, GP, Accounts Ledger, 1829–34 vol.; 1833–34—*Accounts of the Guardians for the Relief and Employment of the Poor …for the Year Ending on the Nineteenth Day of May, 1834* (Philadelphia, 1834); 1835–36—*Pennsylvanian*, 7 December 1837; 1836–37—*Pennsylvanian*, 21 March 1838; 1837–38—*U.S. Gazette*, 17 November 1838; 1838–39—*Pennsylvania Inquirer*, 14 October 1839; 1839–40—PCA, Philadelphia County, Minutes, Board of Auditors, 1836–43 vol., 434–53; 1840–41—*Auditors' Report of the Accounts of the Blockley Alms-House for the Fiscal Year Ending May 17, 1841* (Philadelphia: Mifflin and Parry, 1841); 1841–42—*Pennsylvanian*, 27 January 1843; 1842–43—*Auditors' Report of the Accounts of the Guardians*, 1843; 1843–44—*Auditors' Report of the Accounts of Blockley*, 1844; 1845–46—*Auditors' Report of the Accounts of Blockley*, 1846; 1846–47—*Auditors' Report of the Accounts of Blockley*, 1847; 1847–48—*Auditors' Report of the Accounts of Blockley*, 1848; 1848–49—*Auditors' Report of the Accounts of Blockley*, 1849; 1849–50—*Auditors' Report of the Accounts of Blockley*, 1850; 1850–51—*Auditors' Report of the Accounts of Blockley*, 1851. 1852–54—*Auditors' Reports of the Accounts of Blockley for the Fiscal Years Ending May 21, 1853 and May 21, 1854* (Philadelphia: Crissy and Markley, 1853, 1854); July–December 1854—*Statement of the Accounts of the Guardians of the Poor, July 3 to December 31, 1854* (Philadelphia: Crissy and Markley, 1855).

[a] The tax assessment was usually levied in January for the fiscal year that began in March or May (see notes d and e).

[b] Expenditures are net, meaning that I subtracted from the gross almshouse expenditures income from sources other than taxes. For example, I deducted the value of manufactured goods sold, fees paid by medical students, and board paid for some inmates. Net therefore means the cost of caring for the poor. It does not include salaries paid almshouse employees and the cost of only materials used in the factory.

[c] Expenditures are net, meaning that I subtracted from the gross annual outdoor-relief expenditures income guardians received from sources other than taxes. The largest item deducted was the amount paid by fathers to support their illegitimate children. Total net expenditures include sums spent for outdoor cash aid, medical attendance, and wood as well as for the amount paid in salaries to employees of the guardians of the poor.

[d] From 1800 to 1802, the fiscal year began in March.

[e] Starting in 1803, the fiscal year began in May.

[f] From 1800 to 1802, almshouse figures include the amount paid the Pennsylvania Hospital for boarding some insane patients.

[g] After 1820, I included expenditures for the children's asylum (and for the board of youngsters in the Shelter for Colored Orphans and of the sick in the city hospital) with the almshouse expenditures, although in the annual accounts, they are included with outdoor expenditures. (It seemed more logical to me to group all disbursements for institutions together.)

Appendix 2

Public-Relief Recipients
Philadelphia, 1800–1854

Year	Almshouse and Children's Asylum[a]	Outdoor Pensioners[b]	Total[c]	Medical Aid[d]	Fuel Aid[d]
1800	788	602	1,390	—	—
1801	948	—	—	—	—
1802	804	—	—	—	—
1803	1,101	—	—	—	—
1804	1,196	—	—	—	—
1805	1,270	590	1,180	—	—
1806	1,455	545	2,000	—	—
1807	1,406	—	—	—	—
1808	1,581	—	—	—	—
1809	1,611	—	—	—	—
1810	1,755	745	2,500	—	—
1811	1,796	310	2,106	—	—
1812	1,830	—	—	—	—
1813	1,820	—	—	—	—
1814	1,891	1,254	3,145	—	—
1815	2,254	1,208	3,462	—	—
1816	2,653	1,199	3,852	—	—
1817	2,843	1,239	4,082	—	—
1818	—	1,249	—	—	—
1819	4,049	1,481	5,530	—	—
1820	3,907	1,330	5,237	—	—
1821	3,566	1,268	4,834	—	—
1822	3,897	1,222	5,119	—	—
1823	4,378	1,009	5,387	—	—
1824	3,666	842	4,508	—	—
1825	3,578	1,013	4,591	—	—
1826	4,025	1,034	5,059	—	—
1827	3,411	699	4,110	—	—
1828	4,024	252	4,276	—	—
1829	3,651	709	4,360	2,875	2,128
1830	2,730	720	3,450	—	—
1831	3,501	670	4,171	—	3,197
1832	—	760	—	2,285	3,175
1833	3,400	798	4,198	—	—
1834	—	916	—	—	—

178

Year	Almshouse and Children's Asylum[a]	Outdoor Pensioners[b]	Total[b]	Medical Aid[d]	Fuel Aid[d]
1835	2,512	0	2,512	—	—
1836	2,692	0	2,692	—	—
1837	2,896	0	2,896	—	3,685
1838	2,420	0	2,420	—	2,742
1839	3,008	123	3,131	—	—
1840	2,696	195	2,891	—	2,889
1841	2,985	176	3,161	2,437	4,498
1842	2,869	191	3,060	3,164	7,575
1843	2,958	229	3,187	2,808	6,650
1844	—	—	—	—	—
1845	3,223	252	3,475	3,077	7,040
1846	4,503	307	4,810	3,190	7,720
1847	4,303	217	4,520	2,864	6,903
1848	4,504	271	4,775	2,882	8,868
1849	4,885	261	5,146	3,491	8,821
1850	4,854	187	5,041	—	—
1851	6,719	—	—	—	—
1852	5,017	—	—	—	—
1853	5,407	—	—	—	—
1854	3,244	—	—	—	—

SOURCES: **Almshouse and Children's Asylum Admissions:** For 1800–1802, 1822, and 1830, see PCA, GP, Treasurer, General Ledger, 1789–1803, 1820–30 vols.; for 1803–10, see PCA, GP, Treasurer's "Weekly Entries," 1803–9 and 1809–15 vols.; for 1811–54, see *Poulson's,* 19 November 1812, 19 February 1812, 3 November 1814, 19 October 1815, 19 November 1816, 17 October 1820, 22 May 1822, 16 May 1823, 20 December 1825; *Aurora,* 29 November 1817, 24 September 1818; *Philadelphia Gazette,* 20 December 1825, 7 November 1826, 2 November 1827, 19 January 1830, 12 January 1831, 1 January 1833; *The Pennsylvanian,* 7 December 1837, 21 March 1838, 27 January 1843; *U.S. Gazette* 17 November 1838; *Pennsylvania Inquirer,* 14 October 1839; *Hazard's Register,* 2:101; *Accounts of the Guardians for 1834; Auditors' Reports of the Accounts of Blockley Alms-House for 1841, 1843, 1844, 1846, 1847 to 1854.* In the years when children's asylum admissions were not included with general almshouse admissions, I computed the number who entered the former institution from PCA, MGP, 20 November 1821, 24 May 1822, 20 May 1823, 24 May 1824, 23 May 1825, 6 September 1826, 28 May 1827, 21 May 1828; PCA, GP, Register, Children's Asylum, 1825–35 vol.; *Hazard's Register* 5:345. **Outdoor Pensioners:** For 1800, I took the total number of relief recipients listed in Meredith's report to the state legislature (*Hazard's Register* 2:54) and subtracted those in the almshouse to arrive at the number of pensioners. For 1806, I calculated the total from reports on the number of pensioners in each guardian's district in PCA, MGP, 18 March, 25 March, 1 April, 15 April, 22 April, 6 May, 13 May, 20 May 1806. For 1805, I took the number for 1806 and added the number the guardians dropped from the list in the latter year. For 1810, I subtracted from the total number on welfare listed in Mease, *Picture of Philadelphia,* p. 295, those admitted to the almshouse and arrived at an estimate of the number then on outdoor relief. For 1811, see PCA, Almshouse Admission Book, 1811–14 vol., entry for 23 July 1811. For 1814, see PCA, Register of Relief Recipients, 1814–15. For 1815, I subtracted from the 1814 total the number dropped from the rolls in 1815 as listed in PCA, MGP, 9 May, 16 May, 17 May, 19 May, 22 May, 23 May, 30 May 1815. The number of pensioners in 1816 is an estimate I arrived at by subtracting from the 1815 figure the number taken off the list in 1816 (see PCA, MGP, 2 April, 5 April, 9 April, 16 April, 19 April, 23 April,

3 May, 7 May, 21 May 1816) and adding for each of the thirty-four guardians, two new pensioners. For the 1817, figure see Pennsylvania Society for the Promotion of Public Economy, *Report of the Library Committee*, p. 16. For 1818, see PCA, MAHM, 13 September 1819. For 1819, 1820, and 1822, see *Poulson's*, 17 October 1820, 22 May 1822, 23 February 1825. For 1821, 1823, 1824, 1825, and 1827, see PCA, "Pauper Lists," 1821–29. For 1826, see PCA, MGP, 23 August 1826. For 1828, 1839–50, see PCA, MGP passim (reports of the "visitors of the poor"). For 1829–34, see PCA, MGP, 20 January 1834. **Medical Aid**: For 1829, see PCA, MGP, 8 March 1830; for 1832, see *Hazard's Register* 11 : 364; for 1841–49, see *The Pennsylvanian*, 27 January 1843 and *Auditors' Reports of the Accounts of the Blockley Alms-House for 1843, 1844, 1846, 1847, 1848, 1849.* **Fuel Aid:** For 1829, 1831–32, see *Hazard's Register* 6 : 266–67, 11 : 361, 363; PCA, MGP, 23 May 1838, 20 May 1839, 17 May 1841; *Pennsylvanian*, 27 January 1843 and *Auditors' Reports of the Accounts of Blockley Alms-House for 1843 to 1849.*

ᵃ Almshouse and children's asylum figures are total admission figures for each year. They may be somewhat inflated, because some people were admitted more than once in a year. The children's asylum opened in 1820 and became a division of the new almshouse at Blockley in 1835. From 1800 to 1802, the calandar year used was, from March to March and from 1803 to 1853 it was May to May. With concolidation in 1854, guardians eventually published admission figures only for July through December of that year.

ᵇ Single people and heads of families. The number of children in these families, which is not included in these figures, may have amounted to 40 percent of those on pensions for some years. In years when no numbers are recorded, there were persons receiving outdoor aid, but the number is unknown.

ᶜTotal from columns 2 and 3 when the value of both is known.

ᵈMedical and fuel aid were given annually in most years after 1800, but guardians kept records of the number who received these forms of relief only in the 1830s and 1840s. It would be unwise to total the figures by year, because there is undoubtedly a great deal of overlap. For example, in a given year, possibly all of the outdoor pensioners received fuel and medical aid and/or many of those who obtained medical help also received wood or coal. The overlap is impossible to gage, because there are no surviving lists of the names of recipients of any of this aid.

Notes

Abbreviations used in the notes follow:

GP	Guardians of the Poor (of Philadelphia)
HSP	Historical Society of Pennsylvania
MAHC	Minutes, Almshouse Committee (of Philadelphia)
MAHM	Minutes, Almshouse Managers (of Philadelphia)
MBP	Minutes, Board of Physicians (Philadelphia Almshouse)
MCA	Minutes, Children's Asylum Committee (of Philadelphia)
MGP	Minutes, Guardians of the Poor (of Philadelphia)
MHC	Minutes, Hospital Committee (Philadelphia Almshouse)
MMC	Minutes, Manufacturing Committee (Philadelphia Almshouse)
PCA	Philadelphia City Archives

Introduction

1. Frances Fox Piven, Richard A. Cloward, *Regulating the Poor, the Functions of Public Welfare* (New York: Random House, 1971), pp. 183–338. On the welfare programs of Presidents Nixon, Carter, and Reagan, see *New York Times*, 9 August 1969, p. 1; 16 August 1971, p. 14; 26 May 1974, p. 35; 7 August 1977, p. 1; 13 May 1981, p. 28; 21 September 1981, sec. 4, p. 12.

2. For a report of a recent study on welfare recipients, see *New York Times*, 24 February 1984, p. 1.

3. The most well-known general studies are David Rothman's two books, *The Discovery of the Asylum: Social Order and Disorder in the New Republic* (Boston: Little Brown, 1971) and *Conscience and Convenience: The Asylum and its Alternatives in Progressive America* (Boston: Little Brown, 1980); Robert Bremner, *From the Depths: The Discovery of Poverty in the United States* (New York: New York University Press, 1956). See also Blanche D. Coll, *Perspectives in Public Welfare, A History* (Washington, D.C.: Department of Health, Education, and Welfare, Social and Rehabilitation Service, 1969); Benjamin Klebaner, "Public Poor Relief in America, 1790–1860" (Ph.D. diss., Columbia University, 1952). The newest general study is Michael B. Katz, *Poverty and Policy in American History* (New York: Academic Press, 1983) which was published too recently for me to utilize. For a fine discussion of urban poor relief programs in the colonial era, see Gary B. Nash, *The Urban Crucible: Social Change, Political Consciousness, and the Origins of the American Revolution* (Cambridge: Harvard University Press, 1979). On the same subject, see also Edward Wiberley, Jr., "Four Cities: Public Poor Relief in America, 1700–1775" (Ph.D. diss., Yale University, 1975). Local studies of public welfare include: Raymond Mohl, *Poverty in New York, 1783–1825* (New York: Oxford University Press, 1971); David M. Schneider, *The History of Public Welfare in New York*

State, 1609–1866 (Chicago: University of Chicago Press, 1938); Stephen Anthony Klips, "Institutionalizing the Poor: The New York City Almshouse, 1825–1860," (Ph.D. diss., City University of New York, 1980); Robert W. Kelso, *The History of Public Poor Relief in Massachusetts, 1620–1920* (Boston: Houghton Mifflin, 1920); Susan Grigg, "The Dependent Poor of Newburyport, 1800–1830," (Ph.D. diss., University of Wisconsin, 1978); Eric H. Monkkonen, *The Dangerous Class: Crime and Poverty in Columbus, Ohio, 1860–1885* (Cambridge: Harvard University Press, 1975); Douglas G. Carroll and Blanche D. Coll, "The Baltimore Almshouse: An Early History," *Maryland Historical Magazine* 66 (Summer 1971): 135–52. On Philadelphia, see John K. Alexander, *Render Them Submissive: Responses to Poverty in Philadelphia, 1760–1800* (Amherst: University of Massachusetts Press, 1980) and two articles by Gary Nash, "Poverty and Poor Relief in Pre-Revolutionary Philadelphia," *William and Mary Quarterly* 33 (January 1976): 3–30 and "Urban Wealth and Poverty in Pre-Revolutionary America," *Journal of Interdisciplinary History* 6 (Spring 1976): 545–84.

4. Before the twentieth century, the federal government did provide some relief to veterans (beginning with the Revolutionary War) and freed slaves (the Freedman's Bureau).

5. There are three general bibliographies on Philadelphia's welfare system: Mary Brenz, *The Care of Poor People in Philadelphia from Colonial Times to 1981: An Annotated Bibliography* (Harrisburg: Commonwealth of Pennsylvania, Dept. of Public Welfare, 1972); Pennsylvania Department of Public Welfare, *Public Welfare in Pennsylvania, A Chronology, 1676–1966* (Harrisburg: Commonwealth of Pennsylvania, Dept. of Public Welfare, 1969); Urban Archives Center, Temple University Libraries, *Private Social Services in Philadelphia: A Survey of the Records* (Philadelphia: Temple University Libraries, 1973). Philadelphia's fine collection of government records is beautifully cataloged in John Daly, *Descriptive Inventory of the Archives of the City and County of Philadelphia* (Philadelphia: City of Philadelphia, 1970).

6. Before 1854, there were separate governments in Philadelphia and in each of the surrounding districts, boroughs, and townships in Philadelphia County. Also, before 1854, the city and a few of the districts formed the Philadelphia Poor District to deliver relief to the poor in these areas only through the board of guardians of the poor. (There were small, separate poor districts in the other townships and boroughs throughout Philadelphia County.) Each of the guardians of the poor was appointed by the government of the city or district he represented. The guardians assessed and collected a special tax for the poor and then disbursed to the needy the money they raised. With the consolidation law passed 2 February 1854, the city, district, borough, and township governments (or the city and its surrounding county) became one governmental unit. This unit was divided into twenty-four wards and one guardian of the poor was thereafter elected from each ward. Also, after 1854, guardians no longer raised money for the poor but sought appropriations for poor relief from the new consolidated city government. These issues are also discussed in chapters 1 and 2 and in Charles Lawrence, *History of the Philadelphia Almshouses and Hospitals* (Philadelphia: by author, 1905), pp. 185–86.

7. Bremner, *From the Depths*; Walter I. Trattner, *From Poor Law to Welfare State: A History of Social Welfare in America*, 2d ed. (New York: Free Press, 1979); Walter Friedlander, *Introduction to Social Welfare* (New York: Prentice-Hall, 1955); Nathan E. Cohen, *Social Work in the American Tradition* (New York: Dryden Press, 1958); Frank J. Bruno, *Trends in Social Work, 1874–1956*, 2d ed. (New York: Columbia University Press, 1957).

8. Rothman, *The Discovery of the Asylum*; Mohl, *Poverty in New York*; Nathan Huggins, *Protestants against Poverty, Boston's War on Poverty, 1870–1900* (Westport, Conn.: Greenwood Press, 1970); Anthony Platt, *The Child Savers: The Invention of Delinquency* (Chicago: University of Chicago Press, 1969); Michael B. Katz, *Class, Bureaucracy and the Schools, The Illusion of Educational Change in America* (New York: Praeger, 1971); Piven and Cloward, *Regulating the Poor*.

Chapter 1. The City and Its Poor

1. James Mease, *The Picture of Philadelphia* (Philadelphia, 1811; reprint ed., New York: Arno Press, 1970), pp. 17, 24–25.

2. William S. Hastings, "Philadelphia Microcosm," *Pennsylvania Magazine of History and Biography* 91 (April 1967): 164; George Rogers Taylor, "Comment on Population," in *The Growth of the Seaport Cities, 1790–1825*, ed. David T. Gilchrist (Charlottesville: University Press of Virginia, 1967), p. 39; George Rogers Taylor, "'Philadelphia in Slices' by George G. Foster," *Pennsylvania Magazine of History and Biography* 93 (January 1969): 34–35; *The Stranger's Guide to the Public Buildings, Institutions and Other Objects Worthy of Attention in the City of Philadelphia and its Environs* (Philadelphia: George S. Appleton, 1845), p. 19; Sam Bass Warner, Jr., *The Private City, Philadelphia in Three Periods of Its Growth* (Philadelphia: University of Pennsylvania Press, 1968), p. 51.

3. Warner, *The Private City*, pp. 15–17, 56–77; Norman J. Johnston, "The Caste and Class of the Urban Form of Historic Philadelphia," *Journal of the American Institute of Planners* 32 (November 1966): 342, 345.

4. Warner, *The Private City*, p. 87; Hastings, "Philadelphia Microcosm," pp. 167–68; Bruce Laurie, *The Working People of Philadelphia, 1800 to 1850* (Philadelphia: Temple University Press, 1980), pp. 10–11; *Public Ledger*, 16 March 1842.

5. Boies Penrose and Edward P. Allinson, *Philadelphia, 1681–1887, A History of Municipal Development* (Philadelphia: Allen Lane and Scott, 1887), pp. 63–66; Mease, *Picture of Philadelphia*, p. 95; Warner, *The Private City*, p. 10.

6. Penrose and Allinson, *Philadelphia, Municipal Government*, p. 113. The boards of health and of the guardians of the poor assessed and collected taxes for their own support, and so, too, did county, city, and district officials. Philadelphians paid a confusing array of local taxes as well as a state levy. The amount most citizens contributed depended on the value of the real estate they owned or leased. Because personal estates were rarely taxed in this era, the wealthiest may have escaped large levies. However, propertyless individuals were not exempt from taxation; they paid a flat personal rate. Mease, *Picture of Philadelphia*, pp. 197–98; John Palmer, *Journal of Travels in the United States of North America and in Lower Canada, Performed in the Year 1817* (London: Sherwood, Neely and Jones, 1818), pp. 263–64; Stuart M. Blumin, "Mobility in a Nineteenth-Century American City, Philadelphia, 1820–1860" (Ph.D. diss., University of Pennsylvania, 1968), pp. 43–44; Mathew Carey, "Autobiography," *New England Magazine*, July 1833–December, 1834; (reprint ed., Brooklyn: E. L. Schwaab, 1942), p. 53.

7. Kim Tousley Phillips, "William Duane, Revolutionary Editor" (Ph.D. diss., University of California, 1968), pp. 191, 195, 204–7.

8. Sanford W. Higginbotham, *The Keystone in the Democratic Arch: Pennsylvania Politics, 1800–1816* (Philadelphia: University of Pennsylvania Press, 1952), pp. 115–17, 143–44, 218; Phillips, "William Duane," pp. 456–58, 528–29, 556–609; Warner, *The Private City*, pp. 86–91.

9. Charles M. Snyder, *The Jacksonian Heritage, Pennsylvania Politics, 1838–1848* (Harrisburg: Pennsylvania Historical and Museum Commission, 1958), pp. 26–27, 45; Bruce Laurie, "Fire Companies and Gangs in Southwark: the 1840's," in *The Peoples of Philadelphia: A History of Ethnic Groups and Lower-Class Life, 1790–1940*, eds. Allen F. Davis, Mark Haller (Philadelphia: Temple University Press, 1973), p. 73.

10. Nash, *The Urban Crucible*, pp. 267, 382. On Quaker philanthropy, see Sydney James, *A People among Peoples, Quaker Benevolence in Eighteenth-Century America* (Cambridge: Harvard University Press, 1963). On other religious groups, see Othneil A. Pendleton, Jr., "The Influence of Evangelical Churches upon Humanitarian Reform: A Case Study Giving Particular Attention to Philadelphia, 1790–1840" (Ph.D. diss., University of Pennsylvania,

1945) and Joseph L. Kerlin, *Catholicity in Philadelphia* (Philadelphia: John Joseph McVey, 1909).

11.   James A. Henretta, *The Evolution of American Society, 1700–1815, An Interdisciplinary Analysis* (Lexington, Mass.: D. C. Heath, 1973), pp. 190–92; James W. Livingood, *The Philadelphia-Baltimore Trade Rivalry, 1780–1860* (New York, 1947; reprint ed., New York: Arno Press 1970), p. 24; Herman Le Roy Collins, *Philadelphia, Story of Progress*, 4 vols. (New York: Lewis Historical Publishing Co., 1941), 4:177.

12.   Louis Martin Sears, "Philadelphia and the Embargo, 1808," *Annual Report of the American Historical Association for the Year 1920* (Washington, D.C.: Government Printing Office, 1925), p. 257; Phillips, "William Duane," pp. 288–91.

13.   Donald R. Adams, "Wage Rates in the Early National Period: Philadelphia, 1785–1830," *Journal of Economic History* 28 (September 1968): 415.

14.   Gordon C. Bjork, "Foreign Trade," in Gilchrist, *Seaport Cities*, pp. 58–60.

15.   Samuel Rezneck, "The Depression of 1819–1822, A Social History," *American Historical Review* 39 (1933–34): 28–29; Phillips, "William Duane," pp. 459, 462, 466–67, 471; William A. Sullivan, *The Industrial Worker in Pennsylvania, 1800–1840* (Harrisburg: Pennsylvania Historical and Museum Commission, 1955), p. 51. Quote from Pennsylvania, Senate, *Documents in Relation to the Extent and Causes of the Present General Distress throughout the Commonwealth*, 14 February 1820.

16.   Adams, "Wage Rates in the Early National Period," pp. 415–16.

17.   John Russell Young, *Memorial History of the City of Philadelphia from its Early Settlement to the Year 1895*, 2 vols. (New York: New York Historical Co., 1895), 1:461–65; *Public Ledger*, 7 December 1842; Snyder, *The Jacksonian Heritage*, pp. 35–36, 43, 112, 138, 153, 160–63; Samuel Rezneck, "Social History of An American Depression, 1837–43," *American Historical Review* 40 (July 1935): 664–65; Nicholas B. Wainwright, ed., *A Philadelphia Perspective, the Diary of Sidney George Fisher Covering the Years 1834–1871* (Philadelphia: Historical Society of Pennsylvania, 1967), quote from pp. 134–35, but see also pp. 32, 85, 96, 112, 128, 131–35.

18.   *Public Ledger*, 6 May 1841, 2 September 1842.

19.   Charles Peirce, *A Meteorological Account of the Weather in Philadelphia from January 1, 1790 to January 1, 1847* (Philadelphia: Lindsay and Blakiston, 1847), pp. 20–30, 43–48, 62, 254–56; article signed "Philopenes, No. II," *United States Gazette*, 1 February 1805 and *U. S. Gazette*, 19 January 1821 and "Charitas," *Poulson's*, 29 January 1821; *Public Ledger*, 17 January, 23 January 1840; 9 January, 21 January, 23 April 1841; 9 February, 15 February, 18 February, 2 March, 18 March 1843. Almshouse admission figures are in *Aurora*, 30 August 1805, 1 August 1806, 8 November 1809, 31 October 1810; *Poulson's*, 17 October 1820, 22 May 1822; *Pennsylvanian*, 7 December 1837, 27 January 1843; *Pennsylvania Inquirer*, 14 October 1839. Quote is from *Poulson's*, 20 April 1820.

20.   Guardians of the poor, *The Reply ... to certain remarks made in their presentments by the Grand Inquests inquiring for the County of Philadelphia for February and April sessions, 1849* (Philadelphia, 1849), p. 12; *Public Ledger*, 13 January 1840; Mathew Carey [A Citizen of Philadelphia], *Letters on the Condition of the Poor*, 3d ed. (Philadelphia: Haswell and Barrington, 1836), pp. 5, 7.

21.   *The Philanthropist: Or Institutions of Benevolence by a Pennsylvanian* (Philadelphia: Issac Peirce, 1813), pp. 31–32, 97–98; *The Mysteries and Miseries of Philadelphia* (Philadelphia, 1853), p. 6.

22.   James Robinson, *The Philadelphia Directory, City and County Register for 1803* (Philadelphia: William W. Woodward, 1803), p. 288; J. Thomas Scharf and Thompson Westcott, *History of Philadelphia, 1609–1884*, 3 vols. (Philadelphia: L. H. Everts and Co., 1884), 1:512–19. See Elizabeth Drinker, *Extracts from the Journal of Elizabeth Drinker from 1759 to 1807* (Philadelphia: Lippincott, 1889), pp. 372–76, 381–83, for an example of a family that fled the city one year and then stayed in town the next year and through the next epidemic.

23. *Poulson's*, 29 September 1823; Mathew Carey [Hamilton], "Essays on the Public Charities, No. 3," *U.S. Gazette*, 15 January 1829; Historical Society of Pennsylvania (hereafter referred to as HSP), Roberts Vaux Papers, Robert Evans to Vaux, 2, 4, 9 September 1820; *Philadelphia in 1824* (Philadelphia: H. C. Carey and I. Lea, 1824), pp. 27, 172; Gouverneur Emerson, "Medical Statistics, Consisting of Estimates Relating to the Population of Philadelphia with its Changes as Influenced by the Deaths and Births during Ten Years, Viz from 1821 to 1830 Inclusive," *American Journal of Medical Sciences*, 9 (1831–32): 17–46; *Public Ledger*, 27 May 1840, 22 February 1841, 2 May 1843, 3 November 1845, 28 April 1848.

24. Gouverneur Emerson, "Medical Statistics, Being a Series of Tables Showing Mortality in Philadelphia and Its Immediate Causes," *American Journal of Medical Sciences* 1 (1827): 116–55; *Report of the Joint Committee of Councils Relative to the Malignant or Pestilential Disease of the Summer and Autumn of 1820 in the City of Philadelphia* (Philadelphia: Lydia R. Bailey, 1821), pp. 27–29; *Public Ledger*, 6 November, 29 November, 4 December, 13 December 1847.

25. Philadelphia Board of Health, Sanitary Committee, *Statistics of Cholera ...* (Philadelphia: King and Baird, 1849), pp. 13, 44; *Public Ledger*, 7 September 1849.

26. Female Society of Philadelphia for the Relief and Employment of the Poor, *Report, 1871* (Philadelphia: Wm. K. Bellows, 1871), p. 3; Scharf and Westcott, *Philadelphia*, 2:1483; *Moreau de Mery's American Journey (1793–1798)*, ed. and trans. by Kenneth and Anna M. Roberts (New York: Doubleday, Doran, 1947), p. 293; *Aurora*, 27 January 1805.

27. Robert C. Smith, "A Portuguese Naturalist in Philadelphia, 1799," *Pennsylvania Magazine of History and Biography* 78 (January 1954): 83; Philadelphia City Archives (hereafter referred to as PCA), Minutes of the Guardians of the Poor (hereafter referred to as MGP), 28 April 1812, 21 September, 22 May 1813, 25 January, 1 March, 7 April, 12 October 1814, 15 August, 3 October 1815, 17 September 1816, 21 October, 28 November 1817.

28. PCA, MGP, 21 June 1808, Minutes Almshouse Managers (hereafter referred to as MAHM), 27 June 1808. Some private welfare agencies would not provide aid to poor mothers unless they agreed to indenture their children. See Female Hospitable Society of Philadelphia, *Articles of Association, Act of Incorporation, and Reports Since Commencement* (Philadelphia: Lydia R. Bailey, 1831), p. 9; Female Association of Philadelphia for the Relief of Women and Children in Reduced Circumstances, *Constitution of the Female Association of Philadelphia for the Relief of Women and Children in Reduced Circumstances* (Philadelphia: William Young, 1801), p. 11.

29. Many with such handicaps were listed as being in the incurable wards of the almshouse. PCA, Alms House, Department and Ward Census, 1807.

30. The rest of the Fitzsimmons family also survived, since newspaper publicity resulted in sufficient funds being donated to the family, so that the mother could set up a small store. *Public Ledger*, 10, 13, 21 July 1846.

31. For public-welfare records, see PCA, Guardians of the Poor (hereafter referred to as GP), Treasurer's General Ledger, 1789–1803 vol.; PCA, GP, Treasurer's "Weekly Entries," 1809–15 vol.; *Report of the Committee Appointed to Inquire into the Operation of the Poor Laws, Read, January 29th, 1825, Mr. Meredith, Chairman*, in Samuel Hazard, ed., *Hazard's Register of Pennsylvania*, 16 vols. (Philadelphia: W. F. Geddes, 1828–35), 2:54; Mease, *Picture of Philadelphia*, p. 295; there are only scattered admissions data available for private charities that definitely aided the dependent poor. For Christ Church Hospital, see *Moreau de Mery's American Journey*, p. 356, and Mease, *Picture of Philadelphia*, p. 247; for the Magdalen Asylum, see HSP, Magdalen Society Papers, Minutes of the Board of Managers, 1801–10 vol., 9, 36–37, 53, 57, 63, 65, 74, 83, 87, 89–91, 107–8, 112, 120, 124, 126, 131, 140, 146, 149, 151, 156, 163–64, 167; for St. Joseph's Orphan Asylum, see Kerlin, *Catholicity in Philadelphia*, pp. 192–93 and Scharf and Westcott, *Philadelphia*, 1:537; for the Friends Almshouse, see James, *A People among Peoples*, pp. 46–50; for the Pennsylvania Hospital, see William H.

Williams, *America's First Hospital: The Pennsylvania Hospital, 1751–1841* (Wayne, Pa.: Haverford House, 1976), pp. 114–15, appendix, and Mease, *Picture of Philadelphia*, p. 233.

32. For public-welfare records, see *Poulson's*, 22 May 1822; *Philadelphia Gazette*, 12 January 1831; PCA, MGP, 6 October 1824, and reports of the visitors of the poor, 1829, passim; *Hazard's Register*, 5:345. For private charities, see *Philadelphia in 1824*, pp. 65–66, 68 (Christ Church Hospital, St. Joseph's Orphan Asylum, and Friends' Asylum); *Poulson's*, 21 January 1820, 18 January 1827 (Indigent Widows' and Single Women's Asylum); *Poulson's*, 6 March 1821 and 6 March 1830 (Magdalen Asylum); Thomas Wilson, *Picture of Philadelphia for 1824* (Philadelphia: Thomas Town, 1823), p. 66, and *Poulson's*, 13 January 1830 (Orphan Asylum); *Poulson's*, 1 April 1830 (St. Joseph's Orphan Asylum); *Poulson's*, 3 November 1824 (Shelter for Colored Orphans); Negley K. Teeters, "The Early Days of the Philadelphia House of Refuge," *Pennsylvania History* 27 (April 1960): 179; Thomas Porter, *Picture of Philadelphia from 1811 to 1831* (Philadelphia: Robert Desilver, 1831), p. 77 (Pennsylvania Hospital).

33. For public-welfare records, see the accounts of the guardians of the poor in *The Pennsylvanian*, 27 January 1843, and *Auditors' Report of the Accounts of the Blockley Alms-House for the Fiscal Year Ending May 19, 1851* (Philadelphia: O. I. Search, 1852). For the following charities in 1841: House of Refuge, Friends Almshouse, St. John's and St. Joseph's Orphan Asylums, Friends Asylum, U.S. Naval Asylum, Orphan Asylum, Shelter for Colored Orphans, and Christ Church Hospital, see *Statistics of Philadelphia, Comprehending a Concise View of all the Public Institutions and the Fire Engine and Hose Companies of the City and County of Philadelphia* (Philadelphia, 1842), pp. 4–13. In addition, see "Pennsylvania Hospital Report," *Public Ledger*, 10 June 1846, 13 June 1850; Magdalen Society of Philadelphia, *Report for 1840* (Philadelphia: Joseph and William Kite, 1841), and *Report for 1850* (Philadelphia: Kite and Walton, 1851); Indigent Widows' and Single Women's Asylum, *Report for 1840* (Philadelphia: Lydia R. Bailey, 1841) and "Indigent Widows' and Single Women's Asylum Report," *Public Ledger*, 11 January 1850; "Philadelphia House of Refuge and Colored House of Refuge Reports," *Public Ledger*, 1 January and 28 February 1850; "St. John's Orphan Asylum Report," *Public Ledger*, 25 February 1848; St. Joseph's Orphan Asylum, *Report, 1850–51* (Philadelphia: James Fullerton, 1851); "Friends Asylum Report," *Public Ledger*, 13 June 1850; "Rosine Association Report," *Public Ledger*, 30 May 1849; Moyamensing Union School and Children's Home, *First and Second Annual Reports* (Philadelphia: William F. Geddes, 1850, 1851); Girard College for Orphans, *Report, 1850* (Philadelphia: Crissy and Markley, 1851); for the U.S. Naval Asylum, Orphan Asylum, and Shelter for Colored Orphans at the end of the decade, see R. A. Smith, *Philadelphia As It Is in 1852* (Philadelphia: Lindsay and Blakiston, 1852), pp. 257, 272, 276.

34. Adams, "Wage Rates in the Early National Period," pp. 406, 408–10, 423; Sears, "Philadelphia and the Embargo," 256; *Public Ledger*, 7 December 1842.

35. *Appeal to the Wealthy of the Land, Ladies As Well As Gentlemen, on the Character, Conduct, Situation, and Prospects of Those Whose Sole Dependence for Subsistence Is on the Labour of Their Hands*, 2d ed. (Philadelphia: L. Johnson, 1833), pp. 16–17.

36. *Hazard's Register*, 1:28; David Montgomery, "The Shuttle and the Cross: Weavers and Artisans in the Kensington Riots of 1844," *Journal of Social History* 6 (summer 1972): 418–19; Michael Feldberg, *Philadelphia Riots of 1844, A Study in Ethnic Conflict* (Westport, Conn.: Greenwood Press, 1975), p. 173. Richard McLeod has pointed out to me that the distinction between common laborers and handloom weavers may be an artificial one: most Irish handloom weavers worked in construction during the summer months.

37. Adams, "Wage Rates in the Early National Period," pp. 410, 423.

38. Pennsylvania Society for the Promotion of Public Economy, *Report of the Library Committee . . .* (Philadelphia: Meritt, 1817), p. 13; Mathew Carey, [Hamilton], "Essays on the Public Charities, No. 5," *U.S. Gazette*, 28 January 1829; Carey [C], *Female Wages and Female Oppression* (Philadelphia, 1835), p. 5.

39. For another view of the problem of surplus female labor, see Gareth Stedman Jones,

Outcast London, A Study in the Relationship between Classes in Victorian Society (New York: Oxford University Press, 1971), pp. 84, 125.

40. Carey, *Appeal to the Wealthy*, pp. 13–18.

41. W. E. Burghardt DuBois, *The Philadelphia Negro, A Social Study* (New York: Benjamin Blom, 1899), p. 49; Mease, *Picture of Philadelphia*, p. 35, found fifty-five slaves in 1800 and two in 1810.

42. Quote from George Rogers Taylor, "'Philadelphia in Slices' by George G. Foster," *Pennsylvania Magazine of History and Biography* 93 (January 1969): 62; *Moreau de Mery's American Journey*, pp. 302, 309; DuBois, *Philadelphia Negro*, p. 142; Carol V. R. George, *Segregated Sabbaths, Richard Allen and the Emergence of Independent Black Churches, 1760–1840* (New York: Oxford University Press, 1973), p. 47.

43. Theodore Hershberg, "Free Blacks in Antebellum Philadelphia," in Davis and Haller, *Peoples of Philadelphia*, pp. 113–18, 124; DuBois, *Philadelphia Negro*, p. 32; *Public Ledger*, 3 March 1846; and *Hazard's Register* 9:277.

44. Adam Seybert, *Statistical Annals: Embracing Views of the Population, Commerce, Navigation, Fisheries, Public Lands, Post-Office Establishment, Revenues, Mint, Debt and Sinking Fund of the United States of America: Founded on Official Documents: Commencing on the 4 March 1789 and Ending on 20 April 1818* (Philadelphia: Thomas Dobson and Son, 1818), p. 29; William J. Bromwell, *History of Immigration to the United States* (1856; reprint ed., New York: Arno Press, 1969), pp. 14–15.

45. Edward C. Carter, II, "'Wild Irishman' under Every Federalist's Bed: Naturalization in Philadelphia, 1789–1806," *Pennsylvania Magazine of History and Biography* 94 (July 1970): 342.

46. Theodore Hershberg et al., "A Tale of Three Cities; Blacks and Immigrants in Philadelphia, 1850–1880, 1930 and 1970," in Theodore Hershberg, ed., *Philadelphia: Work, Space, Family, and Group Experience in the Nineteenth Century* (New York: Oxford University Press, 1981), table 1, p. 465.

47. *Public Ledger*, 28 August 1846, 14 July 1847, 6 April 1848; article signed "Richard," *Aurora*, 31 January 1805; Dennis Clark, *The Irish in Philadelphia, Ten Generations of Urban Experience* (Philadelphia: Temple University Press, 1973), p. 85; Feldberg, *Philadelphia Riots of 1844*, pp. 21, 173; Carey, *Letters on the Condition of the Poor*, p. 17; "Essays on the Public Charities of Philadelphia, No. 6," *U.S. Gazette*, 5 February 1829.

48. Montgomery, "Shuttle and The Cross," pp. 420–21; Bruce Laurie, "Fire Companies and Gangs in Southwark," in Davis and Haller, *Peoples of Philadelphia*, p. 73. Quote from Laurie, "'Nothing on Impulse': Life Styles of Philadelphia Artisans, 1820–1850," *Labor History* 15 (summer 1974): 355.

49. Quote from Montgomery, "Shuttle and the Cross," p. 421. See also Laurie, *The Working People of Philadelphia*. The meeting in Kensington in 1844 was conducted by members of an antiimmigrant political party known as the American Republicans. A march led by this party was followed by riots in Southwark. Feldberg, *Philadelphia Riots of 1844*, pp. 96, 99–116, 136–38, 143–59.

50. Peirce, *Meteorological Account of the Weather in Philadelphia*, pp. 20–21; "The Distresses of the Poor by Charitas," *Poulson's*, 29 January 1821; "Howard," *Poulson's*, 30 January 1821.

51. Billy G. Smith, "'The Best Poor Man's Country': Living Standards of the 'Lower Sort' in Late Eighteenth-Century Philadelphia," *Working Papers from the Regional Economic History Research Center*, 2, no. 4 (1979): 31, 49 n.

52. Blumin, "Mobility in Philadelphia, 1820–1860," p. 37. If we assume that there were others besides unskilled laborers among the laboring poor, then perhaps more than one-quarter of Philadelphia's population were in this category by midcentury.

53. Howard P. Chudacoff, *The Evolution of American Urban Society* (Englewood Cliffs, N. J.: Prentice-Hall, 1975), pp. 45, 65; Charles E. Rosenberg, *The Cholera Years* (Chicago:

University of Chicago Press, 1962), pp. 2, 7; Mohl, *Poverty in New York*, pp. 5–6, 17, 20, 29, 83–84, 107–8, 110–11, 114; Bayrd Still, *Urban America: A History with Documents* (Boston: Little Brown, 1974), pp. 127–28.

54. Livingood, *Philadelphia-Baltimore Trade Rivalry*, pp. 11, 22–25; Davis and Haller, *Peoples of Philadelphia*, p. 9.

Chapter 2. Evolution of the Public-Welfare System

1. Nash, "Poverty and Poor Relief," p. 16.

2. Walter Freidlander, *Introduction to Social Welfare* (Englewood Cliffs, N. J.: Prentice-Hall, 1955), pp. 78–80; Marcus Wilson Jernegan, *Laboring and Dependent Classes in Colonial America, 1607–1783* (Chicago: University of Chicago Press, 1931), pp. 175–209.

3. Before this time, justices of the peace provided assistance to the city's indigent. Nash, *The Urban Crucible*, p. 22.

4. Earlier than Philadelphia and New York, Boston experienced economic woes and consequently built its first almshouse in 1685. Ibid., pp. 22, 125–27.

5. Trattner, *From Poor Law to Welfare State*, pp. 9–11, 15–16.

6. On the size of American cities, see Nash, *The Urban Crucible*, pp. 19–54. On the narrow geographical limits of eighteenth-century Philadelphia, see Warner, *The Private City*, pp. 10–19.

7. Nash, *The Urban Crucible*, pp. 247–50, 255.

8. Ibid., pp. 327–31; Nash, "Poverty and Poor Relief," p. 16. In *Render Them Submissive*, Alexander also notes the twin concerns of humanitarianism and social control in public-welfare administration, 1776–1800, but he is convinced that the latter was more important than I think it was. To prove his point, he states that outdoor pensions were suspended for a time in 1793, although he also explains in a footnote that some were still granted, pp. 109–21, n 49. Perhaps economic pressures caused by the yellow fever epidemic of 1793 necessitated suspending pensions for a time. In any case, they were granted again in 1800. On the overall prosperity of the city in the 1780s and 1790s, see Smith, "'The Best Poor Man's Country': Living Standards of the 'Lower Sort' in Late Eighteenth-Century Philadelphia," pp. 17, 20, 22, 24. Smith found that the real wages of Philadelphia's laboring poor (including day laborers, mariners, and cordwainers) improved in the 1780s and rose significantly in the 1790s as war between England and France, beginning in 1793, stimulated American commerce and increased job opportunities in Philadelphia.

9. The names of guardians and the districts they represented are in PCA, MGP, the third week in March and in September for 1800–1802 and the third week in May and November for 1803–54.

10. PCA, MGP, 25 March, 25 September 1800; 25 September 1801; 25 March, 25 September, 4 November 1802.

11. Articles signed "New Market Ward," *Aurora*, 26 January 1802; "D___," *Aurora*, 11 December 1802; "John Douglas, George Bartram," *Aurora*, 29 January 1803; and "Truth," *Aurora*, 16 August, 17 August 1804.

12. There were now thirty rather than twenty guardians. There were similar objections to the undemocratic fashion in which members of the board of health were chosen and similar reforms inaugurated for that board in 1803: *Aurora*, 20 April 1803; William C. Heffner, *History of Poor Relief Legislation in Pennsylvania, 1682–1913* (Cleona, Penn.: Holzapfel Publishing Co., 1913), pp. 164–65.

13. PCA, MAHM, 7 May 1800, 22 March 1801, 12 April 1802, 19 December 1825; Heffner, *History of Poor Relief Legislation in Pennsylvania*, pp. 164–65. In order to assess taxes, almshouse managers had to have the consent of four city aldermen and two justices of the

peace from Southwark as well as two from Northern Liberties. Pennsylvania, *An Act for the Consolidation of the Poor Laws, 1803, Statutes at Large*, 1803, 17:389.

14. I obtained the names of guardians from their minutes in March and September from 1800–02 and in May and November thereafter. I checked their occupations through the city directories. Incidentally, lists of guardians appear occasionally in the city directories, but these lists often contain the names of guardians who served several years before the directories were published. The occupational categories I used were those established by Blumin in "Mobility in Philadelphia, 1820–60," although I compressed his second and third occupational categories into one. Alexander, *Render Them Submissive*, p. 113, also found Philadelphia's welfare officials in the late eighteenth century to be fairly prosperous members of the community.

15. I identified age and some religious affiliations (by burial ground) through Department of Records, City of Philadelphia, *Registration of Deaths Index, 1803–1860*, 15 reels, microfilm (Harrisburg: Pennsylvania Historical Commission, 1962). To determine more accurately which guardians were members of the Society of Friends, I used William Wade Hinshaw's *Encyclopedia of American Quaker Genealogy*, 6 vols. (Ann Arbor, Mich.: Edwards Brothers, 1938), 2:passim. To determine other charitable and governmental commitments of the guardians, I checked the membership lists of the following: Abolition Society; Philadelphia Society for Alleviating the Miseries of Public Prisons; Pennsylvania Hospital; Philadelphia Dispensary; Northern Dispensary; Southern Dispensary; Pennsylvania Infirmary for Eye and Ear Disease; Friends' Asylum; Captain's Society; French Society; German Society; Hibernian Society; St. Andrew's Society; St. George's Society; St. Patrick's Society; Scots Thistle Society; Welsh Society; Musical Fund Society; Savings Fund Society; Fuel Savings Society; St. Joseph's Orphan Asylum; Magdalen Asylum; Philadelphia Society for the Free Instruction of Indigent Boys; Philadelphia Society for the Establishment and Support of Charity Schools; Association of Friends for the Instruction of Poor Children; Benevolent Society (Presbyterian); Hospitable Society (Methodist-Episcopal); Northern Soup Society; Philadelphia Soup Society; Provident Society; House of Refuge; Pennsylvania Institution for the Deaf and Dumb; 1805 Committee of Collection for the Poor; Citizens Meetings, 1821, 1824, 1827, 1829; Benevolent Society of Second Baptist Church, Northern Liberties; Spring Garden Association for Charitable Purposes; Society for the Relief of the Poor, St. John's (Evangelical-Lutheran). Data on governmental officials included those in Philadelphia, Southwark, Northern Liberties, Kensington, Penn Township, Spring Garden, and the justices of the peace and members of the board of health. I am considerably indebted to Richard McLeod, who helped me place many of the guardians in the preceding private and governmental agencies.

16. Wiberley also found that most welfare officials in eighteenth-century Philadelphia remained in office only one term. See his "Four Cities," pp. 173–74. On New York, see Mohl, *Poverty in New York*, pp. 72–73.

17. Eva Tooker, *Nathan Trotter, Philadelphia Merchant, 1787–1853* (Cambridge: Harvard University Press, 1955), pp. 4, 22.

18. On fines, see Pennsylvania, *An Act for the Consolidation of the Poor Laws, 1803, Statutes at Large*, 1803, 17:387.

19. Alexander detailed this conflict in *Render Them Submissive*, pp. 91–94.

20. On passage of the law, see Pennsylvania House of Representatives, *Journal*, 1804–5, 280, 451, 599, 629, 647. On the continuing arguments between welfare officials, see PCA, MGP, 5 July 1816; 3 January 1817; 7 January 1823; 18 May 1825; 10 May, 17 May, 22 May, 24 May 1826; MAHM, 21 May, 17 September 1821; 2 February 1824.

21. PCA, MAHM, passim. At almost every meeting of the managers, the visiting committee for the week reported on the state of the house. PCA, MGP, 25 March, 25 September 1800; 4 November 1802; 31 March 1803; 22 May, 27 November 1820; PCA, GP, Register of Relief

Recipients, 1814–15; Heffner, *Poor Relief Legislation*, pp. 164–65.

22. PCA, MGP, 2 January 1800; 21 January 1801; 7 January, 5 August 1802; 6 January, 18 September 1803; 11 January, 1 February 1804; 5 February, 13 September, 31 December 1805; 7 January 1806; 27 January, 3 February 1807; 9 February 1808; 24 January 1809; 6 February, 18 December 1810; 5 February, 19 March, 11 June, 3 September, 25 November 1811; 27 December 1814; 23 January, 10 December 1816; 7 February 1817; 8 February, 20 February 1818; 4 June 1819; 5 January, 23 January 1821; MAHM, 9 January, 13 August 1804. For a more detailed discussion of outdoor medical aid to the poor, see chapter 3.

23. See appendix 1 and note especially increases in expenditures in the epidemic years of 1802 and 1804.

24. Mohl, *Poverty in New York*, pp. 104–10.

25. PCA, MAHM, 1807–12 vol.: 222–34; *Poulson's*, 19 February 1812, 3 November 1814, 19 October 1815, 19 November 1816; *Aurora*, 29 November 1817, 24 September 1818, 25 October 1819; PCA, GP, Register of Relief Recipients, 1814–15.

26. Female domestics earned $1.25 a week and male day laborers earned $1.00 a day, and here I have assumed they worked six days a week.

27. PCA, MAHM, 2 March 1807, 5 December 1808, 22 July 1811; GP, Treasurer's "Weekly Entries," 1803–9 vol. and Minutes, Manufacturing Committee (hereafter referred to as MMC), 1807–9 vol.: passim. See chapter 4 for a more detailed description of the almshouse factory.

28. Mohl, *Poverty in New York*, pp. 84, 111–12.

29. See appendix 1 and PCA, GP, Register of Relief Recipients, 1814–15; Mohl, *Poverty in New York*, pp. 113–14.

30. Klebaner, "Public Poor Relief in America," pp. 483–563, 395–411.

31. Ibid., pp. 485–530. Often they were simply removed to their last place of residence, and it was up to that community to remove them again if necessary.

32. Piven and Cloward, *Regulating the Poor*, p. 308.

33. Pennsylvania, *An Act for the Consolidation of the Poor Laws, 1803, Statutes at Large*, 1803, 17:395–407. Between 1811 and 1815, one-third of those on outdoor relief were foreign-born, and in 1807, 68 percent of those residing in almshouse wards were recent immigrants (see chapters 3–5).

34. PCA, MAHM, 17 February, 28 April, 12 May 1806; MGP, 22 April, 1 July 1806; 4 February 1812; 2 September, 5 September 1817; 17 March 1818; 3 August, 17 August 1819; 29 June, 3 August 1825; 6 July 1827.

35. Of course the guardians also expected the agent to save them money by administering more efficiently the settlement laws than they could, thereby lessening the number dependent on Philadelphia's poor relief.

36. *Poulson's*, 19 October 1815.

37. Guardians frequently acknowledged in their annual reports that the average cost per pauper was greater for those poor who were institutionalized than those who were not. For example, the guardians noted in 1803 that it cost on the average $1.05 a week to house a person in the almshouse, but just 78¢ a week to assist a poor Philadelphian in her or his own home. *The Accounts of the Guardians of the Poor, and Managers of the Alms-House, and House of Employment, of Philadelphia, from 23rd May 1803 to 23rd May 1804* (Philadelphia: John Geyer, 1804).

38. PCA, MAHM, 30 September 1811; 21 January, 11 March, 18 March 1822; PCA, MGP, 26 March 1811; Klebaner, "Public Poor Relief," pp. 104–15.

39. See appendix 1 and PCA, Poor Tax Duplicates, 1803–11. In 1810, county taxes were $74,541.42, while poor taxes were $78,000. Mease, *Picture of Philadelphia*, p. 198.

40. Articles signed "Truth" in *Aurora*, 16 August 1804 and in *Freeman's Journal*, 17 August 1804.

41. Nash found 30.3 poor per thousand in Philadelphia in 1772–75. See his "Poverty and Poor Relief," table 1, p. 9.

42. See appendix 1 and PCA, Poor Tax Duplicates, 1803–11.

43. *A Plan for the Government of the Alms-House, and for Ordering the Affairs of the Poor in the City of Philadelphia, Township of Northern Liberties, and District of Southwark* (Philadelphia: Kimber, Conrad, and Co., 1805). See also articles in *U.S. Gazette*, 24 January, 25 January, 8 February, 9 February 1805.

44. Pennsylvania House of Representatives, *Journal*, 1807–8, pt. 2:28–29, 46, 163, 416.

45. Citizens on the 1805 committees are listed in *U.S. Gazette*, 24 January 1805. The expansion of almshouse manufacturing and outdoor spinning are described in chapters 3 and 4.

46. PCA, MGP, 22 July 1817; Pendleton, "The Influence of the Evangelical Churches upon Reform," pp. 279–80; Pennsylvania Society for the Promotion of Public Economy, *Report of the Library Committee*, pp. 5–6, 8–9, 12–20.

47. Daniel T. McColgan, *Joseph Tuckerman, Pioneer in American Social Work* (Washington, D.C.: Catholic University of America Press, 1940), pp. 176–77; Schneider, *History of Public Welfare in New York*, pp. 211–12; Blanche D. Coll, "The Baltimore Society for the Prevention of Pauperism, 1820–1822," *American Historical Review* 61 (October 1955): 78–87.

48. J. R. Poynter, *Society and Pauperism, English Ideas on Poor Relief, 1795–1834* (London: Routledge and Kegan Paul, 1969), p. 224; Sidney and Beatrice Webb, *English Poor Law History: Part II: The Last Hundred Years*, 2 vols. (London: Longmans, Green and Co., 1929), 1:40–43.

49. PCA, MGP, 28 December 1819; 8 February, 15 February, 3 March, 7 March, 23 March, 11 April, 9 May, 16 May, 23 May 1820; 30 January, 1 June 1821. MAHM, 3 May 1819, 24 April 1820, 25 June 1821. The only positive action at all out of the ordinary taken by guardians during the depression years early in the decade was to create an employment registry. It opened in the home of Benjamin Kite, who posted lists of jobs available and applicants, including mechanics, laborers, and prospective apprentices. In the first six months, Kite registered the names of 1,418 individuals in need of work but only 1,090 job openings. He kept no record of how many actually found work through the employment registry, but it seemed to be a useful service. Nevertheless, the guardians, giving no explanation for their action, terminated the registry at the end of its first year of operation. PCA, MGP, 27 February, 2 March, 25 September, 26 November 1821.

50. Article signed "Corrector," *Poulson's*, 20 December 1825. In late 1823, the managers found that $91,000 of the $100,000 needed for the poor that year had not yet been collected, PCA, MAHM, 22 December 1823. In 1825, they found that two-thirds of the 1824-tax levy had not yet been collected, PCA, MAHM, 10 January 1825. For other comments critical of rising tax levies, see article signed "Numa" and entitled "Pauperism," *Poulson's*, 8 March 1822, and HSP, Roberts Vaux Papers, Samuel Emlen to Vaux, 10 July 1821. In the 1830s, guardians of that decade commented that citizens were angered by the poor taxes in the 1820s, because they exceeded by $196,000 all other taxes levied for county purposes, PCA, MGP, 9 January 1837. On borrowing, see *Aurora*, 24 September 1818; *Poulson's*, 22 May 1822; *Philadelphia Gazette*, 6 November 1824.

51. Klebaner, "Public Poor Relief in America," pp. 55–56; Schneider, *History of Public Welfare in New York*, pp. 217–29; for a more detailed description of the Pennsylvania state investigation of poverty in 1821, see my dissertation, "The Response to Need: Welfare and Poverty in Philadelphia, 1800–1850," (University of Pennsylvania, 1977), pp. 206–7.

52. Webbs, *English Poor Law History*, 1:7, 12, 22, 44; Poynter, *Society and Pauperism*, p. 296.

53. J. D. Marshall, *The Old Poor Law, 1795–1834* (London: Macmillan, 1968), pp. 13, 20,

25; Webbs, *English Poor Law History*, 1:14–15, 65; Schneider, *History of Public Welfare in New York*, pp. 215–16.

54. First quote is from article signed "Corrector," *Poulson's*, 20 December 1825, and the second is from *Poulson's*, 3 January 1824.

55. HSP, Meredith Papers, Robert Earp to Meredith, 25 January 1827, and James Robertson to Meredith, 18 December 1827. For almshouse-admission figures that include the number admitted from Philadelphia, Northern Liberties, and Southwark, respectively, see *Poulson's*, 22 May 1822; *Philadelphia Gazette*, 6 November 1824, 20 December 1825, 7 November 1826, 2 November 1827, 19 January 1830, 12 January 1831; PCA, GP, Treasurer, General Ledger, 1822 vol.: 56, 58, 60 and 1830 vol.: 176, 178, 180. The only record of outdoor-relief recipients by place of residence is for 1820 when there were 612 in the city and 718 in the districts, *Poulson's*, 22 May 1822. However, for other years, there are records of how much was spent on the outdoor poor by area, and consistently 60 percent or more of the outdoor-relief funds were spent on the poor in Northern Liberties and Southwark. It is probable that since more was spent on the poor in the districts, there were more poor there than in the city who received outdoor aid. For amounts spent on the outdoor poor in the city and districts, see the accounts of the guardians in the *Philadelphia Gazette*, 6 November 1824, 20 December 1825, 7 November 1826, 2 November 1827 and *Accounts of the Guardians of the Poor, and Managers of the Alms-House, and House of Employment, of Philadelphia from 28 May 1822 to 27 May 1823* (Philadelphia, 1823). The political situation in these years is quite confused, but there is no question that for most years, Federalists controlled the city's government, and some faction of the Democratic-Republicans controlled the districts. Phillips, "William Duane," pp. 456–58, 529, 588, 611.

56. Meredith's report was published in the newspapers and *Hazard's Register*, 2:49–69. On his affiliation with the Federalists at this time, see *Poulson's*, 29 September 1823. On the comparative populations of Philadelphia and the districts, see Gilchrist, *Seaport Cities*, table 5, p. 39.

57. PCA, MGP, 26 February 1825; 15 February, 18 October, 24 November 1826; Pennsylvania House of Representatives, *Journal*, 1824–25, pt. 1:492; 1825–26, pt. 1:265, 348. Article signed "G" in *Poulson's*, 14 December 1825; articles signed "Corrector" in *Poulson's*, 20 December 1825, 28 January 1826.

58. PCA, MGP, 18 April, 23 April 1827; *Report of the Committee Appointed by the Board of Guardians of the Poor of the City and Districts of Philadelphia to Visit the Cities of Baltimore, New York, Providence, Boston, and Salem* (Philadelphia, 1827), pp. 23–29. HSP, Meredith Papers, Robert Earp to Meredith, 25 January 1827.

59. Carey [Howard], "Pauperism, nos. 1, 2, 3," *Poulson's*, 14 July, 18 July, 21 July 1827 and 25 July 1827. Carey was not a Federalist, but he did, along with many conservative Philadelphians who opposed the city's welfare system, endorse John Quincy Adams for president in 1828. Phillips, "William Duane," pp. 373–74.

60. *Report of the Committee Appointed at a Town Meeting of the Citizens of the City and County of Philadelphia, on the 23rd of July, 1827, to Consider the Subject of the Pauper System of the City and Districts, and to Report Remedies for its Defects* (Philadelphia: Clark and Raser, 1827), pp. 4–16; the memorial to the legislature is in *Poulson's*, 21 November 1827.

61. PCA, GP, "Pauper Lists," 1823 and 1825; Register of Relief Recipients, 1814–15.

62. *Poulson's*, 21 November 1827; Pennsylvania House of Representatives, *Journal*, 1827–28, pt. 1:11; Pennsylvania, *Laws of the Commonwealth* (1828), secs. 3, 9 of the 1828 poor law, 10:71–72, 78–79.

63. Pennsylvania House of Representatives, *Journal*, 1827–28, pt. 1:301–2 and pt. 2: 931–32; 1828–29, pt. 1:23–24, 455, 583–84.

64. Mohl, *Poverty in New York*, p. 72; Schneider, *History of Public Welfare in New York*, p. 247; Mania Kleinburd Baghdadi, "Protestants, Poverty, and Urban Growth: A Study of the Organization of Charity in Boston and New York, 1820–1865" (Ph.D. diss., Brown

University, 1975), pp. 18–20. The new English system differed from the American in that the former was administered nationally rather than locally and English welfare officials were elected not appointed. Webbs, *English Poor Law History*, 1:61, 63–64, 78–82, 114, 143–45.

65. PCA, MGP, 2 June, 28 May, 29 September 1829. Burden's biography must be pieced together from Warner, *Private City*, pp. 86–91; Snyder, *Jacksonian Heritage*, pp. 58, 86, 77 n., 79 n.

66. The board reorganized annually after the governments of the city and districts chose new guardians. From the minutes of these mid-May meetings, I established a list of guardians who served in 1829–54. I established their governmental and private charity affiliations by checking the membership of the following: **Private charities**: Abolition Society, Colonization Society, Philadelphia Society for Alleviating the Miseries of Public Prisons, Pennsylvania Hospital, Philadelphia Dispensary, Northern Dispensary, Friends' Asylum, German Society, Hibernian Society, St. Andrew's Society, St. George's Society, Musical Fund Society, Savings Fund Society, St. Joseph's Orphan Asylum, St. John's Orphan Asylum, Magdalen Asylum, Lying-In Charity, Provident Society, Union Benevolent Society, Seaman's Friend Society, Philadelphia Society for the Employment and Instruction of the Poor, Grandom Institution, Pennsylvania Institution for the Blind, House of Refuge, Girard College, Philadelphia Association for the Relief of Disabled Firemen, Committee to Aid George St. Fire Victims; **Government**: elected and appointed officials in Philadelphia, Southwark, Northern Liberties, Kensington, Spring Garden, and Moyamensing. I checked the guardians' occupations through the city directories and ranked them by class using Stuart Blumin's scale in "Mobility in Philadelphia, 1820–1860." (This is the same system I used for ranking guardians in earlier decades.) To determine membership in the Society of Friends, I again used Hinshaw, *Encyclopedia of American Quaker Genealogy*.

67. *Public Ledger*, 22 April 1842, 9 July 1845. For the 1841–42 accounts, see *The Pennsylvanian*, 27 January 1843. For some years, the only elected committee of the guardians was the Committee of Supplies, PCA, MGP, 31 May 1841. Later, its activities were divided between the almshouse and hospital committees. *Rules for the Government of the Board of Guardians, its Officers, Business, and Affairs, and for Regulating and Controlling the Alms House Hospital, and House of Employment. Adopted December, 1843* (Philadelphia: J. Perry, 1844), pp. 7, 12.

68. Lawrence, *Philadelphia Almshouse*, pp. 179–84, 198. In the 1840s, the "peculation that filled the pockets" of public-welfare officials was apparently taken for granted, *Public Ledger*, 13 January 1846. As of 1828, guardians of the poor supervised paid employees, and for a time, that was all they did. They lost their old function of levying the poor tax; a few elected officials in the city and districts performed this task. However, the guardians never relished having to apply for funds to these "directors of the poor tax," who frequently asked them uncomfortable questions about how they intended to spend the taxpayers' money. In the early 1830s, directors of the poor tax refused to allow for funds to pay off almshouse-construction loans in the tax levies. Guardians took their case to Harrisburg, and the state legislators passed a law requiring poor-tax directors to raise monies to pay the loans. Conflict between the two sets of officials did not then cease, however. Finally guardians triumphed—on 6 January 1840, the state legislature abolished the directors of the poor tax. Thenceforth, Philadelphia reverted to the customary American practice of having one set of officials both levy and spend poor taxes. PCA, MGP, 1 February 1830; 3 January, 10 January, 17 January, 12 December 1831; 9 January, 13 February 1832; 20 January, 27 January, 1834; 12 January 1835; 1 February 1836.

69. *Rules, Board of Guardians, 1843*, pp. 71–73. Doctors assisted between 2,000 and 3,000 people annually; see appendix 2.

70. PCA, MGP, 18 May, 3 August 1840; 26 July 1841; 21 February, 11 July 1842; 4 September 1843; 2 September 1844; 14 July, 15 December 1845; 2 August 1847; 10 July 1848; 13 August 1849.

71. Schneider, *History of Public Welfare in New York*, pp. 260–62. PCA, MGP, 13

February, 22 May 1837; 29 January, 23 May 1838; 28 January, 20 May 1839; 10 February, 18 May 1840; 18 January, 15 February, 22 February, 17 May, 24 May 1841; 17 January, 14 February, 2 May, 23 May, 30 May, 19 December 1842; 2 January, 6 March, 1 May, 15 May, 22 May, 29 May 1843; 8 January, 22 January, 12 February, 19 February, 26 February, 1 April, 20 May, 27 May, 10 June 1844.

72. In 1840, twelve people in every thousand in Philadelphia were in the almshouse, and in 1850, the proportion rose to only thirteen per thousand. On assistance to blacks during the riots, see PCA, MGP, 18 August 1834.

73. See chapter 5 and PCA, MGP, 11 May, 19 October 1835; 7 June, 12 July 1841.

74. Mathew Carey [C], *From the National Gazette, To the Editor* (Philadelphia, 1839); PCA, MGP, 26 December 1836, 9 January 1837, 19 March 1838, 4 March 1839. Quote is from *Public Ledger*, 13 January 1840. *Rules for the Government of the Board of Guardians, its Officers etc. with the Acts of Assembly Relating to the Relief and Employment of the Poor in the City of Philadelphia, the District of Southwark, and the Townships of Northern Liberties and Penn, Adopted May, 1851* (Philadelphia: King and Baird, 1851), pp. 85–86. For more on outdoor relief, see chapter 3.

75. The old positions of assistant agent, bookkeeper and collector were abolished after 1828. PCA, MGP, 3 November 1834; 15 February, 22 February 1836; 25 January 1841. Philadelphia ship owners did not like the head tax and sought for years to have it repealed. It was declared unconstitutional by midcentury. PCA, MGP, 15 July 1839, 24 January 1842, 12 February 1849; *Rules, Board of Guardians, 1851*, pp. 103–4.

76. On the salaries of the visitors of the poor, see PCA, MGP, 15 February, 22 February 1836; 5 September 1842. On the growth of the social work profession in the late nineteenth century, see Bremner, *From the Depths* and Roy Lubove, *The Professional Altruist, the Emergence of Social Work as a Career, 1880–1930* (Cambridge: Harvard University Press, 1965). On New York, see Mohl, *Poverty in New York*, pp. 72, 103.

77. The new law also allowed the guardian to select the outdoor physician and apothecary in his district. *Rules, Board of Guardians, 1851*, pp. 86, 24–25.

78. Compare the messy lists of outdoor-relief recipients kept by the guardians of the 1820s, PCA, GP, "Pauper Lists," 1821–29, with the neat, clear records kept by the visitors when they took over, PCA, GP, Register of Relief Recipients, 1828–32.

79. PCA, MGP, 21 August 1839, 25 October 1841, 10 August 1846; *Rules, Board of Guardians, 1851*, pp. 23–24. The amounts spent by welfare officials on salaries, pensions, fuel, and other items are listed in the accounts of the guardians, which are cited in full in appendix 1.

80. The yearly average spent by guardians in 1800–10 was $86,861; for 1810–20, $107,697; for 1820–30, $100,072; for 1830–40, $110,117; and for 1840–50, $134,720.

81. The poor-tax rate went up in the 1830s to pay for the cost of constructing the new almshouse. Rates increased from 20¢ in 1830 to 50¢ in 1838. Thereafter, they decreased. *Hazard's Register*, 6:124, 8:88, 10:10, 13:68; *Public Ledger*, 7 April, 5 December 1840, 9 June 1847; PCA, GP, Poor Tax Duplicates, 1804–8.

82. The assessed value of property in the county in 1805 was $7,235,214. See Carey, *Autobiography*, p. 52. The assessment for 1849 was $104,692,036 and for 1838, $49,259,285. See *Public Ledger*, 1 March 1849, 16 May 1840.

83. Note also that the expense of poor relief per thousand Philadelphians increased in the eighteenth century but not in the nineteenth. Compare Nash, "Poverty and Poor Relief," table 1, p. 9, with table 1 in this chapter. See also Nash, pp. 20, 24.

84. On the suspension of cash aid in the 1870s, see Raymond A. Mohl, "The Abolition of Public Outdoor Relief, 1870–1900: A Critique of the Piven and Cloward Thesis," in *Social Welfare or Social Control? Some Historical Reflections on Regulating the Poor*, ed. Walter I. Trattner (Knoxville: University of Tennessee Press, 1983), p. 41. For a more complete

discussion of economic crises from the eighteenth through the twentieth centuries and their effect on public welfare, see chapter 7.

Chapter 3. Outdoor Relief

1. See PCA, MGP, 9 December 1806 for an example of a successful appeal; PCA, MGP, 3 December 1805. Members of one church-sponsored charity complained in 1803 that many honest laborers did not know the proper public officials to appeal to for welfare aid. *The Nature and Design of the Hospitable Society or Sick-Man's Friend* (Philadelphia, 1803), p. 13.

2. HSP, Roberts Vaux Papers, William Savery to Abraham Garrigues, 6 December 1800.

3. Private charities in the nineteenth century also required applicants for aid to present testimonials of their good character. See Charles E. Rosenberg, "Social Class and Medical Care in Nineteenth Century America: The Rise and Fall of the Dispensary," *Journal of the History of Medicine and Allied Sciences* 29 (January 1974): 42.

4. PCA, MGP, 22 February, 21 August 1804; 22 April 1806.

5. PCA, GP, Register of Relief Recipients, 1814–15 is the one extant census.

6. PCA, MGP, 13 February 1821. Officials entered the names in PCA, GP, "Pauper Lists," 1821–29. PCA, MGP, 6 August 1822, 6 May 1823, 25 August 1824, 25 January 1826. PCA, MGP, 2 February, 23 February, 24 May 1808; 24 December 1811; 27 July, 2 August, 16 August, 20 September 1814; 14 February, 28 February, 7 March 1815; 5 August 1817; 31 January, 6 February, 27 March, 17 April 1821; 6 May 1823; 25 August, 1824; 25 January, 15 March, 22 March 1826.

7. Piven and Cloward, *Regulating the Poor*, pp. 169–75. For contemporary exposes of fraud among female recipients of Aid to Families with Dependent Children, see *New York Times*, 10 April 1981, p. 1 and 6 May 1981, p. 25 and CBS Television, "60 Minutes," 21 February 1982.

8. PCA, GP, Register of Relief Recipients, 1828–32.

9. *Rules, Board of Guardians, 1851*, pp. 23–24; PCA, MGP, 21 August 1839.

10. Of course, dishonest officials in this era did manage to profit from the almshouse's supply contracts. See chapter 2.

11. PCA, GP, Register of Relief Recipients, 1814–15; PCA, MGP, 15 February 1820, 30 August 1826; *Pennsylvania Archives*, 4th ser., 5:479; Klebaner, "Public Poor Relief in America," pp. 334, 339; Wiberley, "Four Cities," p. 157.

12. For the sex, race, ethnicity, age, and state of health of those on outdoor relief, see PCA, Almshouse Admission Book, 1811–14; PCA, GP, Register of Relief Recipients, 1814–15 (this is the volume from which examples of applicants were drawn); PCA, MGP, 30 August 1826 and *Hazard's Register*, 6:266. For the proportion of women in nineteenth-century Philadelphia, see Emerson, "Medical Statistics, 1831," pp. 6–7. The figures on AFDC appear in *Congressional Digest*, 57 (May 1978): 135 and Piven and Cloward, *Regulating the Poor*, pp. 193–94. In 1948, the proportion of blacks receiving AFDC was 31 percent, and it rose to 44.3 percent by 1975. In those same years, blacks constituted between 10 and 11 percent of the total population. For nineteenth-century comments on the improvidence of blacks, see Pendleton, "Influence of Evangelical Churches upon Reform," p. 280 and *Report of the Committee Appointed at the Town Meeting* (1827), p. 8.

13. Carey, *From the National Gazette* (1839), p. 2; *Pennsylvania Archives*, 4th ser., 5:479.

14. I am indebted to Piven and Cloward, *Regulating the Poor*, pp. 3–4 and passim for my ideas on the labor-regulating function of public welfare. I do not, however, believe that all of Piven and Cloward's theories on public welfare apply to nineteenth-century Philadelphia; see chapter 7.

15. See chapter 2 for a discussion of welfare crises in the 1760s and 1820s. Quotes are from

PCA, MGP, 16 March 1829 and 25 July 1827.

16. PCA, Register of Relief Recipients, 1814–15; PCA, MGP, 30 August 1826; *Hazard's Register*, 6:266; *Report of the Committee Appointed by the Guardians* (1827), p. 29.

17. *Hazard's Register*, 6:267; PCA, MGP, 8 March 1830.

18. Carey [Hamilton], "Essays on the Public Charities, No. 6," *U.S. Gazette*, 5 February 1829, and untitled article by same author, *U.S. Gazette*, 14 April 1829; Pennsylvania House of Representatives, *Journal*, 1828–29, pt. 1: 587, 646, 909; PCA, MGP, 4 February, 16 March 1829.

19. PCA, MGP, 4 May, 17 August 1835, 23 May 1838, 20 May 1839; Mathew Carey, *From the National Gazette, To the Editor* and by the same author, *The Case of the Out-Door Poor Once More* (Philadelphia, 1838).

20. PCA, MGP, 9 January 1837, 19 March 1838, 20 May 1839; *Rules, Board of Guardians, 1851*, p. 85.

21. PCA, MGP, 31 May 1841, 2 March 1846. Every year from 1845 to 1850, the *Auditors' Reports of the Accounts of Blockley Alms-House* indicate that only poor widows received assistance of 50¢ a week.

22. In 1831–32, there were 2,622 women and 575 men who obtained fuel relief, 1,047 women and 2,091 men admitted to the almshouse, and 670 people (evidently nearly all women) who received outdoor cash pensions. See *Hazard's Register*, 11:363; *Philadelphia Gazette*, 1 January 1833 and PCA, MGP, 20 January 1834.

23. PCA, GP, Steward, Out-Door Spinners Accounts, September 1806–September 1807; Benjamin S. Klebaner, "The Home Relief Controversy in Philadelphia, 1782–1861," *Pennsylvania Magazine of History and Biography* 78 (October 1954): 414.

24. PCA, MAHM, 9 January 1804, 28 October 1805; PCA, MGP, 1 July, 15 July 1806; 20 February, 6 March 1810. On 8 February 1804, guardians commissioned four apothecaries to supply medicine to the outdoor poor but apparently terminated their contracts when the Philadelphia Dispensary took over. On this dispensary, see Rosenberg, "Social Class and Medical Care," pp. 33, 42. PCA, MGP, 8 January, 19 March, 11 June, 3 September, 25 November 1811; 8 April, 16 May 1817.

25. PCA, MGP, 3 January 1815; 4 June 1819; 5 January 1821; 8 March 1830; 5 September 1842; 6 October, 20 October 1845. *Rules, Board of Guardians, 1843*, pp. 71–73.

26. Rosenberg, "Social Class and Medical Care," pp. 39–41; PCA, MGP, 29 March 1826.

27. PCA, MGP, 2 January 1800; 21 January 1801; 7 January 1802; 6 January 1803; 11 January 1804; 5 February 1805; 7 January 1806; 27 January, 3 February 1807; 9 February 1808; 24 January 1809; 6 February 1810; 23 January 1821; 22 January 1822; 24 January 1827; 30 January 1832; 28 February 1842; 13 February 1837; 29 January 1838; 28 January 1839; 10 February 1840; 18 January, 15 February, 22 February 1841; 17 January, 14 February, 19 December 1842; 2 January, 6 March 1843; 8 January, 22 January, 12 February, 19 February, 26 February 1844. See also *Auditors' Report of the Accounts of the Blockley Alms-House for the Fiscal Years Ending May 15, 1843 and May 20, 1844* (Philadelphia: Office of the American Sentinel, 1843 and Mifflin and Parry, 1844).

28. PCA, MAHM, 1807–18 vol.: 222–34; PCA, MGP, 22 May 1826, 28 May 1827; PCA, GP, Treasurers' Accounts, 1829–34 vol.; *Aurora*, 8 November 1809, 31 October 1810, 24 September 1818, 25 October 1819; *Poulson's*, 19 February, 19 November 1812; 3 November 1814; 19 October 1815; 19 November 1816; 29 November 1817; 16 May 1823; *Philadelphia Gazette*, 13 January 1832, 1 January 1833; *Accounts of the Guardians of the Poor, 1822–23; Auditors' Reports of the Accounts of Blockley Alms-House for the Fiscal Years Ending May 17, 1841, May 15, 1843, May 20, 1844, May 18, 1846, May 18, 1847, 1848, 1849, May 21, 1850, May 19, 1851, May 21, 1852, May 21, 1853* (Philadelphia: Mifflin and Parry, 1841, 1844; Office of the American Sentinel, 1843; Daily Sun, 1846; Times and Keystone, 1847; n. pub., 1849; Crissy and Markley, 1851, 1853, 1854; O. I. Search, 1852); *Statement of the Accounts of the Guardians of the Poor, July 3–December 31, 1854* (Philadelphia: Crissy and Markley, 1855).

29. I divided the amount spent for wood by the number of families receiving it each year between 1841 and 1849. For the appropriate citations, see appendixes 1 and 2. For the amounts spent on cash pensions, see n. 21.

Chapter 4. The Almshouse

1. Nash, "Poverty and Poor Relief in Pre-Revolutionary Philadelphia," p. 15; Jean Pierre Brissot de Warville, *New Travels in the United States of America, 1788* (Cambridge: Belknap Press of Harvard University Press, 1964), pp. 173, 175; PCA, MAHM, 28 July 1800; 18 April, 8 June 1803; 4 March, 20 April, 8 July 1805; 13 April, 13 July 1807; 4 April, 11 April, 1808; 25 February,12 August, 9 September, 28 October 1811; 4 January, 25 January 1813; 23 October 1815; 2 July 1827; PCA, MGP, 25 January, 26 January, 7 February, 8 March, 2 April, 7 April 1814; Guardians of the Poor, *Rules and Regulations for the Internal Government of the Almshouse and House of Employment* (Philadelphia: Jacob Frick and Co., 1822), pp. 9–11; Mohl, *Poverty in New York*, pp. 94, 96; Carroll and Coll, "The Baltimore Almshouse," pp. 135–52.

2. Charles E. Rosenberg, "And Heal the Sick: The Hospital and the Patient in Nineteenth Century America," *Journal of Social History* 10 (summer 1977): 428–47. See also his "From Almshouse to Hospital: The Shaping of Philadelphia General Hospital," *Health and Society* 60 (1982): 108–54. PCA, Alms House, Receiving Register, 1800–07 vol., Alms House Admission Book, 1812–13, Alms House, Department and Ward Census, 1807. For details of sample, see n. 56.

3. PCA, Alms House, Department and Ward Census, 1807. See also censuses in minutes, PCA, MGP, 28 July 1821, 25 September 1826.

4. See reports of the visiting committee in PCA, MAHM, 1800–1828, passim; Brissot de Warville, *New Travels in the United States*, pp. 176–77.

5. PCA, Alms House, Department and Ward Census, 1807; PCA, MAHM, 26 December 1808; 1 January, 16 July 1810; 24 July 1811; Mease, *Picture of Philadelphia*, p. 231.

6. PCA, MAHM, 20 October 1806, 18 February 1828. The married ward accommodated no more than ten couples. See PCA, MAHM, 28 July 1821, 25 September 1826. On diet see PCA, MAHM, 19 July 1824 and on the Lighthouses (variously spelled), see PCA, MAHM, 2 July 1821, 23 June 1823, 14 June 1824, 27 June 1825, 19 June 1826.

7. Quote from PCA, MAHM, 8 August 1808. On occasion, managers kept better records of just who was and who was not permitted to leave the asylum. (Customarily, those who returned drunk from leaves were not allowed out again for a month or more.) See PCA, Guardians of the Poor, "Black Book," 1810–20, 1826–34, and Register of "Liberties of the Gate" and Passes from the Grounds, 1823–31. On furniture and dress, see PCA, MAHM, 7 December 1807, 14 November 1808. On diet see PCA, MAHM, 31 December 1804; 23 December 1805; 19 February 1821; 25 August, 6 October 1823; 19 July 1824; 1 August 1825; Wiberley, "Four Cities," p. 38. Alexander also found some dietary restrictions imposed in the 1790s; see his *Render Them Submissive*, pp. 116, 119.

8. All individual examples drawn from PCA, Alms House, Department and Ward Census, 1807. Quotes from *Poulson's*, 21 November 1827, and *The Philanthropist*, p. 36.

9. Rothman, *The Discovery of the Asylum*, pp. 196–97; Klebaner, "Public Poor Relief in America," p. 205.

10. Mohl, *Poverty in New York*, p. 93; Klebaner, "Public Poor Relief in America," p. 245. PCA, MAHM, 22 June 1807, 30 September 1811, 22 March 1813, 2 April 1821, 27 August 1827; "Almshouse," *Poulson's*, 16 March 1830; Female Domestic Missionary Society, *Eleventh Annual Report* (Philadelphia: Wm. F. Geddes, 1827), pp. 5–6; quote from John F. Watson, *Annals of Philadelphia and Pennsylvania in the Olden Times*, 3 vols. (Philadelphia: Leary, Stuart, and Co., 1909), 3:309.

11. PCA, MAHM, 12 January, 25 January 1802; 14 July 1803; 2 July, 6 August 1804; 2 November 1807; 22 January 1810; 23 September 1811; 20 July 1812.

12. First quote from Gerald Grob, *Mental Institutions in America: Social Policy to 1875* (New York: Free Press, 1973), p. 19. See also Williams, *America's First Hospital*, pp. 115–16. Second quote from PCA, MAHM, 19 December 1803.

13. PCA, MAHM, 20 April 1805; 13 July 1807; 11 April 1808; 25 February, 12 August 1811; 4 January, 25 January 1813; 2 July 1827. The fence was originally built in 1789; see Alexander, *Render Them Submissive*, p. 117.

14. In 1812–13, 15 percent of the people admitted to the Philadelphia Almshouse were black. See PCA, Alms House, Admission Book, 1812–13. The absence of segregation early in the century is clear in PCA, Alms House, Department and Ward Census, 1807. For quote, see PCA, MGP, 3 March 1820. On the institution of segregated wards, see PCA, MGP, 28 July 1821, 25 September 1826. On segregation in Baltimore, see Douglas Carroll, "History of the Baltimore City Hospitals," *Maryland State Medical Journal* 15 (May 1966): 85.

15. *Rules Almshouse* (1822), pp. 6, 10–12; PCA, MAHM, 23 February, 7 December 1807; 23 May 1808; 15 July, 22 July 1811; 18 December 1820; 16 October 1826; 27 August 1827; Mohl, *Poverty in New York*, p. 94; Klebaner, "Public Poor Relief in America," pp. 245–48.

16. PCA, MAHM, 26 December 1808, 24 July 1811. Quote from PCA, MGP, 26 March 1811.

17. PCA, MAHM, 22 March, 25 September, 29 September 1800; 25 March, 22 September 1801; 22 March, 25 September 1802; 5 December 1803; 23 May, 31 December 1804; 20 May 1805; 27 January, 21 July 1806; 25 May, 23 November, 7 December 1807; 23 May 1808; 21 May 1810; 16 May 1825; 15 May 1826; 21 May 1827; PCA, MGP, 23 October 1819; Klebaner, "Public Poor Relief in America," pp. 162–65; Mohl, *Poverty in New York*, p. 94.

18. According to PCA, Alms House, Department and Ward Census, 1807, there were 600 inmates and eight employees. A later census made in 1826, PCA, MAHM, 25 September 1826, indicates that there were 956 inmates. In that year, there were thirteen employees. PCA, MAHM, 11 April, 15 May 1826. (I have included among employees the student doctors who lived and worked full-time in the institution, but not the attending physicians and surgeons who, on a rotating basis, visited the Almshouse for just a few hours daily.) On employment and house maintenance in eighteenth- and nineteenth-century American almshouses, see Klebaner, "Public Poor Relief in America," p. 180, and Wiberley, "Four Cities," pp. 45–46, 129–30, 194–95.

19. PCA, MGP, 28 September 1825; PCA, MAHM, Supplement, 16 February 1801; PCA, MAHM, 13 January, 24 February, 15 December 1806; 15 July, 22 July 1811; 19 April 1813; 12 February 1816; 22 January, 12 February, 19 February, 2 April, 24 December 1821; 26 September 1825; Benjamin J. Klebaner, "Poverty and its Relief in American Thought, 1815–1861," *Social Science Review* 38 (December 1966): 382–83; *Report of the Committee Appointed at the Town Meeting* (1827); table 2; Mohl, *Poverty in New York*, p. 94. Quote from Lawrence, *Philadelphia Almshouse*, p. 53.

20. *A Plan for the Government of the Alms-house* (1805); PCA, MAHM, 4 March, 10 November 1806, 2 March 1807; PCA, GP, Treasurer's "Weekly Entries," 1800–1803, 1803–9 vols.; PCA, Minutes, Manufacturing Committee hearafter referred to as MCC, 1807–9 vol.; *Aurora*, 1 August 1806, 8 November 1809. Wiberley found that in the eighteenth century, the same sorts of products were manufactured in the almshouse by inmates and some hired weavers; see his "Four Cities," pp. 115–17.

21. *Freeman's Journal*, 3 February 1809 and article signed "Reality," *Freeman's Journal*, 24 February 1809; *Poulson's*, 19 February, 19 November 1812; Pennsylvania House of Representatives, *Journal*, 1808–9, 463, 562, 580–81; 1809–10, 37, 165–66, 330–31; 1810–11, 389, 402, 566–67; PCA, MAHM, 22 July, 23 September, 2 December 1811; 13 January 1812; 23 October 1815; 20 May 1816.

22. Outdoor spinning ended in 1826. See Klebaner, "Home Relief," p. 414. See the accounts of the guardians printed in the following newspapers for the amount of manufactured goods they sold as well as the value of items made in the factory and consumed in the house: *Aurora*, 29 November 1817, 24 September 1818, 25 October 1819; *Poulson's*, 17 October 1820, 22 May 1822; *Philadelphia Gazette*, 6 November 1824, 20 December 1825, 7 November 1826, 2 November 1827, 13 January 1832, *The Pennsylvanian*, 7 December 1837. On work relief in periods of depression, see Piven and Cloward, *Regulating the Poor*, pp. 22–26, 61–66, 88–100.

23. On eighteenth-century almshouse manufacturing, see Nash, *The Urban Crucible*, pp. 188–93, 332–37, and Wiberley, "Four Cities," pp. 103, 109, 115, and Klebaner, "Public Poor Relief in America," pp. 126–28, 176. PCA, MAHM, 11 March, 18 April, 20 October, 16 December 1823; 21 November 1825; 11 January 1827; PCA, MGP, 15 June, 22 June 1829; 9 August 1830; 12 November 1832; 31 March 1834. On the use of the tread wheel in New York, see Schneider, *Public Welfare in New York State*, pp. 152–55.

24. Average computed from figures in appendix 2.

25. Mohl, *Poverty in New York*, p. 97; Wiberley, "Four Cities," pp. 38–39; Thomas G. Morton, *The History of the Pennsylvania Hospital, 1751–1895* (Philadelphia: Times Printing House, 1895), pp. 440–42, 461, 457, 480; Lawrence, *Philadelphia Almshouse*, p. 43; PCA, MAHM, 15 November 1802; 21 March, 28 July, 8 September 1803; 9 January, 2 April 1804; 14 January, 18 November, 5 December 1805; 9 May, 16 May, 8 August 1808; 1 May 1809; 15 January, 19 November 1810; 6 May 1811; 19 December 1814; 12 April 1819; 30 July, 13 August, 20 August 1821; 21 March, 18 April 1825; 11 April 1826; PCA, Guardians of the Poor, Board of Physicians Minutes (hereafter referred to as MBP), 4 March 1822.

26. PCA, MAHM, 3 September 1804; 23 November 1807; 15 January, 15 April 1816; 24 July, 28 July, 4 August, 18 October, 27 October 1817; 10 December, 24 December 1821; 17 November, 22 December 1823; 19 April 1824; 11 April 1826; 27 August 1827; 10 November 1828; PCA, MBP, 3 July 1835; Guardians of the Poor, *Reply to the Grand Jury* (1849), p. 10.

27. This description of Blockley is taken from Lawrence, *Philadelphia Almshouse*, pp. 135–37; *Hazard's Register*, 16:302–4; *A Guide to the Lions of Philadelphia* (Philadelphia: Thomas T. Ash, 1837), pp. 72–74; PCA, MGP, 12 June 1848.

28. PCA, Guardians of the Poor, Minutes, Hospital Committee (hereafter referred to as MHC), 28 July 1847; PCA, MGP, 19 December 1842, 17 February 1845, 17 September 1849.

29. Guardians of the Poor, *Reply to Grand Jury* (1849), pp. 3–6.

30. Douglas Carroll, "History of the Baltimore City Hospitals," *Maryland State Medical Journal* 15 (April 1966): 65; Mohl, *Poverty in New York*, pp. 84–86.

31. There are very few comments on individual poor people in the minutes of the guardians after 1835, and the one extant account of life in Blockley by a former inmate contains no mention of the guardians of the poor. See Andrew Caffrey, *A Sketch of Blockley Poor-House Hospital About Twelve Years Ago* (1856–61?).

32. No census of the period lists a married ward. On personal belongings, clothes, and leaves, see Caffrey, *Sketch of Blockley; Rules, Board of Guardians, 1843*, pp. 33–34, 51; PCA, MAHC, 10 November 1841; *Public Ledger*, 31 August, 19 October 1843.

33. PCA, MHC, 29 June 1842 and PCA, MGP, 27 October 1834; *Rules, Board of Guardians, 1843*, pp. 54, 62; HSP, Philadelphia Alms-House Statistics, 1837.

34. On arrangement of the wards, see *Guide to the Lions of Philadelphia*, p. 73, and Lawrence, *Philadelphia Almshouse*, p. 136. On diet, see PCA, MGP, 16 April 1849; PCA, MAHC, 28 June 1837; Philadelphia Board of Health, *Statistics of Cholera . . .*, p. 58.

35. For details of the almshouse sample, see n. 56. On hospital procedures and wards, see PCA, MHC, 5 May, 12 May, 19 May, 16 June 1847; 14 June 1848; Smith, *Philadelphia As It Is in 1852*, p. 262; *Hazard's Register*, 16:304; *Report of Robert K. Smith, Chief Resident Physician of the Philadelphia Hospital and Lunatic Asylum* (Philadelphia: Crissy and Markley,

1856), p. 27; *Rules, Board of Guardians, 1843*, pp. 53, 58–64.

36. On moral treatment, see Rothman, *Discovery of the Asylum*, pp. 130–54; Gerald Grob, *The State and the Mentally Ill, A History of the Worcester State Hospital in Massachusetts, 1830–1920* (Chapel Hill: University of North Carolina Press, 1966); Norman Dain, *Concepts of Insanity in the United States, 1789–1965* (New Brunswick: N.J. Rutgers University Press, 1964). Quotes are from PCA, MBP, 9 September 1840; and PCA, MGP, 18 June 1849.

37. "The Insane Poor of Philadelphia," *Journal of Prison Discipline and Philanthropy* 1 (April 1845): 180; *Report on Warming and Ventilating the West Half of the Lunatic Asylum (Female Department) of Blockley Almshouse, Philadelphia, by Birkinbrine, Martin, and Trotter* (Philadelphia, 1850); PCA, MGP, 30 March 1829.

38. PCA, MGP, 9 September 1840; Dorothea Dix, *Memorial Soliciting a State Hospital for the Insane* (Philadelphia: Issac Ashmead, 1845), pp. 41–43; *Public Ledger*, 24 October, 30 November 1844; 3 June, 9 July, 19 August, 6 October 1845; 26 March 1847; *An Appeal to the People of Pennsylvania on the Subject of an Asylum for the Insane Poor of the Commonwealth* (Philadelphia, 1838), p. 12; "Insane Poor of Philadelphia," pp. 180–81; PCA, MGP, 19 March 1849.

39. PCA, MGP, 30 March, 21 September 1846, 31 January 1848, 9 April 1849; PCA, MHC, 8 January, 15 January 1845; 24 March 1847; 20 April 1849; PCA, MAHC, 22 July, 24 July, 28 October 1846; *Public Ledger*, 20 March, 1 December 1846. For the superior classification methods used in other mental hospitals of the day, see Rothman, *Discovery of the Asylum*, pp. 147–48.

40. First quote, PCA, MGP, 18 June 1849, and last quote, MBP, 9 September 1840. See also PCA, MGP, 24 March, 14 April 1845; 8 May, 25 September 1848; 19 March, 26 March, 16 April, 10 September, 17 September 1849; 14 June 1850; PCA, MHC, 20 January 1847; Guardians of the Poor, *Reply to the Grand Jury* (1849), pp. 9–11; Reverend Edward C. Jones, *An Account of the Mission in the Insane Department and Children's Asylum of Blockley Almshouse, Philadelphia* (Philadelphia: King and Baird, 1855), pp. 2–3, 6.

41. On movement inside Blockley, see *Hazard's Register*, 16:302, 304, and *Guide to the Lions of Philadelphia*, p. 73, and Caffrey, *Sketch of Blockley*. On Campbell, see PCA, MAHC, 24 July 1846.

42. Guardians of the Poor, *Reply to Grand Jury* (1849), p. 11.

43. The almshouse census in PCA, MGP, 21 October 1839, indicates that there were 1673 inmates; there were probably nineteen employees then. See *Rules, Board of Guardians, 1843*, pp. 44–52, 61. The census made in 1848, PCA, MGP, 12 June 1848, indicates that there were 1558 people in the almshouse at that time; there were then eighteen employees. See *Rules, Board of Guardians, 1843*, pp. 44–52, and PCA, MGP, 15 September 1845. (As before, I have included student doctors, and by 1848, the chief resident physician, among employees, but not attending physicians and surgeons.)

44. PCA, MGP, 2 August 1841; 23 February, 23 March 1846; PCA, MAHC, 1848, 1849 passim; Caffrey, *Sketch of Blockley*; *Public Ledger*, 11 March 1844.

45. PCA, MGP, 8 November 1847; 14 August 1848; 23 April, 17 September 1849; PCA, MAHC, 12 May 1848; Caffrey, *Sketch of Blockley*. Nancy Tomes also found in her study of the Pennsylvania Hospital for the Insane, much "irregularity and spontaneity of behavior." See "The Pervasive Institution: Thomas Story Kirkbride and the Art of Asylum-Keeping, 1841–1883" (Ph.D. diss., University of Pennsylvania, 1978), p. 291.

46. The consistent success of the farm as well as the failure of the factory are evident from accounts by the guardians; see *The Pennsylvanian*, 7 December 1837, 21 March 1838; *U.S. Gazette*, 17 November 1838; *Pennsylvania Inquirer*, 14 October 1839; and *Auditors Reports of the Accounts of Blockley Alms-House, 1841, 1843, 1845, 1846, 1847, 1848, 1849, 1850 to 1854*. On closing the factory, see PCA, MGP, 19 December 1842: Klebaner, "Public Poor Relief in America," p. 178.

47. Dix, *Memorial Soliciting a State Hospital for the Insane*, p. 41; PCA, MGP, 19 December 1842, 17 February 1845, and PCA, MMC, 1844–54, passim; Guardians of the Poor, *Reply to Grand Jury* (1849), pp. 10–14.

48. PCA, MGP, 22 August (first two quotes); 24 October 1836 (last quote).

49. PCA, MAHC, 21 August 1835, 10 March 1848 and 1846, 1848, and 1849 entries, passim; PCA, MGP, 31 August 1840, MMC entries for 1850; *Auditors' Report of the Accounts of Blockley Alms-House, 1850–51:* Klebaner, "Public Poor Relief in America," pp. 166–68.

50. Averages computed from the almshouse's admission figures in appendix 2. Of course, 1820 was a depression year and 1850 was not. But even if we compare inmates per 1000 in the city's population in 1840 (another depression year) to 1820, in 1840 there were just 12 per 1000.

51. Quotes from Guardians of the Poor, *Reply to Grand Jury* (1849), pp. 9–11, 13–14.

52. Quote from *Public Ledger*, 27 September 1847; see also 9 July 1845. PCA, MBP, 1 July 1845. Beginning in 1848, guardians no longer paid salaries to the consulting doctors but instead paid them $5.00 a visit. PCA, MGP, 17 January 1848.

53. PCA, MGP, 21 July 1845.

54. The first chief resident physician was Dr. Henry S. Patterson, whom the Guardians found unsatisfactory, because he divided his time between the almshouse and the medical department of the University of Pennsylvania, where he was an instructor. He resigned, and the guardians appointed Dr. Nathan Benedict in his place in 1846. Dr. Benedict served until Dr. William S. Haines took over in 1849. *Public Ledger*, 8 October 1845, 5 November 1846, 27 November 1849; PCA, MGP, 12 January, 19 January 17 August 1846; 20 November 1848.

55. PCA, MGP, 30 August, 13 September, 20 September 1847; 23 October 1848; *Public Ledger*, 25 September 1847, 16 November 1848; D. Hayes Agnew, "The Medical History of the Philadelphia Almshouse" in John Welsh Croskey, *History of Blockley, A History of the Philadelphia General Hospital from its Inception, 1731–1928* (Philadelphia: F. A. Davis Co., 1929), pp. 39–41.

56. The list of all people admitted in 1812–13 is in PCA, Alms House Admission Book, 1812–13. In it are listed the age, sex, color, and previous admissions of each inmate. There is no other clear, usable source of almshouse-admission data until 1828, when officials began to keep registers for male and female admittants. See PCA, Alms House Hospital, Female Register, 1828–54, and PCA, Alms House Hospital, "Men's Register," 1828–54. Despite their titles, these records contain data on all people admitted to the almshouse in these years; records are arranged alphabetically by years. For my sample of 600 (250 men, 250 women, 100 children under the age of 16), I drew names from all years and all letters of the alphabet. However, I gave appropriate extra weight to years when the most people were admitted and to letters of the alphabet under which most names fell. In making all statistical analyses, I weighted men, women, and children in relation to their actual proportions of the almshouse's population in the years studied. I have defined the young as those under 16 and the old, as those over 50. These admissions books list the same information for each inmate as is in the 1812–13 admission book as well as data on date of admission and discharge, reason for discharge, ethnicity, occupation, marital status, and state of health.

57. Descriptions of these inmates are in PCA, Alms House Admission Book, 1812–13.

58. In the 1812–13 Almshouse Admission Book, officials often left blank the column for "result," or how the inmate left the asylum. However, internal evidence suggests that they did consistently record escapes and left result blank only for inmates who were officially discharged. In other words, it was hardly necessary to record official discharges, since they were the rule, but it was necessary to record escapes, because they were the exception.

59. This disparity is not due to an increase in the actual number of venereal patients in the almshouse hospital. They occupied 5 percent of the hospital beds both in the Bettering House, 1812–13, and Blockley, 1828–50. Moreover, venereal patients did not have a great number of

previous admissions. Like the majority of inmates, 1828–50, most VD victims had never been in the institution before, and of those suffering from venereal disease who escaped, well over half had never been in the asylum before.

60. At Blockley, those people most likely to be forced to stay to work in the asylum were venereal patients and people who frequently sought readmission to the poor house. PCA, MAHC, 1837–49, passim.

61. On the 1832 cholera epidemic in the almshouse, see PCA, MGP, 30 July – 3 September 1832, passim. Figures released to the newspapers by the guardians indicate that the death rate in the old almshouse from 1804–16 was just 10 percent, and from 1818 to 1821, it was 13 percent. However, these figures are definitely understatements, for they include only those who died in hospital wards and not all who died in the institution. Given the erratic classification scheme of the almshouse at this time, ill people were often placed, and perhaps subsequently died, in other than hospital wards. The 1828–50 death rate is based on the sample drawn from all people admitted to all almshouse wards in these years. For the guardians' figures on the number who died in the almshouse between 1804 and 1821, see *Aurora*, 30 August 1805, 1 August 1806, 8 November 1809, 31 October 1810, 25 October 1819, and *Poulson's*, 19 February, 19 November 1812; 3 November 1814; 19 October 1815; 19 November 1816; 17 October 1820; 22 May 1822.

62. Statistics on the cholera epidemic of 1849 in Blockley can be found in PCA, MGP, 24 December 1849.

63. Baltimore, Trustees for the Poor of Baltimore City and County, *Report of the Trustees for the Poor of Baltimore City and County to the Mayor and City Council for the Year Ending 31 December 1849* (Baltimore: James Lucas, 1850), table *C*, p. 11.

64. PCA, Alms House Hospital, "Men's Register," 1828–34 vol. under letter *L*, entry for 11 November 1830, and PCA, Alms House Hospital, Female Register, 1848–54 vol. under letter *W*, entry from 2 March 1850.

65. Klips, "Institutionalizing the Poor: The New York City Almshouse," pp. 159–64.

66. PCA, Alms House Hospital, "Men's Register," 1834–36 vol. under letter *J*, entries for 5 March 1830 and 27 July 1833.

67. Douglas Carroll, "History of the Baltimore City Hospitals," *Maryland State Medical Journal* 15 (April 1966): 67, and Klips, "Institutionalizing the Poor: The New York City Almshouse," p. 179.

68. Douglas Carroll, "History of the Baltimore City Hospitals," *Maryland State Medical Journal* 15 (January 1966): figure 2, 89; Louis J. Piccarello, "Social Structure and Public Welfare Policy in Danvers, Massachusetts: 1750–1850." Paper delivered at November 1980 meeting of Social Science History Association.

69. Ibid. Piccarello did find that in the late eighteenth and early nineteenth centuries when Danvers was still an agricultural community, most almshouse inmates were very young or very old and they did stay for long periods of time in the poorhouse. He found that once shoemaking came to Danvers, it attracted large numbers of migrants who could not always find work. Most were able-bodied men in the middle years of their lives who ended up in the almshouse for short periods of time between jobs. Of course, Philadelphia and Baltimore were not agricultural communities even in the late eighteenth century; they, like Danvers later on, were magnets for foreign and native migrants who could not always find work and subsequently entered the almshouse for short stays. There is some indication that before the upheavals of the Seven Years' War in the 1760s, the Philadelphia Almshouse did accommodate more elderly and helpless people than it did later. See Nash, "Poverty and Poor Relief," p. 12.

70. PCA, Alms House Hospital, "Men's Register," 1836–43 vol. under letter *Mc*, entry for 27 September 1839; PCA Alms House Hospital, Female Register, 1828–35 vol. under letter *C*, entry for 4 December 1832; PCA, Alms House Hospital, Female Register, 1835–42 vol. under

letter *C*, entry for 31 January 1840; PCA, Alms House Hospital, "Men's Register," 1843–47 vol. under letter *R*, entry for 23 November 1846; PCA, Alms House Hospital, "Men's Register," 1828–34 vol. under letter *B*, entry for 3 November 1829; PCA, Alms House Hospital, Female Register, 1828–35 vol. under letter *A*, entry for 27 July 1829; PCA, Alms House Hospital, "Men's Register," 1836–43 vol. under letter *G*, entry for 2 April 1838.

71. The other low-paying jobs included mariner, weaver, shoe and leather worker, porter, textile worker, waterman, waiter, metal worker and peddler. Almost all who were not in this low-wage category were artisans of some sort. Given the marital status of most almshouse inmates, it is not surprising to find that most were childless.

72. *Appeal on Behalf of the Sick* (Philadelphia: Lindsay and Blakiston, 1851), p. 21; PCA, Alms House Hospital, "Men's Register," 1828–34 vol. under *B*, entry for 20 January 1831, and in 1836–43 vol. under letter *R*, entry for 18 January 1837. For another composite picture of a somewhat different inmate population in this era, see Tomes, "The Pervasive Institution," pp. 45–50, 238–55.

Chapter 5. Children and Welfare

1. Rothman, *Discovery of the Asylum*, pp. 206–10; Homer Folks, *The Care of Destitute, Neglected, and Delinquent Children* (New York: 1902; reprint ed., New York: Johnson Reprint Corp., 1970), pp. 12–42; Trattner, *From Poor Law to Welfare State.*

2. New York City charities included the Society for the Relief of Poor Widows with Small Children, the Orphan Asylum, and the Roman Catholic Orphan Asylum. Baltimore charities included the Baltimore Orphan Asylum, St. Mary's Female Orphan Asylum, and St. Paul's Orphan Asylum. Boston charities were the Boston Female Asylum and the Boston Asylum for Indigent Boys. Mohl, *Poverty in New York*, pp. 148–49, and Folks, *The Care of Destitute Children*, p. 52.

3. On St. Joseph's, see Kerlin, *Catholicity in Philadelphia*, pp. 192–93. On the Orphan Asylum, see Pendleton, "The Influence of Evangelical Churches Upon Reform," pp. 262–64. For an explanation of Philadelphia's female charities, see chapter 6. For the figures on public poor relief, see table 2.

4. See table 1 and PCA, Guardians of the Poor, Register of Relief Recipients, 1814–15.

5. PCA, Guardians of the Poor, "Nurse Book," 1806. See chapter 4 on the almshouse's lying-in ward. On fathers and support payments, see PCA, MGP, 7 May 1801; 1 April, 28 October 1802. Family members' obligation to support their children is first stated in "An act for the Consolidation of the Poor Laws, 1803" in Pennsylvania, *Statutes at Large* (1802–5), 17:407–9.

6. PCA, Alms House, Department and Ward Census, 1807.

7. Ibid. and PCA, MAHM, 9 June, 29 September 1806; 14 August 1820; 29 January, 2 April 1821; 23 October 1826; PCA, MGP, 21 June 1808, 23 February 1822; Mohl, *Poverty in New York*, pp. 93, 98. Quote from PCA, MAHM, 22 December 1815.

8. PCA, MGP, 15 February 1820, 30 August 1826; quote from Philadelphia Guardians of the Poor, *Report of the Committee to Visit Other Cities* (1827), p. 29. On reductions in cash relief made by female charities, see chapter 6.

9. Outdoor cash aid was restored in Philadelphia in the 1840s, but there is no record that any of it went to poor children. Instead, it seems to have gone largely to single, indigent widows. PCA, MGP, 31 May 1841, 2 March 1846 and *Auditors Reports of the Accounts of Blockley Alms-House*, 1845–54.

10. Teeters, "Early Days of the House of Refuge," 166–73.

11. Scharf and Westcott, *History of Philadelphia*, 2:1455, 1483; *Poulson's*, 3 November 1824. There is one other asylum founded in this era that I have not included in this list of

children's charities. It is the Pennsylvania Institution for the Deaf and Dumb founded in 1821. The asylum was actually funded by the state, and because it admitted handicapped children from all social classes, I do not think it should be classed as an asylum for indigent children. See Pendleton, "The Influence of Evangelical Churches Upon Reform," pp. 265–67.

12. PCA, MGP, 23 February 1822.

13. PCA, MGP, 12 March, 16 March, 23 March, 6 April, 7 May, 18 May 1819; 18 April 1820. At the same time (in the 1820s), when children were being segregated by race in Philadelphia's public institutions, so, too, were adult paupers; see chapter 4. On public institutions for poor children in other cities, see Folks, *The Care of Destitute Children*, p. 16, and Klebaner, "Public Poor Relief in America," pp. 213–14.

14. PCA, Guardians of the Poor, Children's Asylum Register, 1820–33. Note also that many children in the almshouse were ineligible for admission to the children's asylum, because they were either too old, ill, or nonwhite.

15. Quote from PCA, MGP, 12 March 1819. See also PCA, Minutes, Children's Asylum Committee (hereafter referred to as MCA), 12 April 1820; 23 January, 6 March, 19 June, 6 October 1821; 26 March 1822; 10 February, 17 February, 17 March, 22 December 1823; 12 February, 1 April, 3 May, 17 May 1824; 10 February, 4 April, 20 May, 11 July 1825; 15 May 1826; 1 October 1828.

16. PCA, MCA, 28 April 1820; 23 January, 9 February 1826; 19 February 1827; PCA, MGP, 19 November 1822, 6 September 1826, 21 May 1828, 29 August 1827; *Poulson's*, 28 July 1827; *Hazard's Register*, 5:345. From 1829, there was no resident student in the children's asylum either. PCA, MCA, 23 January 1833.

17. Quote from PCA, MCA, 19 March 1822. See also PCA, MGP, 12 January, 2 February 1825.

18. PCA, MCA, 23 January, 23 October 1821; 14 April 1823; 21 March 1825; Teeters, "The Early Days of the House of Refuge," p. 171.

19. *Hazard's Register*, 5:345–46. Quotes from PCA, MGP, 24 May 1822. See also PCA, MCA, 9 January 1821; 19 March, 26 March 1822; 12 May, 16 December 1823; PCA, MGP, 12 May 1820, 12 May 1824, 6 September 1826. Teeters, "The Early Days of the House of Refuge," pp. 173–81. On discipline and routine in other children's institutions of the era, see Rothman, *Discovery of the Asylum*, pp. 206–36.

20. Of the remainder, 15 percent were still in the institution; 4 percent had been discharged; 5 percent died; and 3 percent escaped. PCA, MGP, 6 September 1826. On parental objections to public indenturing, see Philadelphia Society for the Promotion of Public Economy, *Report of the Library Committee*, 1817, p. 21.

21. PCA, MGP, 28 May 1827; Pennsylvania, *Laws of the Commonwealth*, 1828, 10:82.

22. PCA, MCA, 17 December 1828; 12 May 1830.

23. PCA, MGP, 1 December 1834. After 1834, Bostonians, like Philadelphians, cared for youngsters in separate buildings adjacent to the house of industry, which was located first in South Boston and later on Deer Island. Baltimore did not establish a separate public asylum for poor youngsters but accommodated them inside the city's almshouse alongside adult paupers. On the other hand, Charleston's children's asylum did remain distinct from its almshouse. Folks, *The Care of Destitute Children*, pp. 16, 19–20, 30–33.

24. PCA, Alms House, "Men's Register," 1836–43 vol. under letter *Mc* entry for 5 October 1840; PCA, Alms House, Female Register, 1835–42 vol. under letter *R*, entry for 21 October 1839; PCA, Alms House, "Men's Register," 1843–47 vol. under letter *L*, entry for 7 May 1844, and under letter *S*, entry for 6 February 1844.

25. Figures on the racial and ethnic composition of the almshouse population are drawn from a sample of that population described in chapter 4.

26. Martha Dungan was hired in 1825 and served as matron of both the children's asylum and the women's almshouse from 1841–43. When she departed, Eliza Mathews, and later

Anne Robinson, succeeded her as head of the children's asylum. PCA, MCA, 20 May 1825; MGP, 1 November 1841, 4 September 1843, 24 June 1844, 13 September 1847, 28 October 1850. Quotes from *Guide to the Lions of Philadelphia*, p. 74. On Murray, see PCA, MCA, 1 August 1832.

27. *Hazard's Register*, 11:333, 16:303. Quote from *Public Ledger*, 30 May 1845.

28. First and last quotes from PCA, MGP, 27 April 1835. See also PCA, MGP, 4 May 1835, 12 July 1841; *Public Ledger*, 9 March 1849.

29. Dix, *Memorial Soliciting a State Hospital for the Insane*, p. 41; PCA, MAHC, 19 January, 26 January 1849.

30. In this analysis, I have not included the number of youngsters who lived in families that received an occasional load of wood from public authorities or a visit from a doctor, because such forms of aid were so minimal in comparison to cash pensions or institutionalization.

31. *The Laws Relating to the Relief and Employment of the Poor in the City of Philadelphia, the District of Southwark, and the Townships of Northern Liberties and Penn* (Philadelphia: Thomas Kite, 1828), p. 20. (Section 15 of 1828 poor law.)

32. Klebaner, "Public Poor Relief in America," pp. 215–16. Unless otherwise noted, the information on indentures that follows is based on the records of all children indentured in 1805, 1810, 1820, 1828, 1840, and 1850. See PCA, Guardians of the Poor, Indentures Made, vols. for 1804–12, 1819–25, 1825–28, 1837–49, 1850–74.

33. Catherine Catharell's records are in PCA, GP, Indentures Made, 1804–12, vol.

34. PCA, GP, Indentures Made, 1850–74 vol.

35. Curtis P. Nettels, *The Emergence of a National Economy, 1775–1815* (New York: Holt, Rinehart and Winston, 1962), p. 266; David Montgomery, "The Working Classes of the Pre-Industrial City, 1780–1830," *Labor History* 9 (Winter 1968): 6–7; Carl F. Kaestle, *The Evolution of an Urban School System, New York City, 1750–1850* (Cambridge: Harvard University Press, 1873), p. 97; Sharon V. Salinger, "Colonial Labor in Transition: The Decline of Indentured Servitude in Late Eighteenth Century Philadelphia," *Labor History* 22 (Spring 1981): 165–91.

36. *Hazard's Register*, 11:332; PCA, MGP, 27 May 1839, 17 May 1841; PCA, GP, Register, Children's Asylum, entries for 17 May 1848–17 May 1849 in 1848–52 vol.

37. Figures for Boston are in *Annual Report of the Directors of the Houses of Industry and Reformation, 1856* (Boston: Geo. C. Rand, Avery, 1856), p. 23, and Folks, *The Care of Destitute Children*, p. 32. Figures for Baltimore are in Trustees for the Poor of Baltimore City and County, *Report, 1849*, table C, p. 11. Figures for New York are in Klips, "Institutionalizing the Poor: The New York City Almshouse," pp. 159–61.

38. St. Joseph's (Catholic) and the Orphan Asylum (Protestant) were the two agencies for children in Philadelphia in 1820. By 1830, they were joined by the House of Refuge, the Shelter for Colored Orphans, and St. John's Orphan Asylum. By 1850, there were these five children's agencies plus Girard College, the Southern Home for Destitute Children, and the Foster Home Association. In 1833, the Pennsylvania Institution for the Blind was opened in Philadelphia, and it admitted children between seven and sixteen. However, it was funded by the state, in large part, and admitted blind children whether or not they were poor, so I have not included it in this list of private charities for indigent youngsters. See Pendleton, "The Influence of Evangelical Churches Upon Reform," pp. 268–69.

39. On St. John's, St. Joseph's, Girard College, the Orphan Asylum, and the Shelter for Colored Orphans, see Smith, *Philadelphia As It Is in 1852*, pp. 119–31, 272–76. House of Refuge, *Twenty-Second Annual Report* (Philadelphia: T. K. and P. G. Collins, 1851); Moyamensing Union School and Children's Home, *First and Second Annual Reports*. The Foster Home Association was the same as the Temporary Home Association, which provided a temporary home for unemployed women seeking work (see chapter 6). *Public Ledger*, 10 December 1850.

40. St. Joseph's and St. John's indentured perhaps six children a year. St. Joseph's Orphan Asylum, *Annual Report, 1850–51* and St. John's Orphan Asylum, *Annual Reports, 1845, 1850*. Girard College, *Fourth Annual Report* (Philadelphia: Crissy and Markley, 1852). The Orphan Asylum indentured on the average about ten children a year in the 1840s. Orphan Asylum, *Twenty-Fifth* through *Thirty-Sixth Annual Reports* (Philadelphia: Lydia R. Bailey, 1840–51). House of Refuge, *Twelfth* through *Twenty-Second Annual Reports* (Philadelphia: E. G. Dorsey, 1840–45; by contributors, 1846; T. K. and P. G. Collins, 1847–50).

41. New York charities were Society for the Relief of Widows and Small Children (1797), Orphan Asylum Society (1806), Roman Catholic Orphan Asylum (1817), House of Refuge (1824), Leake and Watts Orphan Asylum (1831), Society for Half Orphan and Destitute Children (1835), Colored Orphan Asylum (1836), Institution of Mercy (1846), Society for the Relief of Destitute Children of Seamen (1846), the Five Points House of Industry (1850). Boston charities were Boston Female Orphan Asylum (1800), the Boston Asylum for Indigent Boys (1813), House of Reformation (1826), St. Vincent's Orphan Asylum (1831), Farm School Society (1832), Children's Friend Society (1833), Infant School and Children's Home Association (1833), Nickerson Home (1835), Temporary Home for the Destitute (1847), Children's Mission to the Children of the Destitute (1849). Baltimore charities were St. Paul's Orphanage (1799), the Orphan Asylum (1807), St. Mary's Female Orphan Asylum (1817), St. Vincent de Paul Male Orphan Asylum (1840), Christ Church Asylum for Female Children (1840), St. Peter's Asylum (1845), Manual Labor School for Indigent Boys (1845), St. Patrick's Orphan Asylum (1848), House of Refuge (1849). Folks, *The Care of Destitute Children*, pp. 52–53.

Chapter 6. The Private-Welfare System

1. David Owen, *English Philanthropy, 1600–1960* (Cambridge: Harvard University Press, 1964); M. H. Heale, "Patterns of Benevolence: Charity and Morality in Rural and Urban New York, 1783–1830," *Societas—A Review of Social History* 3 (Autumn 1973): 341. Although in this chapter I discuss only charities designed primarily to aid adults, in computing the number of charities in the city and the amounts spent by all, I have included charities for children as well.

2. James, *A People among Peoples*, pp. 46–50; Alexander, *Render Them Submissive*, p. 128; David S. Forsythe, "Friends' Almshouse in Philadelphia," *Bulletin of Friends Historical Association* 16 (Spring 1927): 22.

3. Benjamin Dorr, *An Historical Account of Christ Church, Philadelphia from Its Foundation, A.D. 1695 to A.D. 1841* (Philadelphia: Burns and Sieg, 1859), pp. 335–36; Alexander, *Render Them Submissive*, pp. 128–29.

4. HSP, Collections of the Genealogical Society of Pennsylvania, vol. 297, "First Baptist Church Philadelphia, vol. 2, Minutes, 1760–1850," passim.

5. Alexander, *Render Them Submissive*, pp. 125, 129; Scharf and Westcott, *History of Philadelphia*, 2:1464–68; Mease, *Picture of Philadelphia*, pp. 280, 285–86; HSP, Hibernian Society, Minute Book, 1813–1852; John Hugh Campbell, *History of the Friendly Sons of St. Patrick and of the Hibernian Society for the Relief of Emigrants from Ireland, March 17, 1771–March 17, 1892* (Philadelphia: Hibernian Society, 1892), p. 155; HSP, Welsh Society of Pennsylvania, Minute Book for 1798–1839; Scots Thistle Society of Philadelphia, *Constitution of the Scots Thistle Society of Philadelphia* (Philadelphia: John Bioren, 1799), pp. 15–16; Harry W. Pfund, *A History of the German Society of Pennsylvania, Bicentenary Edition, 1764–1964*, 2d rev. ed. (Philadelphia: German Society of Pennsylvania, 1964), pp. 8, 26; Society of the Sons of St. George, Philadelphia, *History of the Society of the Sons of St. George, Philadelphia* (Philadelphia: Theodore C. Knauff, 1923), pp. 32–37.

6. Alexander, *Render Them Submissive*, p. 124; Mease, *Picture of Philadelphia*, pp. 267–73; HSP, Society for the Relief of Poor and Distressed Masters of Ships, Their Widows and Children, Minute Book, 1806–16. There were also special mutual benefit societies formed by blacks. See DuBois, *Philadelphia Negro*, pp. 23, 222. On mutual benefit societies in New York, see Heale, "Patterns of Benevolence, " p. 341.

7. Alexander, *Render Them Submissive*, pp. 137–39; Margaret H. Bacon, *History of the Pennsylvania Society for Promoting the Abolition of Slavery; the Relief of Free Negroes unlawfully held in Bondage; and for Improving the Condition of the African Race* (Philadelphia: Pennsylvania, Abolition Society, 1959), pp. 6–7, 10. On New York charities for blacks, see Carroll Smith-Rosenberg, *Religion and the Rise of the American City; The New York City Mission Movement, 1812–1870* (Ithaca: Cornell University Press, 1971), pp. 27, 44, 93–94, 137.

8. Keith Melder, "Ladies Bountiful: Organized Women's Benevolence in Early Nineteenth Century America," *New York History* 48 (1967): 232–34, 237–38.

9. Pendleton, "Influence of Evangelical Churches upon Reform," p. 276; Female Society of Philadelphia for the Relief and Employment of the Poor, *Report* (1871), pp. 4–10.

10. Female Association of Philadelphia for the Relief of Women and Children in Reduced Circumstances, *Report, January 1st, 1803* (bound with *Constitution*, Philadelphia: Jane Aitken, 1803), pp. 12–18; *History of the Female Association of Philadelphia for the Relief of Women and Children in Reduced Circumstances* (Philadelphia, 1965), pp. 3–15.

11. Female Hospitable Society of Philadelphia, *Articles of Association and Reports, 1808–1830*, pp. 5–51; Mease, *Picture of Philadelphia*, p. 249; Pendleton, "Influence of Evangelical Churches upon Reform," pp. 277–78.

12. Quote from Magdalen Society of Philadelphia, *Constitution of the Magdalen Society of Philadelphia* (Philadelphia, 1809), pp. 3–6; Pendleton, "Influence of Evangelical Churches upon Reform," pp. 270–71; Magdalen Society, *Report, 1847* (Philadelphia: Jos. Rakestraw, 1848); *Freeman's Journal*, 2 December 1807.

13. Smith-Rosenberg, *Religion and the Rise of the American City*, pp. 27, 44; Huggins, *Protestants against Poverty*, pp. 83–110; Morton, *Pennsylvania Hospital*, pp. 440–41; Mease, *Picture of Philadelphia*, pp. 235, 229; Williams, *America's First Hospital*, pp. 132, 134–36, 290–91.

14. Rosenberg, "Social Class and Medical Care," pp. 32–36, 40; *Gazette of the United States*, 24 December 1802; Smith, *Philadelphia As It Is in 1852*, p. 268. In 1837, the Philadelphia Dispensary added an obstetric department and later cooperated with a lying-in and nurse charity to attend poor pregnant women in their own homes. Philadelphia Lying-In Charity and Nurse Society, *Report, 1851* (Philadelphia: Jos. Rakestraw, 1852).

15. *Friends' Asylum for the Insane, 1813–1913; A Descriptive Account from its Foundation, List of Managers and Officers from the Beginning, Facts and Events in its History, with Appendix* (Philadelphia: J. C. Winston Co., 1913), pp. 13–17, 66–72.

16. On Rush, see N. G. Goodman, *Benjamin Rush, Physician and Citizen, 1746–1813* (Philadelphia, 1934). On Girard, see John B. McMaster, *The Life and Times of Stephen Girard, Mariner and Merchant* (Philadelphia: Lippincott, 1918). An occupational analysis for the years 1800–1820 of leaders of the following charities indicates that over one-third were merchants and most of the rest were lawyers, doctors or prosperous artisans: French Benevolent Society, German Society, Philadelphia Dispensary, Scots Thistle Society, St. George's Society, St. Andrews' Society, Hibernian Society, Abolition Society, Methodist-Episcopal Benevolent Society, Magdalen Society, Pennsylvania Hospital, St. Joseph's Orphan Asylum, Welsh Society.

17. For the managers of the Pennsylvania Hospital, see Morton, *Pennsylvania Hospital*, pp. 405–6; PCA, MAHM, 14 May 1804; 14 January 1805; 15 November, 22 November 1813; 12 December 1814; 15 May, 26 June 1815.

18. On the relations between public and private welfare in other cities, see Klebaner, "Public Poor Relief in America," pp. 473, 476–79. Female Association for the Relief of Women and Children in Reduced Circumstances, *History* (1965), p. 9; PCA, MGP, 3 January 1809, 18 December 1810, 5 February 1811, 29 December 1812, 14 December 1813, 27 December 1814, 23 January 1816, 7 February 1817. HSP, Magdalen Society Papers, Minutes, Board of Managers, 1801–10 vol: 74, 89, 91, 98–99, 112, 126, 131, 149, 156, 163, 164, 167.

19. Female Society of Philadelphia for the Relief and Employment of the Poor, *Report* (1871), p. 3; *The Nature and Design of the Hospitable Society*, p. 9.

20. In addition to the relief in kind provided by the city's major charities, there was also some free food distributed by a small soup society in 1803 and some free wood handed out by a small charity called the Fund for Supplying the Necessitous Poor of the City of Philadelphia with Fuel. Alexander, *Render Them Submissive*, pp. 124–25; Mease, *Picture of Philadelphia*, pp. 340–41.

21. Female Hospitable Society, *Reports* (1831), p. 6; Female Association for the Relief of Women and Children in Reduced Circumstances, *Report, 1803*, p. 13, and *Constitution, 1801*, p. 11; Female Society for the Relief and Employment of the Poor, *Constitution, By-Laws, and Rules, 1815* (Philadelphia: Jos. Rakestraw, 1836), p. 12; Magdalen Society of Philadelphia, *To The Members* (Philadelphia, ca. 1818), p. 3.

22. Female Association for the Relief of Women and Children in Reduced Circumstances, *Report, 1803*, p. 17; Female Society for the Relief and Employment of the Poor, *Report* (1871), p. 3; HSP, Minutes of the Magdalen Society, 1801–17, passim.

23. For some charities, financial records for 1810 were unavailable, so I used records for the next closest year. Mease, *Picture of Philadelphia*, pp. 239, 246, 286 (Philadelphia Dispensary, Magdalen Asylum, Scots Thistle Society); Female Hospitable Society, *Report* (1831), p. 12; HSP, Society for the Relief of Poor and Distressed Masters of Ships, Their Widows and Children, Minute Book, 4 April 1811; Female Association for the Relief of Women and Children in Reduced Circumstances, *Report, 1803* (Philadelphia: Jane Aiken, 1803), p. 14, figure for 1802–3; *Centennial History of St. Joseph's Orphan Asylum, 1814–1914* (Philadelphia, 1914), p. 17, figure for 1814; HSP, Minute Book of the Welsh Society, 2 March 1801, figure for 1800; Scharf and Westcott, *History of Philadelphia*, 2:1467, has an average of the dollars spent by the Society of the Sons of St. George for 1813–21. The five charities for which there is no financial record for 1810 or thereabouts are the Pennsylvania Hospital, the Friends' Almshouse, Christ Church Hospital, the Female Society for the Relief and Employment of the Poor, and the Abolition Society. For the amounts spent by public authorities in 1810, see appendix 1.

24. It is very difficult to measure how many people were assisted by private charities, because few lists of recipients of aid from these agencies are extant. My best guess is that private charities may have, throughout the first half of the nineteenth century, annually cared for more poor than did public-welfare officials, but the amount of charity aid granted needy supplicants was, typically, extremely small—much smaller than the amount of aid (whether indoor or outdoor) commonly extended to public-relief recipients.

25. Phillip Schuyler Benjamin, "The Philadelphia Quakers in the Industrial Age, 1865–1920" (Ph.D. diss., Columbia University, 1967), p. 307. Quote from *Poulson's*, 21 January 1820. Carole Haber, "The Old Folks at Home: The Development of Institutionalized Care for the Aged in Nineteenth-Century Philadelphia," *Pennsylvania Magazine of History and Biography* 101 (April 1977): 240–45. The Indigent Widows' Asylum opened in a building on Market Street vacated by the Orphan Asylum, another charity founded by churchwomen in 1815 to help indigent children, many of them orphaned by the war (see chapter 5). Later in 1820, the asylum for the elderly moved to a new building adjacent to the Orphan Asylum on Cherry St. *Poulson's*, 21 January 1820, 18 January 1827.

26. Scharf and Westcott, *History of Philadelphia*, 2:1470–71; *Poulson's*, 13 November 1823.

27. *Philadelphia in 1824*, p. 62.

28. *Poulson's*, 12 November 1822 (Dorcas Societies); Pendleton, "The Influence of Evangelical Churches upon Reform," p. 283, and *Poulson's*, 28 January, 20 March 1824 (Provident Society).

29. Female Association for the Relief of Women and Children in Reduced Circumstances, *History* (1965), p. 15; *Poulson's*, 19 January 1828.

30. *Poulson's*, 18 January 1823 (Indigent Widows' and Single Women's Asylum), 24 February 1824 (Magdalen Asylum); Female Hospitable Society, *Twenty-Second Annual Report*, p. 49; *Poulson's*, 8 January 1820 (Orphan Asylum), 4 February 1830 (Provident Society). On the loss of subscribers, see *Poulson's*, 14 January 1821 (Female Association for the Relief of Women and Children in Reduced Circumstances), 7 January 1828 (Orphan Asylum), 24 January 1825 (Indigent Widows' and Single Women's Asylum), 25 December 1823 (Philadelphia Dispensary), 24 December 1824 (Southern Dispensary), 8 September 1823 (Northern Dispensary).

31. When records for 1825 were not available, I used the financial accounts for the next closest year and have indicated it. Since, in most cases, I used a year earlier in the decade, I may actually have overstated expenditures for 1825, because most charities spent more in the early 1820s and less as the decade progressed. *Poulson's*, 18 January 1827 (Indigent Widows' and Single Women's Asylum), 29 December 1825 (Philadelphia Dispensary), 24 December 1825 (Southern Dispensary), 20 January 1826 (Northern Dispensary), 27 March 1826 (Southern Dorcas Society), 7 January 1826 (Orphan Asylum), 12 May 1827 (Captain's Society), 20 April 1820 (Northern Soup Society; figure for 1820), 7 April 1821 (Western Charitable Association, a soup society; figure for 1821), 13 November 1823 (Southern Soup Society; figure for 1821), 24 February 1824 (Magdalen Society; figure for 1823), 14 December 1821 (Female Association for the Relief of Women and Children in Reduced Circumstances; figure for 1821); Scharf and Westcott, *History of Philadelphia*, 2:1467 (Sons of St. George; figure for 1820); *Hazard's Register*, 3:54 (Female Society for the Relief and Employment of the Poor, Shelter for Colored Orphans, St. Joseph's Orphan Asylum, Abolition Society; figures for 1828); Edwin Wolf and Maxwell Whiteman, *The History of the Jews of Philadelphia from Colonial Times to the Age of Jackson* (Philadelphia: Jewish Publication Society of America, 1957), pp. 278–79 (United Hebrew Beneficent Society; figure for 1822, when first formed to provide relief to poor Philadelphia Jews). The charities for which financial records are missing are the Pennsylvania Hospital, the Provident Society, the Friends' Almshouse, and Christ Church Hospital. For public welfare expenditures in 1825, see appendix 1.

32. *Poulson's*, 13 November 1823, 31 December 1828, 24 January 1824. Soup society and dispensary officials also enforced control by granting food or medical aid only to poor people who had been recommended by a public- or private-welfare official.

33. *Poulson's*, 19 December 1821, 28 January 1824; Carey, "Essays on the Public Charities, No. 7," *U.S. Gazette*, 19 May 1829.

34. *U.S. Gazette*, 7 May, 11 May 1829; Carey [Hamilton], "To the Public," *U.S. Gazette*, 19 May 1829; M. Carey "To the Public," *U.S. Gazette*, 22 June 1829; HSP, Simon Gratz Collection, Carey to Stephen Van Renssalaer, 21 November 1833, and 4 December 1833.

35. Smith, *Philadelphia As It Is in 1852*, pp. 263–65.

36. *Hazard's Register*, 9:8, 15:224. In 1844, the two charities merged. Philadelphia Lying-In and Nurse Charity, *Report, 1851*.

37. Benjamin, "The Philadelphia Quakers in the Industrial Age," p. 303.

38. All quotations from Paul Boyer, *Urban Masses and Moral Order in America, 1820–1920* (Cambridge: Harvard University Press, 1978), pp. 5, 89, 90.

39. *Hazard's Register*, 8:284–85, 9:278–79; Eudice Glassberg, "Philadelphians in Need: Client Experiences with two Philadelphia Benevolent Societies, 1830–1880" (Ph.D. diss., Temple University, 1979), pp. 147–87. On the New York Association for Improving the Condition of the Poor, see Boyer, *Urban Masses and Moral Order in America*, pp. 92–94.

40. Scharf and Westcott, *History of Philadelphia*, 2:1478.

41. Philadelphia Society for Bettering the Condition of the Poor, *First Annual Report* (Philadelphia: Wm. Stavely, 1830) and *Constitution* (Philadelphia: Clark and Raser, 1829); Scharf and Westcott, *History of Philadelphia*, 2:1471. On New York's city missions, see Smith–Rosenberg, *Religion and the Rise of the American City*.

42. *Hazard's Register*, 8:285. On religious charity and social control, see also Clifford S. Griffin, *The Ferment of Reform, 1830–1860* (New York: Thomas Y. Crowell, 1967); Mohl, *Poverty in New York*; Lois W. Banner, "Religious Benevolence as Social Control: A Critique of an Interpretation," *Journal of American History* 60 (June 1973): 23; and Boyer, *Urban Masses and Moral Order in America*, pp. 56–62. I agree with Banner and Boyer that a mixture of motives characterized the founders of religious charities in the antebellum period, but I do not believe that the desire of these charity leaders to exert social control over the poor was in any sense insignificant.

43. *Public Ledger*, 3 March, 22 April 1846; 21 January, 28 January, 2 February, 9 February, 27 February 30 March, 13 November 1847; 11 January, 30 December 1848; 1 January, 11 April, 21 April, 11 June 1849; 10 January, 18 April 1850; Glassberg, "Philadelphians in Need," pp. 258–76.

44. *Public Ledger*, 11 November 1841; 30 November 1843; 20 May, 9 December 1847; 30 April 1850.

45. Scharf and Westcott, *History of Philadelphia*, 2:1479; Grandom Institution, *Report, 1850* (Philadelphia: T. and G. Town, 1850).

46. St. Anne's Widow's Asylum, *Act of Incorporation, By-Laws, and Terms of Admission* (Philadelphia: L. B. Corzet, 1850); Clark, *The Irish in Philadelphia*, pp. 99, 102; *Public Ledger*, 2 December, 15 December 1848; 27 July 1849; 10 September 1850.

47. Smith, *Philadelphia As It Is in 1852*, pp. 253–55, 268–71; *Public Ledger*, 29 November, 6 December 1848.

48. Melder, "Ladies Bountiful," pp. 238–45. For an especially clear discussion of the "separate sphere," see Carl Degler, *At Odds, Women and the Family in America from the Revolution to the Present* (New York: Oxford University Press, 1980), pp. 73, 283, 302–5; *Public Ledger*, 6 December 1847; 5 May 1848; 4 January, 30 May 1849.

49. *Public Ledger*, 5 February 1847; 31 January, 4 February, 9 February 1848; 9 July 1849; 10 December 1850; Northern Association for the Relief and Employment of Poor Women, *Reports, 1846, 1848–50* (Philadelphia: T. Ellwood Chapman, 1846, 1848–50).

50. Smith, *Philadelphia As It Is in 1852*, p. 257; Edward Shippen, "Some Account of the Origin of the Naval Asylum at Philadelphia," *Pennsylvania Magazine of History and Biography* 7 (1883): 117–42.

51. *Public Ledger*, 10 March, 6 April 1848; 26 May 1849; 18 May, 8 June 1850.

52. In Boston and New York, a few charities, organized along bureaucratic lines, appeared in the 1840s and 1850s, although all continued to use unpaid volunteer visitors in addition to a few paid workers. See Baghdadi, "Protestants, Poverty, and Urban Growth," pp. 142–49.

53. Orphan Asylum, *Twenty-Sixth Annual Report* (Philadelphia: Lydia R. Bailey, 1841); Northern Dispensary, *Report, 1842* (Philadelphia: J. Richards, 1843); Female Association for the Relief of Women and Children in Reduced Circumstances, *History* (1965), p. 15; Provident Society, *Report, 1844* (Philadelphia: Jos. and Wm. Kite, 1844); Union Benevolent Association, *Report, 1840* (Philadelphia: Jos. and Wm. Kite, 1840).

54. Quotation from Boyer, *Urban Masses and Moral Reform in America*, p. 15. Boyer is describing leaders of moral-reform societies in the midnineteenth century, but his description is applicable to most of Philadelphia's charity leaders at this time. On the control of private charities by the elite in this era, see Edward Pessen, *Riches, Class, and Power before the Civil War* (Lexington, Mass.: D. C. Heath, 1973), pp. 251–68, and Glassberg, "Philadelphians in Need," pp. 154, 269–70.

55. *Public Ledger*, 11 April 1849 (Houses of Industry), 11 November 1841 (Pennsylvania Seaman's Friend Society), 9 July 1849 (Temporary Home Association); Magdalen Asylum, *Report, 1849* (Philadelphia: Issac Ashmead, 1850); Union Benevolent Association, *Report, 1849* (Philadelphia: Merrihew and Thompson, 1849).

56. When reports of expenditures for 1850 were unavailable, I used figures for the next closest year and have indicated it. *Public Ledger*, 10 December 1850 (Temporary Home Association), 9 April 1850 (Pennsylvania Institution for the Blind), 20 April 1850 (Moyamensing Soup Society), 18 April 1850 (Moyamensing House of Industry); Girard College, *Report, 1850*; Philadelphia Lying-In and Nurse Charity, *Report, 1851*; Philadelphia Dispensary, *Report, 1850* (Philadelphia: Jos. Rakestraw, 1851); Northern Association for the Relief and Employment of Poor Women, *Report, 1850*; Orphan Asylum, *Thirty-Sixth Annual Report* (Philadelphia: Lydia R. Bailey, 1851); St. John's Orphan Asylum *Report, 1850* (Philadelphia: Peter McKenna, 1851); Moyamensing Union Home and Children's Home, *First and Second Annual Reports*; Union Benevolent Association, *Report, 1850* (Philadelphia: Merihew and Thompson, 1850); Association for the Care of Colored Orphans. *Report, 1850* (Philadelphia: Jos. Rakestraw, 1851); Philadelphia City Mission, *Thirteenth through Eighteenth Annual Reports* (Philadelphia: Stavely and M'Calla, 1850), average amount spent, 1843–49; Northern Dispensary *Report, 1849* (Philadelphia: Jos. Rakestraw, 1849), figure for 1849; Female Hospitable Society, *Report, 1846* (Philadelphia: Lydia R. Bailey, 1846), figure for 1846; Female Society for the Relief and Employment of the Poor, *Report, 1840* (Philadelphia: Jos. Rakestraw, 1841), figure for 1840; *Public Ledger*, 6 April 1848 (amount spent by all immigrant-aid societies, of which there were about ten in 1847), 28 February 1850 (House of Refuge for 1849), 11 January 1850 (Indigent Widows' and Single Women's Asylum for 1849), 9 December 1847 (Female and Male Branches of the Seaman's Friend Society, 1847), 27 February 1849 (amount spent on poor patients in 1849 in the Pennsylvania Asylum for the Insane), 6 June 1849 (amount spent on poor patients in the Pennsylvania Hospital, 1848), 25 February 1847 (Pennsylvania Institution for the Deaf and Dumb, 1846), 30 May 1849 (Rosine Association, 1848), 13 November 1847 (Northern Liberties House of Industry, 1847); Magdalen Asylum, *Report, 1846* (Philadelphia: Jos. and Wm. Kite, 1847), figure for 1846. The ten charities for which accounts are missing are Wills Hospital, Friends' Almshouse, Christ Church Hospital, Home Missionary Society, Naval Asylum, St. Anne's Widow's Asylum, St. Joseph'a Hospital, the Western House of Employment, the Provident Society, and the Female Association for the Relief of Women and Children in Reduced Circumstances. For public welfare expenditures in 1850, see appendix 1.

57. PCA, MGP, 14 August 1821; 16 April, 24 May 1822; 30 September 1823; 7 January, 28 July, 13 October 1824; 18 May, 19 May, 12 October 1825; 11 January, 27 January, 12 April, 8 September 1826; 17 January, 18 April, 5 July, 26 November 1827; 16 January, 16 April 1828; 19 October 1829; 26 November, 31 December 1832; 11 July, 1 August 1836; 12 March, 9 April 1838; 17 June 1839.

58. PCA, Guardians of the Poor, Indentures Made to Girard College, 1847–48, 1848, 1849–50, 1850–53 vols.

59. Bremner, *From the Depths*, pp. 51–57; Lubove, *The Professional Altruist.*

Chapter 7. Nineteenth-Century Welfare: The Broader Perspective

1. Mohl, "The Abolition of Public Outdoor Relief," in Trattner, *Social Welfare or Social Control?*, pp. 36–39.

2. Piven and Cloward, *Regulating the Poor*, pp. 45–119. Mohl argues in the article cited in n. 1 that the contraction of public welfare in the face of massive protests by the poor in the late nineteenth century refutes the Piven and Cloward thesis. The two latter writers disagree: "We

never said, 'if mass disorder, then mass relief.' What we did say is, 'if mass relief, then mass disorder preceded.' These are quite different statements." "Humanitarianism in History: A Response to the Critics," in *Social Welfare or Social Control?*, pp. 131–36.

3. *America's Struggle against Poverty, 1900–1980* (Cambridge: Harvard University Press, 1981), pp. 38–42, 52–53, 56–57.

4. Ibid., p. 57. Piven and Cloward are less willing to see the expansion of relief as a humanitarian gesture, and this is one area in which I disagree with them. In the discussion that follows, I rely principally on Piven and Cloward and on Patterson, because they are currently the most influential interpreters of this era in welfare history. A whole book has recently been published on the Piven and Cloward thesis, and its editor acknowledges that Patterson is their most recent and trenchant critic. Trattner, *Social Welfare or Social Control?*, pp. 6–8, 156.

5. Piven and Cloward, *Regulating the Poor*, pp. 95–97.

6. Patterson, *America's Struggle against Poverty*, quotes from pp. 60, 61, 62.

7. *Regulating the Poor*, pp. 200–340.

8. *America's Struggle against Poverty*, pp. 113–14, 127–37; quote, p. 135.

9. Ibid., pp. 128–29, 133, 136, 151. First quote, p. 164; last quote, p. 151.

10. An interesting critique of Reagan's program is Piven and Cloward's *The New Class War: Reagan's Attack on the Welfare State and its Consequences* (New York: Pantheon Books, 1982).

11. On AFDC see *Congressional Digest* 57 (May, 1978): 135. On Medicaid and food stamps see U.S. Bureau of the Census, Current Population Report P60, #136, *Characteristics of Households and Persons Receiving Selected Non Cash Benefits, 1981* (Washington, D.C.: U.S. Government Printing Office, 1981), pp. 41, 20. On old age insurance see *Statistical Abstract of the United States* (Washington, D.C.: U.S. Government Printing Office, 1978), p. 341. On unemployment compensation and worker's compensation see U.S. Bureau of the Census, Consumer Income Series P60, #18, *Money Income in 1977 of Families and Persons in the United States* (Washington, D.C.: U.S. Government Printing Office, 1978), pp. 204, 206.

12. Mark H. Leff, "Consensus for Reform: The Mothers'-Pension Movement in the Progressive Era," *Social Service Review* 47 (September 1973): 397–415. Some women are also eligible for the social insurance and public aid programs previously mentioned as being accessible today to men.

13. *New York Times*, 16 April 1977, p. 30.

14. Ibid. 1977 was the first year of the previous ten in which over half of those who obtained AFDC were *not* black.

15. Food stamps first faced severe criticism when food prices rose sharply in the late 1970s and early 1980s. As people lined up to pay high bills in grocery stores, they noted with resentment their fellow shoppers who paid with food stamps. Hence, when President Reagan proposed cutting food stamps along with other welfare programs, many Americans endorsed his suggestion. So, too, did Congress. *New York Times*, 4 April 1981, p. 11; 13 May 1981, p. 28; 21 September 1981, sec. 4, p. 12.

Select Bibliography

Manuscript Sources   The most useful records to me were those in the Archives of the City and County of Philadelphia. Most are cataloged in John Daly, *Descriptive Inventory of the Archives of the City and County of Philadelphia* (Philadelphia: City of Philadelphia, 1970). For a more detailed description of city archival materials concerning the poor from the late eighteenth century to 1887, see my article, "Paupers and Public Relief Studying the Poor in Nineteenth Century Philadelphia," *News Letter, Philadelphia City Archives* 34 (June, October 1978).

In the city archives, the best source of information on Philadelphia's public welfare in the nineteenth century is undoubtedly the Minutes of the Guardians of the Poor, 1788–1887, and the Minutes of the Almshouse Managers, 1788–1828. Some years after the demise of the almshouse managers in 1828, an almshouse committee was formed, and its minutes (1837–62), though less complete than the managers', are nevertheless useful. There were four other committees concerned with various facets of the almshouse. The Board of Physicians Minutes, 1809–45, are extremely brief and sketchy, but the Hospital Committee Minutes, 1836–87, are more detailed. The Minutes of the Committee on Manufacturing, 1807–87, are largely a catalog of the number of inmates employed at various tasks. The Minutes of the Children's Asylum Committee, 1820–33, 1857–66, are fairly comprehensive.

The administration of the almshouse can also be studied through sources other than committee minutes. There is one good Alms House Department and Ward Census for 1807 and an Alms House Admission Book for 1812–13. Otherwise, almshouse admissions can be traced through two volumes marked Almshouse Hospital, Female Register, 1803–88, and Almshouse Hospital, "Men's Register," 1828–88, which are actually alphabetical lists of all inmates in all wards in the institution (and not just those in the hospital section) as of 1828 and those admitted thereafter. The Daily Occurrence Docket, 1787–1888, is extremely confusing and has many overlapping volumes. The almshouse's "Examinations of Paupers," 1820–44, is interesting but only contains information about those inmates adjudged non-Philadelphia residents. For the almshouse factory, see Steward, Manufactory Accounts Ledger, 1808–10 and Weekly Statements of Manufactory Production, 1835–44. On punishment of inmates, see "Black Book," 1810–87.

Records of outdoor relief in Philadelphia's city archives are sketchy. The best is the Register of Relief Recipients for 1814–15. Guardians of the poor kept lists of their outdoor pensioners in the 1820s, but these pauper lists are confusing and difficult to read. Note also that the new visitors of the poor compiled a Register of Relief Recipients in 1828–32.

In the Historical Society of Pennsylvania, there are several useful collections of papers of midnineteenth century reformers, including the William M. Meredith Papers, the Roberts Vaux Papers, the Simon Gratz Collection (for Mathew Carey). There are also some manuscripts pertaining to private charities, including the Hibernian Society Minute Book; the Magdalen Society Papers; the Society for the Relief of Poor and Distressed Masters of Ships, Their Widows and Children Minute Books; and the Welsh Society of Pennsylvania Minute Books.

Newspapers   These provide much valuable information about disputes over welfare, public and private, as well as the published annual reports of guardians of the poor and many private charities. I used *The Aurora*, 1800–5; *The Freeman's Journal*, 1804–10; *Poulson's American Daily Advertiser*, 1820–30; *The Public Ledger*, 1840–50; and *The United States Gazette*, 1802–10, 1820–21, 1828–29.

Printed Records   The published accounts of the guardians of the poor, 1804, 1823, 1834, and 1841–54 are invaluable for understanding both the money spent on the poor and their numbers. A fine source of information on both public and private welfare in Philadelphia is Samuel Hazard, ed., *Hazard's Register of Pennsylvania*, 16 vols. (Philadelphia: W. F. Geddes, 1828–35). Also of use are the many published reports by private charities and the city directories.

Books by Contemporaries   There are two guidebooks to the city that provide useful information about welfare. They are James Mease, *The Picture of Philadelphia* (Philadelphia, 1811; reprint ed., New York: Arno Press, 1970) and R. A. Smith, *Philadelphia As It Is in 1852* (Philadelphia: Lindsay and Blakiston, 1852). Other books about welfare and the city's poor are *The Philanthropist: or Institutions of Benevolence by a Pennsylvanian* (Philadelphia: Issac Peirce, 1813) and the many pamphlets written by Mathew Carey, including *Appeal to the Wealthy of the land, Ladies as well as Gentlemen, on the Character, Conduct, Situation, and Prospects of Those Whose Sole Dependence for Subsistence is on the Labour of their Hands* (Philadelphia: L. Johnson, 1833), *Female Wages and Female Oppression* (Philadelphia: Carey, 1835), *From the National Gazette, To the Editor* (Philadelphia: Carey, 1839), and *The Case of the Out-Door Poor Once More* (Philadelphia: Carey, 1838). The only extant published account of life in the Philadelphia Almshouse from the perspective of a former inmate is Andrew Caffrey, *A Sketch of Blockley Poor-House Hospital about Twelve Years Ago* (1856–61?). There are also two old histories of the almshouse that are, in all but name, accounts by contemporaries. These histories do contain much useful information; see John Welsh Croskey, *History of Blockley,* ˆ*A History of the Philadelphia General Hospital from Its Inception, 1731–1928* (Philadelphia: F. A. Davis, 1929) and Charles Lawrence, *History of the Philadelphia Almshouses and Hospitals* (Philadelphia: by author, 1905).

Secondary Published Materials   The books I found most useful in providing a general background on welfare in America in the nineteenth century are Paul Boyer, *Urban Masses and Moral Order in America, 1820–1920* (Cambridge: Harvard University Press, 1978); Robert H. Bremner, *From the Depths, the Discovery of Poverty in the United States* (New York: New York University Press, 1956); and David J. Rothman, *The Discovery of the Asylum, Social Order and Disorder in the New Republic* (Boston: Little Brown, 1971).

To understand the general history of Philadelphia in the last century, I consulted J. Thomas Scharf and Thompson Westcott, *History of Philadelphia, 1609–1884*, 3 vols. (Philadelphia: L. H. Everts and Co., 1884), an old, but invaluable source; and David T. Gilchrist, ed., *The Growth of the Seaport Cities, 1790–1825* (Charlottesville: University Press of Virginia, 1967); Sam Bass Warner, Jr., *The Private City, Philadelphia in Three Periods of Its Growth* (Philadelphia: University of Pennsylvania Press, 1968). Useful for a somewhat later period is Theodore Hershberg, ed., *Philadelphia: Work, Space, Family, and Group Experience in the Nineteenth Century* (New York: Oxford University Press, 1981).

On poverty and welfare in Philadelphia in the colonial era, there are several intriguing books and articles: John K. Alexander, *Render Them Submissive: Responses to Poverty in Philadelphia, 1760–1800* (Amherst: University of Massachusetts Press, 1980); Gary B. Nash, *The Urban Crucible: Social Change, Political Consciousness, and the Origins of the American Revolution* (Cambridge: Harvard University Press, 1979); and by the same author, "Poverty and Poor Relief in Pre-Revolutionary Philadelphia," *William and Mary Quarterly* 33 (January 1976): 3–30; and "Urban Wealth and Poverty in Pre-Revolutionary America," *Journal of Interdisciplinary History* 6 (Spring 1976): 545–84.

On ethnic groups and the laboring poor in nineteenth-century Philadelphia, I found most helpful: Dennis Clark, *The Irish in Philadelphia, Ten Generations of Urban Experience* (Philadelphia: Temple University Press, 1973); Allen F. Davis and Mark Haller, eds., *The Peoples of Philadelphia; A History of Ethnic Groups and Lower Class Life, 1790–1940* (Philadelphia: Temple University Press, 1973); Michael Feldberg, *The Philadelphia Riots of 1844, A Study in Ethnic Conflict* (Westport, Conn.:

Greenwood Press, 1975); Bruce Laurie, *The Working People of Philadelphia, 1800–1850* (Philadelphia: Temple University Press, 1980); and two articles by David Montgomery, "The Working Classes of the Pre-Industrial American City, 1780–1830," *Labor History* 9 (Winter 1968): 3–22; and "The Shuttle and the Cross: Weavers and Artisans in the Kensington Riots of 1844," *Journal of Social History* 6 (Summer 1972): 412–46.

Of particular use on the economy of early nineteenth-century Philadelphia are Donald R. Adams, "Wages Rates in the Early National Period: Philadelphia, 1785–1830," *Journal of Economic History* 28 (September 1968): 404–26; James Weston Livingood, *The Philadelphia-Baltimore Trade Rivalry, 1780–1860* (New York: Arno Press, 1970); and two articles by Samuel Rezneck: "The Depression of 1819–1822, A Social History," *American Historical Review* 39 (1933–34): 28–47 and "Social History of an American Depression, 1837–1843," *American Historical Review* 40 (July 1935): 662–87.

I puzzled together the political situation of the era with the help of Sanford W. Higginbotham, *The Keystone in the Democratic Arch: Pennsylvania Politics, 1800–1816* (Philadelphia: University of Pennsylvania Press, 1952) and Charles M. Snyder, *The Jacksonian Heritage, Pennsylvania Politics, 1833–1848* (Harrisburg: Pennsylvania Historical and Museum Commission, 1958).

There are several books that gave me a background in English poverty and welfare, including Gareth Stedman Jones, *Outcast London, A Study in the Relationship between Classes in Victorian Society* (New York: Oxford University Press, 1971); J. D. Marshall, *The Old Poor Law, 1795–1834* (London: Macmillan, 1968); J. R. Poynter, *Society and Pauperism, English Ideas on Poor Relief, 1795–1834* (London: Routledge and Kegan Paul, 1969); Sidney and Beatrice Webb, *English Poor Law History*, 2 vols. (London: Longmans, Green, and Co., 1929).

Of the various books and articles on poverty and welfare in cities other than Philadelphia in the nineteenth century, I liked best Raymond Mohl, *Poverty in New York, 1783–1825* (New York: Oxford University Press, 1971); Carroll Smith-Rosenberg, *Religion and the Rise of the American City, The New York City Mission Movement, 1812–1870* (Ithaca: Cornell University Press, 1971); and Charles E. Rosenberg, "And Heal the Sick: The Hospital and the Patient in Nineteenth Century America," *Journal of Social History* 10 (Summer 1977): 428–47.

Dissertations   Of most use to me were: Stuart M. Blumin, "Mobility in a Nineteenth Century American City, Philadelphia, 1820–1860" (University of Pennsylvania, 1968); Benjamin S. Klebaner, "Public Poor Relief in America, 1790–1860" (Columbia University, 1952), Othneil A. Pendleton, Jr., "The Influence of the Evangelical Churches upon

Humanitarian Reform: A Case Study Giving Particular Attention to Philadelphia, 1790–1840" (University of Pennsylvania, 1945); Kim Tousley Phillips, "William Duane, Revolutionary Editor" (University of California, Berkeley, 1968); and Stephen Edward Wiberley, Jr., "Four Cities: Public Poor Relief in Urban America, 1700–1775" (Yale University, 1975).

Index